# The Einstein Vendetta

*Also by Thomas Harding*

# The Einstein Vendetta

*Hitler, Mussolini and a True Story of Murder*

## THOMAS HARDING

MICHAEL JOSEPH

PENGUIN MICHAEL JOSEPH

UK | USA | Canada | Ireland | Australia
India | New Zealand | South Africa

Penguin Michael Joseph is part of the Penguin Random House group of companies
whose addresses can be found at global.penguinrandomhouse.com

Penguin Random House UK
One Embassy Gardens, 8 Viaduct Gardens, London SW11 7BW

penguin.co.uk

Penguin
Random House
UK

First published 2025

001

Set in 13.5/16pt Garamond MT Std
Typeset by Jouve (UK), Milton Keynes
Printed and bound in Great Britain by Clays Ltd, Elcograf S.p.A.

The authorized representative in the EEA is Penguin Random House Ireland,
Morrison Chambers, 32 Nassau Street, Dublin D02 YH68

A CIP catalogue record for this book is available from the British Library

HARDBACK ISBN: 978-0-241-65848-2
TRADE PAPERBACK ISBN: 978-0-241-65849-9

Penguin Random House is committed to a sustainable future
for our business, our readers and our planet. This book is made from
Forest Stewardship Council® certified paper.

For Christoph Partsch, for making it possible

*Vendetta*: Revenge, which can affect both the direct offender or any member of their family.

– Grande Dizionario Italiano (Italy)

*Vendetta*: (Italian) Blood revenge.

– Meyer's Encyclopaedia (Germany)

# Contents

PART ONE

## Crime

# CONTENTS

# CONTENTS

# Cast of Characters

## Einstein Family

| | |
|---|---|
| Robert Einstein | – Nina's husband, father to Luce and Cici |
| 'Nina' (Agar) Einstein | – Robert's wife, mother to Luce and Cici |
| Luce Einstein | – Robert and Nina's daughter |
| 'Cici' (Anna Maria) Einstein | – Robert and Nina's daughter |
| Seba Mazzetti | – Nina's sister |
| Anna Maria Boldrini | – Robert and Nina's niece and god-daughter |
| Lorenza Mazzetti | – Robert and Nina's niece, sister of Paola |
| Paola Mazzetti | – Robert and Nina's niece, sister of Lorenza |
| Maja Einstein | – Robert's first cousin, sister of Albert |
| Albert Einstein | – Robert's first cousin, brother of Maja |

## Il Focardo

| | |
|---|---|
| Orando Fuschiotti | – estate manager, or *fattore* |
| Erenia Fuschiotti | – wife of Orando |

'Pipone' (Egisto) Galante – deputy estate manager
Giulia Galante         – wife of Pipone

## Investigators

| | |
|---|---|
| Milton Wexler | – war crimes commissioner: New York, USA |
| Carlo Gentile | – historian: Cologne, Germany |
| Judge Thomas Will | – war crimes investigator: Ludwigsburg, Germany |
| Hubert Ströber | – public prosecutor: Frankenthal, Germany |
| Marco De Paolis | – military prosecutor: La Spezia and Rome, Italy |
| Barbara Schepanek | – TV journalist: Munich, Germany |
| Brian Dalrymple | – forensic expert: Toronto, Canada |

Germany and Italy, 2 August 1944

*Baltic Sea*

*North Sea*

Hamburg

Amsterdam
NETHERLANDS

Berlin

Poznań

POLAND

GERMANY

Brussels
BELGIUM

Cologne

Wrocław

LUXEMBOURG

Frankenthal

Ludwigsburg

Stuttgart

Prague

CZECHOSLOVAKIA

Paris

Munich

Vienna

AUSTRIA

HUNGARY

Zurich    LIECHTENSTEIN
SWITZERLAND

FRANCE

Vichy

Milan

Verona    Venice

ITALY    Ferrara

Sant'Anna
di Stazzema    Parma    Bologna

YUGOSLAVIA

Pisa    Florence
Livorno    Arezzo

**ALLIED
ADVANCES TO
2 AUGUST 1944**

Siena

*Adriatic Sea*

CORSICA

Rome

**BRITISH
EIGHTH
ARMY**

*Mediterranean Sea*

Anzio

**US FIFTH
ARMY**

Naples
Salerno

SARDINIA

*Tyrrhenian
Sea*

Axis areas

Allied areas

Palermo

*Ionian
Sea*

SICILY

0    100    200 miles

0    100    200    300 kilometres

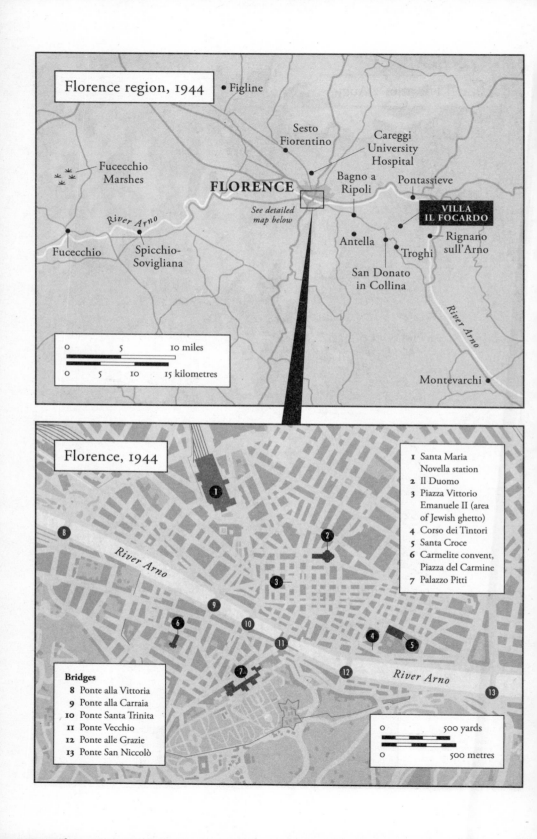

Florence region, 1944

• Figline

Sesto
Fiorentino •

Careggi
University
Hospital

**FLORENCE**

Bagno a
Ripoli

Pontassieve •

*See detailed
map below*

**VILLA
IL FOCARDO**

*River Arno*

Antella •

Troghi •

Rignano
sull'Arno

Fucecchio •

Spicchio-
Sovigliana

San Donato
in Collina

*River Arno*

Fucecchio
Marshes

0        5        10 miles

0     5     10     15 kilometres

Montevarchi •

Florence, 1944

1  Santa Maria
   Novella station
2  Il Duomo
3  Piazza Vittorio
   Emanuele II (area
   of Jewish ghetto)
4  Corso dei Tintori
5  Santa Croce
6  Carmelite convent,
   Piazza del Carmine
7  Palazzo Pitti

*River Arno*

*River Arno*

**Bridges**
 8  Ponte alla Vittoria
 9  Ponte alla Carraia
10  Ponte Santa Trinita
11  Ponte Vecchio
12  Ponte alle Grazie
13  Ponte San Niccolò

0                500 yards

0                500 metres

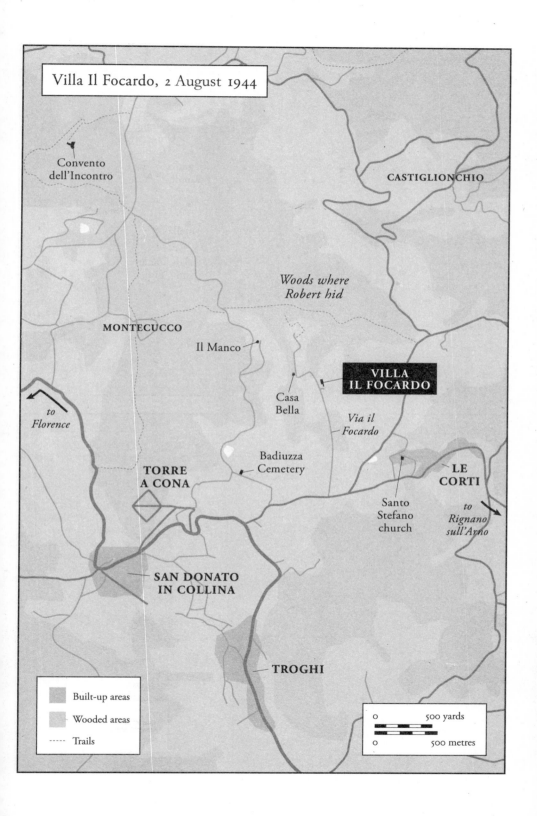

Villa Il Focardo, 2 August 1944

Convento
dell'Incontro

CASTIGLIONCHIO

*Woods where
Robert hid*

MONTECUCCO

Il Manco

*to
Florence*

Casa
Bella

**VILLA
IL FOCARDO**

*Via il
Focardo*

Badiuzza
Cemetery

LE
CORTI

TORRE
A CONA

Santo
Stefano
church

*to
Rignano
sull'Arno*

SAN DONATO
IN COLLINA

TROGHI

Built-up areas

Wooded areas

----- Trails

0          500 yards

0          500 metres

# Einstein Family Tree

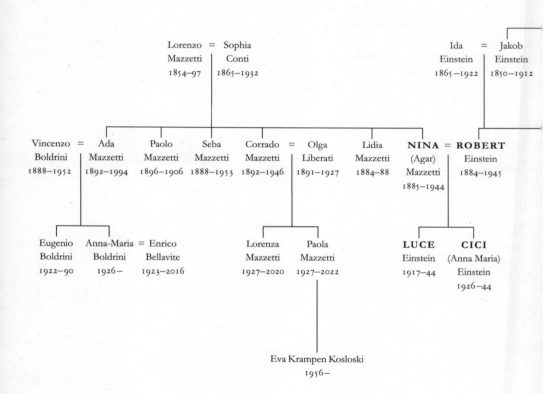

Lorenzo = Sophia
Mazzetti | Conti
1854–97 | 1865–1932

Ida = Jakob
Einstein | Einstein
1865–1922 | 1850–1912

Vincenzo = Ada
Boldrini | Mazzetti
1888–1952 | 1892–1994

Paolo
Mazzetti
1896–1906

Seba
Mazzetti
1888–1953

Corrado = Olga
Mazzetti | Liberati
1892–1946 | 1891–1927

Lidia
Mazzetti
1884–88

NINA = ROBERT
(Agar) | Einstein
Mazzetti | 1884–1945
1885–1944

Eugenio
Boldrini
1922–90

Anna-Maria = Enrico
Boldrini | Bellavite
1926– | 1923–2016

Lorenza
Mazzetti
1927–2020

Paola
Mazzetti
1927–2022

LUCE
Einstein
1917–44

CICI
(Anna Maria)
Einstein
1926–44

Eva Krampen Kosloski
1956–

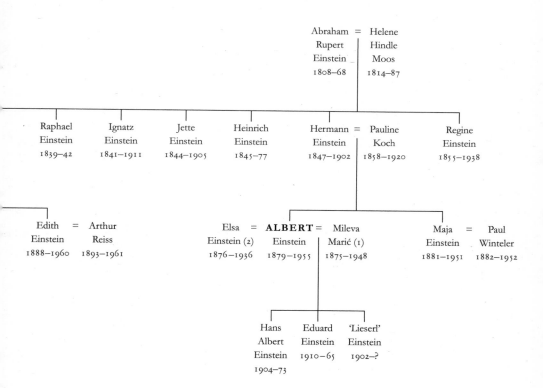

Abraham = Helene
Rupert   Hindle
Einstein  Moos
1808–68   1814–87

Raphael        Ignatz         Jette          Heinrich       Hermann = Pauline      Regine
Einstein       Einstein       Einstein       Einstein       Einstein   Koch         Einstein
1839–42        1841–1911      1844–1905      1845–77        1847–1902  1858–1920    1855–1938

Edith  = Arthur                    Elsa      = ALBERT = Mileva              Maja     =  Paul
Einstein   Reiss                   Einstein (2)  Einstein   Marić (1)        Einstein    Winteler
1888–1960  1893–1961               1876–1936     1879–1955  1875–1948        1881–1951   1882–1952

Hans      Eduard      'Lieserl'
Albert    Einstein    Einstein
Einstein  1910–65     1902–?
1904–73

# Author's Note

This is a work of non-fiction. As such, I have relied on investigative reports, written testimonies, letters, official records, photographs and other archival documents. I was also granted the rare opportunity to go beyond the public record. After winning a court case in Germany, I received a copy of the prosecutor's files, the first time a journalist has gained access to such documents. And I was privileged to speak to various eyewitnesses, including many who were in their nineties, providing me with details that only those who have experienced an event first-hand can provide.

Ever since the events in this book took place, there have been numerous attempts to get to the bottom of what happened. As new information became available, opinions changed, the history was revised and then revised again. In Italy, there are two words for memory: *ricordo* and *memoria*. The first includes the word *cor* which means 'heart', and describes a more emotional, personal and fluid memory; the second comes from the Latin word *mens*, which means 'mind', and is more objective, collective and stable. This book attempts to capture both *ricordo* and *memoria*, in an effort to reach for the complete truth.

# PART ONE
# Crime

It was such a night that one knew that human eyes
would not witness it and survive.

— Primo Levi

# 1. Il Focardo, 1944

Robert Einstein was hiding in the woods, fifteen miles southeast of Florence, away from his house, away from his family. For two weeks now, he had remained holed up, within sight of his villa but concealed. All he had with him was a blanket and a book that he had quickly grabbed from his library. Some nights, he slept on the ground beneath the cypress, oak and hazelnut trees. Other nights, he found refuge with a local farmer. Afraid his whereabouts might be revealed to the Nazis who were looking for him, he never stayed in one place for more than twenty-four hours.

Two weeks earlier, members of the Hermann Göring Division had knocked loudly on his front door and demanded to see him. Luckily, he had been working in the fields at the time and the German visitors had been sent away. Later, he sat with his wife, Nina, and their two adult daughters, Luce and Cici, and discussed what to do. Was it safer to stay together or to separate? In the end, they had agreed that it would be best to separate: the women would remain in the villa and he would find somewhere close by and lie low. After all, it was Robert who was the target, and so it must be Robert who must hide. If the Germans came back to the villa, the women would say that he was away. It had worked once already, why not again? As for Nina, Luce and Cici, they were Christian, this would surely insulate them from any possible violence.

But ever since he had said goodbye, giving a long hug to his daughters, kissing his wife on the cheek, he had worried that they'd made the wrong decision. Had they considered all the options? Were Nina, Luce and Cici in fact safe? Being apart made him feel powerless. Powerless to respond to changing circumstances. Powerless to protect his family. More than once, he had considered returning to the villa. At least then they would be together, able to face whatever adversity came their way. But then he remembered the reasons why they had separated in the first place, and so, reluctantly, he stuck with the plan: they would remain apart until conditions changed.

For two weeks, therefore, he had waited in the shadows, paralysed with anxiety, hoping that something would shift. As an engineer, he thought of himself as a man of reason. He did not rely on faith or superstition, nor was he one to pray. He assessed a situation according to the facts, so when he came across someone in the woods – a farmer travelling to one of the local villages, a band of partisans on their way from one action to the next, a black marketeer trading cigarettes, eggs or cheese – he pressed them for the latest news. Mostly, however, he was by himself. And so he listened intently to the noises around him, the boom boom of artillery shells getting closer and closer, the reverberant rumbling of B-24 and other Allied bombers flying more frequently overhead, the rat-tat-tat of machine-gun fire growing louder and more

4

frequent in the hills around. From all this, he concluded that the American and British ground forces would soon arrive in Florence and, with their superior resources, drive the dreaded Germans away from the region, and at last he would be able to reunite with his family. They would be safe.

Occasionally, and best of all, Robert was sometimes able to gather information from a source even more welcome, his dear wife. So it was that, at seven in the morning of 3 August 1944, Robert Einstein was standing at the edge of the wood, listening out for her footsteps. Though this visit was prearranged, they had agreed that it should be cancelled if Nina perceived any cause for concern, so her arrival remained uncertain. The minutes ticked by in relative quiet, too late for night-time aerial bombardments and too early for close-quarters combat. Occasionally, the tense silence was punctured by the cry of an unseen bird or the scuffle of some small mammal scurrying through the undergrowth.

Then Robert heard the crunch of footsteps approaching. Though quiet – whoever was coming was making an effort to keep the noise down – in the dry summer air, the sound echoed dangerously off the rocky path below. He caught some whispered words. Recognizing his wife's voice, he called out her name, and a few moments later he saw her face; she was carrying a small package, and her forehead was beaded with sweat. Deep into the Tuscan summer, it was already swelteringly hot, but here in the shade it was mercifully cooler. It was also out of view, which is why they had chosen this place to meet.

Careful not to draw attention to themselves, and standing close, they greeted each other in hushed tones. Nina shared the latest news, that the girls were doing fine, that the peach harvest had started on the estate, that according to the previous evening's report on BBC radio the Allied forces were only twenty miles south of Florence. How long would he have to remain in the woods? Perhaps not too long. From what Nina was saying, the British and American forces were even closer than he had hoped. After four years of war and eleven months of German occupation, it might soon all be over, maybe as early as this week. Perhaps even as soon as tomorrow. It looked like the decision to split the family, with Nina and the girls staying in the villa and Robert hiding in the woods, had paid off.

As she spoke, Robert looked at his wife. Nina was fifty-nine years old, with almond-shaped eyes, thin lips and shoulder-length dark hair. She still had her northern Italian accent despite decades of living in Rome and Tuscany. Indeed, Nina had hardly changed since they had first met more than thirty years earlier and their love had only grown with age. As for Robert, though his beard and hair were flecked with white, he felt younger than his sixty years. All those seasons working in the fields alongside the *contadini*, or farmworkers, had given him vitality and stamina. And, having grown up in Munich, he also had an accent, though he wasn't sure his Teutonic roots were now a hindrance or a benefit.

They continued to catch up, careful to avoid certain subjects. Nina didn't want to know where Robert would be staying that night in case she was questioned. Nor was there a need to discuss the protocols in case of an emergency. They had been over these many times. If Nina came looking for him at a time not previously agreed, then he was to remain hidden. On no account would he reveal himself, even if she appeared desperate.

They were coming to the end of their conversation when they heard a tremendous crashing sound coming from the direction of the villa. It sounded like something massive had been broken. Unsure what it could be, and now anxious, Nina quickly said goodbye to her husband and hurried away. Robert watched as she disappeared down the sandy track.

Nina ran the whole way, holding up her long country dress as she went. It took five minutes to reach the tall wrought-iron gates of their villa – Il Focardo.

She turned up the cypress-lined drive until, panting and drenched in sweat, she reached the main entrance and immediately saw what had caused the noise. The front doors had been smashed open. It would have taken tremendous force to break these solid timbers. She clambered over the splintered ruins and into the hallway. There she was confronted with the source of the destruction. In front of her stood seven heavily armed German soldiers.

Nina demanded to know what was going on. She spoke in fluent German, having lived for years in Bavaria with Robert. Ignoring the question, the commander asked for her name, to which she replied she was Nina Einstein. He then asked where her husband was, and Nina said she did not know. The commander persisted. They had orders to arrest him, he said, and was confident Robert was hiding nearby. It was useless to deny it. Where was he? Nina kept her silence.

The stand-off was interrupted by the arrival of the rest of the household. First came Nina's two daughters. Luce, the oldest, was twenty-seven and in her final year of medical school at Florence University. She was tall and slender, with dark, shoulder-length hair like her mother, and also like her mother she liked to wear practical country clothes. Cici, the youngest, was eighteen years old. She attended the Michelangelo High School in Florence, one of the best in the city, where she was achieving mostly good grades, excelling in religious studies, Italian and history, but, according to her teachers, needing to improve in mathematics and physics. She was a head shorter than Luce, with blond, curly hair and a dimpled chin; unlike her more serious sister, she tended to wear shorter, fashionable dresses that were cut just above the knees. With them was Ali, the family's black-and-white sheepdog, who padded around the room, sniffing the black boots and starched uniforms, curious about these strangers with their unfamiliar smells. Moments later, Nina's younger sister, Seba, walked in, followed by Anna Maria (the eighteen-year-old daughter of Nina's other sister, Ada) and the twins, Lorenza and Paola (the seventeen-year-old daughters of Nina's brother Corrado). The hallway was now crowded. The seven Italian women stood near the entrance. Seven German soldiers faced them.

The commander asked Nina again for the whereabouts of Robert Einstein. The German, Nina was able to observe, was in his thirties, had a scrawny face and wore round metal glasses. She did not reply. This had been the agreement. If soldiers came looking, they had decided the best thing was to keep silent.

The commander had another go, his voice now rising. Where was her husband? Where was the cousin of Albert Einstein?

# 2. Munich, 1884

Robert Einstein was born at 8.30 in the morning on 27 February 1884 at his parents' home in Munich, Germany. According to his birth certificate, the religion of his mother Ida and that of his father Jakob was 'Mosaic' (Jewish). They lived with Jakob's brother, Hermann Einstein, and his wife Pauline, along with their two children: two-year-old Maja and four-year-old Albert.

The two families lived together in the same building at Müllerstrasse 3, just south of the Old Town. A year after Robert's birth, they built a two-storey house at Rengerweg 14 (later Adlzreiterstrasse), a quiet street three miles southwest of the city centre. They were the only residents, often cooking for each other and socializing as a single unit. According to one chronicler, the Einsteins were solidly upper middle class.

By the autumn of 1888, there were four small children in the house, Ida having given birth to a girl, who they called Edith. And while young Albert tended to keep himself to himself – later he would say that he had been 'inwardly inhibited and alienated' – he spent considerable time with his cousin Robert. The families also studied together, Jakob in particular helped Albert with his mathematics. There was music in the house: Pauline, who was a fine pianist, taught Robert and Maja the piano, while Albert played Mozart and Beethoven sonatas on the violin. The children played together too. One of their favourite spots was under the magnificent row of tall trees which grew outside the house. In all, Robert and Albert would live in the same property for eleven years. And while Robert was four years younger than Albert, they held a deep affection for each other. They were close; some might call them brother-cousins.

Robert's father and uncle ran an electrical engineering company called 'J. Einstein & Co.' which made equipment for the electrification of public spaces. Their factory stood just a few hundred feet from their home on Adlzreiter-strasse. Trained as an engineer, Jakob was responsible for the scientific aspects of the business, while Hermann focused on the commercial side, including employment, marketing and accounting. Their personalities, however, were not necessarily suited to these tasks. Hermann 'owing to his contemplative nature may have lacked the qualities required of a businessman', Maja later recalled, whereas Jakob was 'constantly seeking novelty and change and unable to learn from any failure, and was an over-eager and even stubborn optimist'. But for a while, at least, the enterprise thrived. By 1890, the number of employees had risen from twenty to 200. Projects included the electrification of the Munich Okto-berfest on Theresienwiese, the provision of street lights in Schwabing (a suburb outside Munich) and the installation of lighting in numerous cafés, a maze and a shooting gallery. By any measure, the company was a success.

Robert's parents and uncle and aunt were fairly relaxed

when it came to their Judaism. 'A liberal spirit, undogmatic in matters of religion prevailed within the family,' Maja wrote. 'There was no discussion of religious matters or rules.' That is not to say that the Einsteins rejected their Jewish heritage. On the contrary, they followed many of the religious trad- itions. When he was a baby, Robert was circumcised; and later, as a young child, he was instructed in the basic tenets of Judaism. Each spring, he would gather with the rest of the family around the table at home to celebrate Seder and recount the story of the Jews' escape from slavery in Egypt. The family also belonged to the Jewish community associ- ation in Munich, which was just a fifteen-minute walk from where they lived. Robert and the others would dress up in their best clothes and attend the most important annual ser- vices, including Yom Kippur and Rosh Hashanah.

When Robert was six, his cousin Albert grew intensely interested in Judaism. As a result, Maja remembered, Albert became 'so zealous in his religious feeling that he strictly adhered to all the details of religious regulations'. Provid- ing one example, Maja said that her brother stopped eating pork. It is probable that he also stopped eating shellfish and encouraged his family to purchase their meat from a kosher butcher. Pauline or Ida would have been unwilling to prepare separate meals, so the entire family now had to follow young Albert's diet. It wasn't long, however, before Albert's grow- ing interest in science put an end to his religious exuberance. At this point, much to everyone's relief, the family's eating habits returned to normal.

In the spring of 1894, when Robert was ten years old, the family suffered financial calamity. Jakob and Hermann's busi- ness was already overextended, its investments in machinery and salaries considerably exceeding its income, and when the company lost a crucial contract to provide public lighting for Munich's city centre, matters reached breaking point. In a dramatic move, the brothers decided to close down their company in Munich, liquidate its assets, and start again in the heavily industrialized region of Milan in northern Italy. Robert had to say goodbye to his friends, his teachers, and the city which had always been his home.

There is no record of the emotional impact on Robert of the family's sudden change in fortunes. Nevertheless, we know from Maja that the move was difficult. She recalled that while they were waiting to be relocated to Italy, she, Robert and the other children watched the family's land being sold to make way for new tenement buildings. In the process, the cherished trees outside their house were cut down. 'Until it was time to move,' Maja remembered, 'we had to watch the destruction of our favourite memories from our home.' The collapse of the family business also had a dramatic effect on Robert's older cousin: Albert's 'discomfort spiraled toward depression', reported his biographer Walter Isaacson, 'perhaps even close to a nervous breakdown'.

Upon arrival in Italy, Robert was enrolled in a local school. He found himself in a strange new place, without friends and where the people spoke a foreign language (he didn't know Italian). The two families once again lived together. First in Milan, and then, soon after, in an apartment at Via Foscolo 11 in Pavia, a town twenty miles south of Milan. While the apartment was smaller than their Munich home, they had use of a cloistered courtyard that provided shade in the summertime and a small garden that boasted lemon and sweet gum trees. As for Albert, who was now fifteen years old, his parents decided, much to his chagrin, that it was best if he stayed behind in Germany to continue his studies. When he came home to Pavia for Christmas, Albert made it clear that he would not be returning to Munich. He spent the next ten months living with Robert and the others, during which he prepared his application to the polytechnic in Zurich and wrote his first essay on theoretical physics.

Their lives were just beginning to feel stable when, in 1896, the Einstein brothers' business took another bad turn. After failing to win a contract to electrify the town of Pavia, their company again went bankrupt. This second financial collapse was perhaps even more painful than the first. Not only was the inheritance of Robert's aunt Pauline lost in the venture but also significant donations from other relatives. 'The family,' Maja later wrote, 'was left with hardly anything.' From this point forward, the two brothers split their financial affairs. Hermann set up a business in Milan, while Jakob worked first in Lecce, a small city in southern Italy, and then in Genoa, in the country's northwest, where he secured a job as an engineer for a large company. As for Robert, he stayed with his uncle, aunt and cousins in Milan for a year, attending the Giuseppe Parini High School, before joining his parents in Genoa. This would be the fourth time Robert had moved in three years; it was also the first time in his life that he would be living away from his cousins.

Things finally settled down in Genoa. The family's income stabilized, the stress of running a business was behind them and they had all improved their Italian language skills. Indeed, they were increasingly enjoying Italian culture, food and attitudes. Robert, in particular, fell in love with the Italian countryside, and whenever he could he spent time in nature.

It was around now, after turning thirteen in the spring of 1897, that he probably performed his bar mitzvah at a synagogue in Genoa. Sometime soon after, he decided that, though he belonged to the Jewish culture and cherished its traditions, he did not believe in the existence of God. It did not agree with his rational proclivities. Following the example of his cousin Albert, he was, he concluded, an atheist.

Over the next few years, Hermann tried one enterprise and then another, but none found great success. He died in Milan in 1902 of heart failure, aged fifty-five (Maja blamed his death on years of financial worries). Seven years later, Robert's parents divorced and, three years after that, on 8 September 1912, Jakob also died from a heart attack, aged sixty-two, in Vienna. According to the death notice posted in the local newspaper, Robert and Edith were 'deeply shocked to announce the passing of their dearly loved and unforgettable father'.

At the time of his father's death, Robert was twenty-eight years old and had left Genoa. Following in his father's footsteps, he had studied to become an electrical engineer, and, after graduating, he had moved to Rome. It was there that he met Nina Mazzetti. On the surface, they had little in common. While her family went back generations in northern Italy, his roots were German. She belonged to the Protestant Waldensian Church while his family were Jewish. Yet they shared numerous interests that brought them together. They both liked to read, adored classical music and enjoyed taking walks in the countryside. They also shared aspirations. They both wanted to live on a farm where they could keep animals and grow their own food, and they both wanted to start a family. They also both knew hardship. When Nina was three, her older sister Lidia died; when she was twelve, her father died, leaving her mother to take care of her and her four siblings; and when she was twenty-one, her younger brother Paolo died. Through these connections, and more, Nina and Robert formed a tight bond.

So it was that, on 13 October 1913, Robert and Nina were married in a civil ceremony in Rome. Not long after the wedding, Robert said he wanted to return to Munich to see if he could resurrect the family engineering business. It was almost twenty years since his father and uncle had been forced to flee the city in humiliation. And so, at the start of 1914, full of the spirit of optimism and resilience, the newly-weds moved to Germany to build a new life for themselves.

Their hopes for calm domesticity were dashed, however, on 1 August, when Germany declared war on Russia. At this point, Robert could have found a way to return to Italy with his young wife. Instead, just seven days after the start of the war, the thirty-year-old Robert Einstein enlisted in the army. His father, Jakob, had served as an engineer in the Franco-Prussian War of 1870–71, and now it was his turn to do his duty. Like the majority of assimilated German Jews, Robert considered himself to be German first. It was normal, therefore, for a Jew such as himself to enlist, just as it was for the rest of the population. Indeed, it was mandatory for all German men aged seventeen to forty-five. This did not stop accusations circulating in the media that Jews were cowards and lacked patriotism. Such attacks prompted the military to conduct a count of the number of Jews in its ranks and it was found that over 100,000 Jewish soldiers served in the German Army, roughly the same proportion as the general population. This finding, however, was never made public. Robert would have been extremely aware of the antisemitism pervasive in the German Army and would have wanted to keep a low profile. The fact that he was living in a majority Catholic region of Germany is probably why it was recorded on two of his military documents that his religion was Catholic.

Robert was assigned to the reserves of the Royal Bavarian Light Infantry Regiment and, after a brief period of training in Munich, he was deployed to France. There he endured more than twelve months of brutal trench warfare, including the gruelling battle at Verdun. Though he did not suffer a major injury, it is probable that – as has been recorded in the diaries, poems and letters of so many other combatants – the physical and psychological toll was severe.

As for Robert's cousin Albert, he had been a Swiss citizen since 1901 and had long relinquished his feelings of German patriotism. 'I'm curious what our cousin Robert will say when we get to see him again,' Albert wrote in a letter to his sister Maja. 'He was not as careful as I was in choosing his fatherland.'

Occasionally, Robert was able to obtain leave from his military duties and returned home to Munich to see Nina, who was living by herself in a boarding house at Martiusstrasse 8. It was during one of these visits, in the summer of 1916, that Nina became pregnant. Nine months later, at 1.30 p.m. on 19 April 1917, Nina gave birth to a baby girl. They called her Luce, meaning 'light' – a moment of hope, maybe, during the dark times of war. On the birth certificate, the mother's religion was given as Protestant. The father's was assigned once again as 'Catholic'.

By late 1917, Robert had risen to the most senior rank of

non-commissioned officer, a position known as 'officer-in-waiting', and received the Bavarian King Ludwig Cross. The following summer, August 1918, he was injured. Though the nature of his wound went unrecorded, it was significant enough that he had to return to his regiment's home base in Bad Tölz, thirty miles south of Munich, to convalesce. After he had fully recovered, he was assigned to the 30th Royal Bavarian Light Infantry Regiment and deployed to Arlon in Belgium. This is where he was stationed when the war came to an end in November 1918.

Once Robert was demobilized, he returned to Munich, and he and Nina had a long conversation about their future. Should they stay in Germany and try once again to re-establish an electrical engineering firm with the Einstein name? If so, they would have to deal with the chaos of post-war Germany and face the growing antisemitism that was being stoked by politicians and journalists. Or perhaps they should return to Rome? If they went back, Robert could reach out to old business contacts and Nina could ask her family to help with their very mobile toddler. Rome was also more tolerant of Jews, though this could change at any time. Perhaps more than anything, after four long years in war-torn Germany, Nina was missing home. In the end, they made the decision: they would return to Italy.

# 3. Rome, 1921

Like Germany, Italy was reeling following the end of the First World War. In 1915, it had signed a treaty in London in which it agreed to fight alongside the Allies. This treaty guaranteed that after the war's end Italy would receive several important territories, including parts of South Tyrol, the Istrian peninsula on the Adriatic Sea and the city of Fiume. By the time Austria–Hungary and Italy signed an armistice on 3 November 1918, more than 650,000 Italian men had been killed and a million wounded. This cost was made even harder to bear when Italians learned that they would not be receiving the territories they had been promised after all. The combination of grief, diplomatic betrayal and wounded national pride provoked widespread discontent and anger. The mood was made worse by rampant inflation and job shortages. Workers occupied factories in Milan, Turin and other cities. There was fighting in the streets between rival political gangs. The poet Gabriele D'Annunzio and 200 armed supporters seized the city of Fiume. Talk of revolution was in the air.

This was the context to which Robert and Nina returned

when they arrived back in Rome. They rented a small apartment away from the city centre and reconnected with old friends. Robert started a new engineering business and worked hard to support the family financially. Nina, meanwhile, joined a nearby church and Luce started at a local kindergarten. After more than six years out of the country, it was hard to adjust, but they pushed through.

Then, in the autumn of 1921, their mood picked up when they heard that Maja was also coming back to Italy. She would be with her husband, Paul Winteler, and would be renting a house in Fiesole, just outside Florence. While it was a seven-hour train journey from Rome, it would be possible to see each other more often. Soon after Maja's arrival there was more good news. Albert would be visiting Florence. In a postcard to Maja, he wrote that he would be 'travelling incognito' with his teenage son Hans Albert. They arrived on 17 October and remained for three days, before heading off to present a lecture in Bologna. It is likely that Robert spent time with his cousin during his stay, after all they had not seen each other since before the war. Six months later, Robert and Nina travelled to Berlin, where they probably saw Albert again. And in their letters, Maja and Albert mentioned Robert to other people. They even had a nickname for him: 'Bubi', meaning little boy. It appeared that the childhood affection between the cousins had continued into adulthood.

Meanwhile, politics in Italy reached boiling point. On 24 October 1922, the head of the National Fascist Party, Benito Mussolini, announced in front of up to 40,000 supporters in Naples that it was time to seize power. The following week, thousands of armed blackshirts headed towards the nation's capital. This so-called 'March on Rome' provoked terror among the ruling class, who feared that the country was close to a civil war, prompting King Vittorio Emanuele III to invite Mussolini to become prime minster and form a new government. Over the next few months and years, Il Duce, as Mussolini liked to be known, consolidated his power by making himself no longer answerable to parliament, so that he could be removed only by the king. And as his control over the levers of government grew, he rolled out a radical agenda, including large-scale infrastructure development, centralization of the education system and an aggressive foreign policy.

Despite the rapid change in the political climate, Maja decided she wanted to remain in Italy for the long term, so she and her husband Paul purchased a house with money borrowed from Albert (she also borrowed from Robert's sister Edith, though it is not clear if she also used this to purchase the house). Their new home was in Sesto Fiorentino, just to the northwest of Florence, and they called it 'Samos' after the Greek island which was the birthplace of the philosopher Pythagoras. This marked the start of the Einstein family's more permanent connection with Florence.

A few months later, Nina became pregnant and, on 23 February 1926, she gave birth to a second daughter, Anna Maria, who they called Cici. The family was soon to grow still further. On 26 July 1927, a little over a year after Cici was born, Nina and Robert received some shocking news from Nina's brother Corrado. His wife Olga had given birth to identical twins, Lorenza and Paola, before dying soon after from labour-related complications. Over the next few years, Nina and Robert watched as Corrado tried his best to look after his two girls, while holding down his job as an insurance agent. Nina helped whenever she could, though she had two daughters of her own. Others also lent a hand, including friends, neighbours and a nurse, but it was clear to Nina that her brother was finding the responsibility overwhelming. Finally, in 1934, after years of sleepless nights and unsatisfactory childcare, Corrado told Nina that he did not think he was providing the parenting his daughters needed. Would she be able to look after the twins? After discussing it with Robert, Nina agreed to take them in.

The Einsteins now had four girls to raise in their modest Rome apartment: Luce, who was by then almost eighteen; Cici, who was eight; and Lorenza and Paola, who were seven. It soon grew a little cramped. Fortunately, Robert's career as an electrical engineer was going well. This allowed them to look for a larger home with some land, away from the busy capital. The following year, 1935, they moved to a horse farm near the medieval village of Corciano, halfway between Rome and Florence. The house was situated in wooded hills, with stunning views of the valley below. It was a rambling stone farmhouse, with large rooms and plenty of space to work and play without stumbling over each other. It was also just ten miles from Perugia University, where Luce would shortly start her first year of medical studies. Robert purchased a car so that he could drive her to classes each day. All in all, it was a big change from life in Rome, but it was a change that everyone in the family welcomed.

Robert in particular enjoyed living out in the countryside. On 22 December 1935, he wrote to a friend providing him with an update. 'Here life continues as usual,' he said. 'Now we are pressing the olives, which unfortunately were few this year.' The sowing of the fields was complete and once the weather improved they would start work on repairing the farm tracks. He concluded by wishing his friend a happy Christmas and a prosperous New Year.

As the months progressed, the integration of Paola and Lorenza into the family went better than anyone could have expected. And while there was some tension from the daughters, particularly jealousy from Cici, who was close to the twins in age, it was clear that the four girls were fond of each other. The twins soon came to see Nina as a second mother. She brushed Paola's and Lorenza's hair and cooked their favourite dishes, just as she did with her own daughters. She helped them complete their homework and taught them English and French. She showered them with praise and encouraged them to improve themselves. She believed that girls should receive the same education as boys and hoped that Luce's example would serve as an inspiration. She also urged them to explore their creative selves, to paint and play music. Soon the twins had taught themselves the accordion, and after dinner they would entertain the others by playing songs in the living room. Most of all, Nina wanted the girls to enjoy the stunning natural surroundings in which they lived. One of their favourite activities was to go out into the fields with Ali the family dog to pick broom and cornflowers. Later, they would arrange vases of pretty wildflowers around the house.

The girls also loved Robert. He made time in his busy schedule to be with them. He invited them to join him as he walked around the estate, inspecting the crops or petting the horses. They accompanied him on thrilling trips to town. And in the evening, when it was dark, they sat at his feet in the living room while Beethoven pulsed excitedly out of the radiogram (a large wood-panelled piece of furniture that included both a radio and a record player). And while they didn't like it when he lost his temper after they had broken a vase or tracked dirt into the house (for which he made them write out lines), he was good at setting boundaries, which the children found reassuring. 'To bed, to bed! Everyone in bed!' he would shout adamantly at the end of a long evening filled with noise and frolicking, 'Oh yes, worthwhile fun is short-lived. Now all to bed. Silence!'

The horse farm, however, proved too much for Robert and Nina to manage. There was no one to help take care of the animals and they were expensive to maintain. It also felt a little remote. After a few months, therefore, Robert started looking for a new family home. In the summer of 1937, he found somewhere that might work. It was just fifteen miles southeast of Florence and was called Il Focardo.

Postcard of Villa Il Focardo, 1924.

It was through his network of acquaintances that Robert first heard that Il Focardo was being put up for sale and, even more interestingly, that its owner was in financial trouble. Enrico Bürgisser had inherited the estate from his eminent father, the great Rodolfo Arnoldo Bürgisser, who had founded one of the largest banks in Tuscany and was known for being discreet, sober and thrifty. Which was why Enrico was such an embarrassment. After struggling to study in Pisa and then Freiburg, Enrico had returned to Florence, where he drank heavily, partied hard, purchased expensive cars and engaged in gambling. Facing economic collapse, he felt forced to sell the property.

On a warm summer's day, Robert drove from Perugia to have a look at Il Focardo. Having parked the car in the narrow cypress-lined gravel driveway, he took some time to survey what was on offer. At the centre of the 250-acre estate was the villa itself, an elegant, beige-stuccoed building, whose windows were framed by handsome green shutters. To one side stood a chapel with its own access to the driveway. Inside the villa, with its high ceilings, plentiful windows and stone floors, the rooms were cool, light and airy. The ground floor had eight rooms, including a large living room (called the 'Sala Rossa' because of the red fabric covering its walls), a dining room capable of seating sixteen guests, a kitchen, a laundry and various storerooms. A wide staircase took him upstairs, where he found six bedrooms and a bathroom. The villa would be more than sufficient to accommodate his family.

Going outside, Robert inspected the ten farmhouses which came with the sale, each just a short walk from the villa. These were where the *contadini*, or farmworkers, lived with their families. Their contribution would be crucial to the successful management of the estate. As with the other nearby farms, the work here was organized along the medieval principle of the *mezzadria*, or 'halving', a form of sharecropping whereby, in return for their labour, the *contadini* received 50 per cent of the produce, and the rest went to the landowner. In addition, the workers enjoyed free housing and a modest payment at the year's end. They also kept their own animals, including bees, cows, sheep, chickens and pigs.

Behind the villa, towards the wood-lined hills, Robert came across the peach orchard for which the estate was best known. There was a handful of *contadini* standing on ladders leaning against the trees. Each had a reed basket in hand and was carefully gathering the yellow and red peaches hanging plump and soft after months of warm sun. Other men and women were carrying full crates to a nearby shed to be stored, where the air was thick with a sweet, sticky scent. In a day or so, the ripe peaches would be driven to the market. Below the orchard, the estate extended down the hillside. First, came acres of olive trees, then there were fields of wheat and, beyond that, a small vineyard, its ancient vines running down the slope in neat, parallel lines.

From his time in Perugia, Robert was familiar with how the calendar turned for an estate such as this. In September and October it would be time for the *vendemmia*, the grape harvest. Then, in the last weeks of October and early November, the olives would have to be picked, just as they were becoming soft and ripe, but before the insects laid their eggs in the black fruit. He knew that for the best results, the crates of olives should be quickly taken to the *frantoio*, the olive press. Starting in January, manure would have to be spread in the olive groves and vineyards, and then in March, as the peach trees blossomed pink and white, it would be time to prune the olive groves. Finally, in July and August, the wheat would need to be cut, dried and threshed. After that, the cycle would start all over again.

Robert looked out over the view across the Arno valley, a swathe of mustard yellows, russet browns and olive greens, each earthy tone melting into the next, dotted with stone cottages, churches and farm buildings that blended into the landscape. Straight ahead, to the south, was Troghi, the near-est village, with a few shops and a café. To his left, to the east, stood the tiny hamlet of Le Corti and then the town of Rignano sull'Arno, the centre of the local municipality. To his right, to the west, was the neighbouring estate of Torre a Cona; and then, on the other side of the hill, just fifteen miles from the villa, lay the Renaissance jewel of Florence.

The estate was exactly what Robert was looking for. It was close to Florence, which had a top medical university that would allow his daughter Luce to continue her studies (she had completed her first year in Perugia). The city's schools were well regarded and of high quality, making them suitable for his second daughter Cici and his two nieces, Lorenza and Paola. They would also be closer to Maja, so they could see each other more frequently.

As an engineer, Robert valued the estate's efficiency as a working farm. As a romantic, he savoured its architectural beauty and gorgeous setting. And as a businessman, he liked the price. So it was that, on 15 October 1937, Robert signed the contract to purchase Il Focardo for 600,000 lire (equivalent to £515,000 today), of which 450,000 lire was paid in cash, with the rest taken as a loan with the seller. The estate was theirs.

Soon after moving into Il Focardo, Robert rented an apart-ment at Corso dei Tintori 21 in Florence, just steps from the basilica of Santa Croce. Situated in a large building owned by one of the city's most powerful families, the apartment would offer a refuge during the cold winter months when the villa would be challenging to heat. It would also allow Luce to remain in Florence during the week so she could attend her medical studies, and it would afford the family an opportunity to enjoy the city's cultural riches. As was common for the most affluent Florentine families, the Einsteins now had the use of two residences, one in the country and one in the city. From the very start, however, they considered Il Focardo to be their home.

For Robert, the purchase of Il Focardo was the culmination of fifteen years' hard work. Since childhood, he had lived in the wake of his twice-bankrupt father's financial ruin. This had resulted in instability and distress that had long tainted his life. As soon as he had arrived at Il Focardo, Robert felt that he had finally found a place of tranquillity and gentle beauty. A home where his soul could mend and where his wife, daughters and nieces could thrive.

As for the rest of Robert's extended family, they were scattered across the world. Though his cousin Maja and her husband Paul were nearby in Sesto Fiorentino, just outside Florence, his cousin Albert was living in the USA, while Albert's eldest son, Hans Albert, was also in the USA, and his youngest son, Eduard, and Robert's sister Edith were in Switzerland. With Adolf Hitler's and Benito Mussolini's growing friendship, it was unlikely that any of the family would be travelling to Italy any time soon.

For now, at least, the villa Il Focardo provided an oasis for Robert, Nina and the girls, away from the politics of hate broiling in Rome and Berlin, and away from the growing drumbeat of war.

# 4. Il Focardo, 1944

Once again, the commander demanded to know the whereabouts of Nina's husband. Where was the cousin of Albert Einstein? Once more, Nina and the others refused to reply. Realizing that the women were not going to cooperate, the commander ordered everyone into the cellar. It was safer there, he said, because of the likely Allied air raids. This made some sense, given that in the past few days British and American planes had dropped bombs on nearby villages including Pontassieve, Incisa, Figline Valdarno and Troghi.

The Germans pushed the women through the hallway and into a narrow corridor. They bunched up behind Nina's sister Seba, who had a bad hip and shuffled along slowly. As they were moved along the passage, the women had time to observe their captors. The soldiers were all in their twenties and thirties. Their uniforms were made of grey-green wool and were noticeably clean, as if they had just been issued. They called the commanding officer with the round metal spectacles 'captain'. There was also a junior officer, perhaps a lieutenant.

At the end of the corridor, a heavy metal gate was swung

open and behind that a door. The women were now guided past the gate, through the door and ordered to descend the flight of steep wooden stairs into the cellar. For Seba in particular, the climb down was slow and painful. Once they were all below, they heard a double clank: first the door being closed and then the metal gate, followed by the squeak of a key being turned. They were locked in.

It was cold, dark and frightening down in the cellar. Nina and her sister tried to comfort the five young women. After a few moments, as their eyes adjusted, they realized that there were others with them, perhaps as many as fifteen women, men and children. Apparently the *contadini* had come down here for safety after hearing the German soldiers arrive.

Nina was reassured to see that among them was the familiar face of Orando Fuschiotti, the *fattore*, or estate manager. Orando's parents had also been *contadini*; as such, farm life was in his blood. At high school he had mastered mathematics, allowing him to manage the estate's accounts and negotiate with local suppliers. He was also good with people. He liked to tell jokes; the *contadini* thought him extremely funny. Most of all, he was a man of integrity, someone you could trust. Which was why Robert had asked him to manage his estate.

Nina was fond of Orando. He was thirty-seven years old, short and plump, with a high forehead and dark brown hair. He was always friendly and polite to her. As was Erenia, his wife, who was standing next to him. Less outgoing than her husband and somewhat taller, she had sleepy oval eyes and wore her brown hair pinned back. It amused Nina that, to avoid showing Orando up, she didn't wear heels. The couple lived at the back of the villa, with only a single door separating their side from the Einstein family. With Orando and Erenia were their four-year-old daughter and nine-month-old son. Seeing Nina, the girl ran over for a hug. Over the past few weeks, there had been several times when Nina had comforted the child by playing the piano when artillery fire or exploding bombs were heard nearby.

Also down here in the cellar were the deputy estate manager, Pipone, and his family. Nina knew that it was with the tall, dark-haired and moustachioed Pipone that Robert had the tighter relationship. At forty-six years old, Pipone was nearer in age to her husband and had a passion for Il Focardo. They had another thing in common too: a shared appetite for self-improvement. Having received little formal education, Pipone had asked Robert to teach him how to read and write, and then, after the deputy *fattore* was proficient, the *padrone* – the owner of the estate – arranged for him to attend a diploma course on advanced farming practices. At night, Robert would come over to Pipone's pink-painted house, Casa Bella; there, overlooking a garden bursting with peas, tomatoes, cucumbers and peppers, the two men would sit, drinks in hand, discussing astronomy, culture and politics.

In an attempt to capture the essence of his friend Robert Einstein – and this was the word he used, 'friend' – Pipone liked to give two examples. Once, when visiting the orchard, Robert had picked up a peach lying on the ground. When Pipone urged him to take a fresh one from the tree, Robert demurred, saying that the best fruit should be sold at market and he did not want to detract from the *contadini*'s income. Pipone also thought it remarkable that Robert opened his private chapel to Pipone and the other *contadini*, even though he wasn't Christian.

For her part, Nina was closer to Pipone's wife, Giulia, who was comforting her three children a few steps away. Giulia came daily to the villa to assist Nina with the girls. She helped prepare the food, clean the villa and was responsible for the laundry. Sometimes the children would be at the villa. At others they would be at Pipone and Giulia's Casa Bella.

Nina knew that Orando, Pipone and the other *contadini* valued her family. That they considered the Einsteins to be far better than the estate's previous owners. She also knew that they loved her girls and the feelings were mutual. Most of all they respected Robert as the *padrone*. After seven sowings and seven harvests, they considered him to be fair and thoughtful. He had, they said, a *cuore d'oro*, a heart of gold.

Such were the relationships that were in place on 3 August 1944 when the women were pushed down the stairs and into the cellar. The new arrivals now told Orando, Pipone and the others what they had learned upstairs. There were at least seven German soldiers in the house. A captain was in charge. They were looking for Robert. Nina reassured everyone that this incident would soon be over. The Germans would leave the house, and then they would all laugh at this, the last unpleasantness of this long and terrible war.

But even as Nina spoke, the question of why the Germans were there remained. After all, weren't the soldiers themselves in danger? Just the night before, she and the others had heard on the radio that the Allies would shortly arrive in the area. Surely it would be foolish for the German soldiers to wait around.

Which raised the question: how had the Germans found them in the first place? The Einstein villa was located at the end of a long lane. Not somewhere you would come to unless you were expressly looking for it. Someone must have betrayed them. But who? The *contadini* were loyal, as were the priest and their neighbours. But even if they were betrayed by an Italian, this didn't explain why the German soldiers had stormed into the villa. Given that the Allied forces were so close, they should be either defending their positions or retreating. This couldn't be part of some general rounding up of Jews. That had stopped months ago, as the Germans had turned their attention to the fast-approaching enemy. It had to be something more targeted, something related to this family in particular. As Nina pondered this, she realized with mounting concern the seriousness of their predicament.

# 5. Il Focardo, 1938

For years now, Nina and Robert had agreed that they would take a broad-minded approach when it came to their girls' religion. Nina had grown up in the Protestant Waldensian community and she and her husband would encourage their daughters Luce and Cici to follow suit. Meanwhile, they would continue to raise Lorenza and Paola as Catholics, following their father Corrado's wish. It was left to Pipone's wife Giulia to instruct them about Catholic rituals, the Virgin Mary, the saints and the martyrs. As for Robert, while he was open about his family's Jewish roots, he remained both a committed atheist and also tolerant towards all faiths. Indeed, it gave him pleasure to offer the villa's chapel to the local community. Regardless of these personal beliefs and habits, however, the entire family was considered by most of the local community to be Jewish.

Before the Second World War, there were 44,500 Italian Jews living in Italy. There were, in addition, around 10,000 non-Italian Jews resident in the country. The largest concentration of Jews was in Rome, but sizeable populations also lived in Bologna, Livorno, Milan, Turin and Venice. As for

Florence, it was home to more than 3,000 Jews, around 1 per cent of the city's population. There had been Jews living in Italy since Roman times, nevertheless hatred of Jews was buried deep within the nation's psyche. Over the centuries, various popes, bishops, priests and others in power had blamed the Jews for the killing of Jesus Christ (even though the Bible reported it was the Romans who killed him), leading to waves of pogroms, segregation and persecution. Yet, by the start of the twentieth century, it was possible for Jews to reach the highest positions in Italy; indeed, in the early 1900s, two of the country's prime ministers were Jewish and a third was of Jewish descent.

When Mussolini had taken power in 1922, Robert would have been pleased, like most businesspeople, by the National Fascist Party's focus on enterprise and government investment. As for being a Jew, he would have remained unconcerned, since Mussolini was no more antisemitic than the wider society at that time. Indeed, Mussolini had attracted sizeable Jewish support. Between October 1928 and October 1933, just over 10 per cent of the total Jewish population joined the National Fascist Party, which was roughly proportionate to non-Jewish party membership. Jews also held top posts in Mussolini's government. His undersecretary for the interior, Aldo Finzi, for instance, was a Jew. As were Guido Jung (finance minister), Dante Almansi (deputy chief of police) and Maurizio Rava (governor of Libya). In addition, Margherita Sarffati, Il Duce's long-time mistress, was brought up Jewish. This did not stop Mussolini from publicly expressing tenets of antisemitic ideology. On 4 June 1919, for instance, he wrote an article in *Il Popolo d'Italia* that stated 'World finance is in the hands of the Jews. Whoever owns the people's vaults controls their politics. Behind the puppets of Paris, there are the Rothschilds, the Warburgs, the Schyffs, the Guggenheims, who have the same blood as the rulers of Petrograd and Budapest.'

Mussolini's ill will towards the Italian-Jewish population intensified with Adolf Hitler's visit to Florence in May 1938. Desperate to impress his visitor, the Italian leader spent vast amounts of money cleaning up the buildings, the parks and the streets. He then gave the Führer a no-holds-barred guided tour of the city. Travelling in a twenty-car motorcade, they were cheered on by tens of thousands of flag-waving Italians, right arms raised to the sky in the fascist salute. Mussolini escorted his guest to the Piazzale Michelangelo Park high above the city, where Hitler was said to have been impressed by its magnificent view, and to the basilica of Santa Croce, home to memorials of many of the nation's heroes: Dante Alighieri, Niccolò Machiavelli, Leonardo da Vinci, Galileo Galilei and Guglielmo Marconi. Given that the Einstein family's apartment on Corso dei Tintori was just 200 feet from Santa Croce and that the university term was still in session, Luce undoubtedly saw the cavalcade as it passed by. Certainly she and the rest of the family would have been aware of the details of Hitler's visit, as it was extensively covered in the newspapers.

Six months later, on 11 November 1938, and much to the shock of Robert Einstein and the rest of his family, Mussolini announced the introduction of his Racial Laws. Jewish children were now forbidden to attend public schools and universities. Jews who had become Italian nationals after 1919 were stripped of their citizenship. Jews could no longer work in banks, insurance companies or local government.

They could not marry non-Jews, nor could they manage factories related to military production, own more than 125 acres of land, serve in the army or be members of the Fascist Party. Once the legislation had been approved by parliament, King Vittorio Emanuele III signed it into law.

The implications for the Einstein family were varied. Robert was stripped of his Italian citizenship, even though Italy had been his home since the 1890s. Luce and Cici also lost their citizenship, despite their Christian beliefs and the tradition that Jewish identity was passed down from the mother. As for Nina, she retained her citizenship as she was born in Italy and was a practising Christian. Yet, at least for now, the changes had little practical impact on the family. Robert was able to keep control of Il Focardo, even though it exceeded the 125-acre limit, and his professional status as an engineer remained unchecked. Luce and Cici were able to continue with their university and high school studies. But though the Racial Laws were not consistently enforced, the sense of state menace was real. So much so that Luce wrote on her annual University of Florence enrolment form that she was 'di razza Ariana', or 'of Aryan race'. The following year, she went further and said she was an 'Italian national, Aryan race'. The authorities, however, were aware of Luce's background. A handwritten note in her university file recorded that she was an 'Israelita', or a Jew.

Quite a few of the Jews in Florence were unwilling to take the risk of waiting to see what happened next. One of these was Robert's cousin Maja. A few months after the enactment of the Racial Laws, she decided to leave Florence and purchased a boat ticket to the USA. Her husband Paul would return to Switzerland. Robert stayed in touch with his two cousins who, with Maja's arrival in America in February 1939, were now both safely ensconced on the other side of the Atlantic. On Albert's sixtieth birthday, on 14 March that year, he sent a telegram: '*Infiniti auguri e ricordi Roberto*', or 'Infinite good wishes and memories Robert'.

It was Robert's sincere hope that the anti-Jewish laws in Florence would not get any worse. After all, calamity had happened here before.

In 1567, after years of relative tolerance and harmony, the second Duke of Florence, Cosimo I de' Medici, announced a law for the Jews living in Tuscany: from that point forward, Jewish men would have to wear a mark of yellow cloth on their tunics and Jewish women would have to wear a yellow sleeve. Three years later, on 26 September 1570, Cosimo I issued a further law, entitled the Decree and General Edict on the Jews. From this point, Jews were no longer allowed to own real estate, employ Christian servants, socialize with Christians, work on Christian holidays or provide medical care to Christians. In addition, all the Jews in Tuscany (apart from Livorno and Pisa) would immediately have to relocate into a single ghetto in Florence.

The site selected for this ghetto was the Mercato Vecchio (Old Market), situated less than 200 yards from the city's cathedral of Santa Maria del Fiore (commonly referred to by Florentines as 'Il Duomo'), whose vast red-brick dome towered over the streets far below. Uniquely among the ghettos then in existence – such as the one in Venice (established in 1516, the first in the world) and the one in Rome (established in 1555) – the enforced segregation in Florence would be a profit-making exercise, for Cosimo would own the buildings and the Jews would have to pay him rent for their accommodation. By the year's end, more than 700 Jews were crammed into the enclosure.

The ghetto was approximately 200 yards wide and fifty yards long. It contained around 40 four- and five-storey buildings, two synagogues, two public squares, a public well, a ritual bath (*mikveh*) and a maze of paths, vaulted alleyways and rambling staircases. Access to the outside city was only possible through two large gates that were locked at sunset.

Trade inside the ghetto was restricted. Permitted occupations included kosher butchers, bakers and the selling of second-hand clothes (*strazzaria*). The Jews were no longer allowed to run their own banks. Money-lending, which had long been at the centre of Jewish business in Tuscany, was now severely limited. As the decades progressed, the ghetto became increasingly crowded, impoverished, fetid and foul-smelling.

In 1705, after more than a century of the ghetto's existence, the then Grand Duke of Tuscany, Cosimo III, decreed that the ghetto would be enlarged and that any Jews who had managed to live outside it would be forced back inside. By 1715, the New Ghetto (as it was called) was completed next to the old structure, with some of the buildings seven storeys tall. There were now more than 1,600 Jews incarcerated behind the high stone walls.

By the time of Italy's unification in 1870, the ghetto had been abandoned; then, as part of Florence's period of *Risanamento* (redevelopment), it was torn down between 1892 and 1895 and replaced by a large square named after the king: Piazza Vittorio Emanuele II (today, Piazza della Repubblica). On one side, an enormous arch was erected, and on its façade was written the legend: 'The ancient city centre, from centuries of squalor, to new life restored'. No mention was made of the Jews who had been forced to live on this exact spot for more than 250 years. And it was here, on this same square, that Mussolini had thrown a mass rally in honour of his guest, Adolf Hitler, on 9 May 1938.

For the Jews of Florence, the fact that celebrations for the Nazi leader took place on the site of the ghetto was not only a reminder of past trauma, it also served as a stark warning that their persecution could easily be repeated.

# 6. Florence, 1943

At 6 p.m. on 10 June 1940, Benito Mussolini walked out on to the balcony of the Palazzo Venezia in Rome. He was dressed in a military jacket and trousers, with a wide belt across his stomach and a peaked cap on his head. In front him, in the square below, stood tens of thousands of supporters, waving flags and chanting 'Il Duce, Il Duce, Il Duce'. Mussolini began his speech: 'Fighters of land, sea and air! Black shirts of the revolution and legions! Men and women of Italy, the empire and the kingdom of Albania! Listen! An hour marked by destiny strikes in the sky of our homeland.' These words were greeted with raucous cheers. Mussolini then told the crowd that he had declared war against Britain, France and their allies. Italy would be joining his great ally, Adolf Hitler. The crowd responded with even louder approval. 'We shall win!' Mussolini roared. 'We shall finally provide a long period of peace and justice to Italy, to Europe, and the world. Italian people! Run to your arms, and show your tenacity, your courage and your valour!'

In the following days, it was announced that men of fighting age must immediately join the army. For his part, Robert was too old to enlist and so he remained at Il Focardo to manage the estate. Each night, he and the rest of the family gathered around the radiogram in the Sala Rossa to listen to the news. There, surrounded by family treasures, including Nina's beloved grand piano and an oil painting of Robert's cousin Albert above the fireplace, they tracked the progress of the war as it spread across Europe and then beyond. As the months and years progressed, they saw the impact of the hostilities in their daily lives. Prices of food and farm materials climbed steeply. There were fewer and fewer young men available to work in the vineyards and orchards. And when they travelled into Florence, the Einsteins noticed that there were increasing numbers of Jews in the city, apparently having concluded that Italy was a relative haven compared to France, Belgium and Czechoslovakia. For even though Mussolini had enacted his Racial Laws, they continued to be rarely enforced and were therefore considered by the refugees to pose less of a risk than the situation back in their home countries.

This sense of relative safety, however, was not to last. During the summer and early autumn of 1943, a series of events unfolded, one following inexorably on to the next, leading to a dramatic shift in the circumstances for Robert Einstein and the tens of thousands of Jews still living in Italy. On 10 July, the Allied forces landed in Sicily and prepared to attack the Italian mainland. Two weeks later, sensing defeat, the Grand Fascist Council passed a motion of no confidence in prime minister Benito Mussolini. The following day, 25 July, King Vittorio Emanuele III dismissed Mussolini and had him arrested. Fascist rule appeared to be over.

Then, on 31 August 1943, the Allies dropped more than 400 tons of bombs on Pisa. It was the heaviest aerial attack so far on Italy. The city was chosen as a target because it lay at the heart of the country's rail network. At least 950 civilians were killed. Living in Pisa at this time was Nina's sister Ada, along with her husband and two children. None of them was injured in the air raid; but in the hours that followed, Ada decided they must immediately evacuate the children. She sent her son Eugenio, who was ill with pneumonia, to a hospital in Sondrio in northern Italy, where he could be treated. And her daughter Anna Maria was despatched to the girl's godparents Nina and Robert Einstein at Il Focardo.

On 8 September, the new prime minister, Pietro Badoglio, announced that the king had signed an armistice with the Allies. At the news, the church bells in the towns and villages near Il Focardo – Le Corti, Troghi, San Donato in Collina and Rignano sull'Arno – rang out in celebration. Hearing the happy tolling, the *contadini* ran out of their homes, shouting with joy. But German forces were already sweeping into northern Italy. This prompted the king and most of the rest of the government to abandon Rome and flee to safety in southern Italy, which was controlled by the Allies. Just three days later, at 9 a.m. on 11 September, German tanks, assault guns, ammunition wagons, armoured cars and other vehicles were seen rumbling along the main road near Il Focardo. By lunchtime, they had occupied Florence. The following day, 12 September, Mussolini escaped prison in an audacious raid carried out by German paratroopers and SS commandos. He was transported to Berlin for a meeting with Hitler and then on to northern Italy, where, on 18 September, he announced the creation of the new Italian Social Republic, which he would head. With German soldiers walking the streets of Florence, and Mussolini back in power, Robert and Nina had decided it was no longer safe to spend time at their apartment in the city.

Their timing was fortuitous. On 16 October, less than three weeks after moving full-time to their home at Il Focardo, they heard that over a thousand Jews had been subject to a *razzia*, or 'raid', in Rome. These men, women and children were put on a train and deported to Eastern Europe. Three weeks later, on 5 and 6 November, Italian police and paramilitary gangs rounded up hundreds of Jews in Florence and the Tuscan towns of Siena and Montecatini. Many of them were taken to Villa La Selva, a large house less than fifteen minutes' drive from Il Focardo. They too were soon loaded on to trains to the East.

Then word of another local *razzia* reached Nina and Robert. At 3 a.m. on 27 November 1943, a group of around thirty armed men arrived at the Carmelite convent on Piazza del Carmine in Florence. The building was located twenty steps from the Brancacci Chapel, home to the world-renowned frescoes painted by the Renaissance masters Masaccio and Masolino. Half the raiding party were German soldiers, the rest were Italian fascists. At that moment, there were as many as fifty Jewish women and children hiding inside the convent. One of these was Wanda Pacifici, the wife of the Rabbi of Genoa. Hearing a warning bell from the night porter, the nuns remained in their rooms, as they had been instructed if a raid was to take place. Meanwhile, the intruders cut the telephone lines and searched the premises for Jews. When they found them, they herded them into a meeting room on the convent's ground floor. Somehow, during these chaotic moments, between twelve and twenty Jews managed to avoid capture. One hid under a bed, a second pretended to be a nun, while a third, a baby boy, was surreptitiously handed to a nun who agreed to take care of him.

After arriving in the meeting room, the hostages were told to hand over their jewellery, money and anything of value. If they refused, they were told, they would be shot. They were then individually questioned. Their papers were checked and rechecked. They underwent repeated medical examinations. Many were subject to sexual violence. A few were able to persuade their captors that they were not in sufficient health to be deported. One proved that she had appendicitis and another that she suffered from psychological ailments. The women and girls were held for four long days. Finally, on 1 December, the armed men took twenty-six women and girls and left the convent by the back exit on Via del Leone. The prisoners were transported to a camp near Verona before being sent on to Auschwitz. Later, it was learned that only one person survived. It was one of the worst attacks on Jews in Tuscany.

If such individual actions were not proof enough that awful things were taking place in Italy, what happened next would remove any doubt. On the same day that the Jewish women were transported from the Carmelite convent in Florence, the minister of the interior Buffarini Guidi appeared on national radio and announced a set of instructions for police officers across the country to arrest all Jews and put them in special detention camps:

The following Police Order Number 5 is hereby communicated for immediate execution, to be applied throughout the entire nation:

   1. All Jews who live in the national territory, no matter their nationality, must be sent to concentration

camps. All their property, both movable and immovable, must immediately be seized pending confiscation in the interests of the Italian Social Republic, which will use it for the benefit of the destitute left behind by enemy air raids.

2. All those born in mixed marriages who were recognized as belonging to the Aryan race in Italy's Racial Laws must be subject to special vigilance by police organizations.

In the meantime, the Jews are to be moved to provincial concentration camps while waiting to be assembled in special concentration camps.

Nina and Robert listened in horror as Police Order Number 5 was read out on the radio. In the weeks that followed, the Einsteins learned of other Jews being rounded up in Florence, as well as in the Tuscan towns of Prato and Arezzo. It was then, in early December 1943, that they seriously discussed fleeing Italy. They had two options. The first was to travel south until they reached territory controlled by the Americans. But to do so they would have to find a way through hundreds of thousands of German and Italian soldiers and then cross an active conflict zone beset by intense fighting between the Allies and Nazis. Perhaps a better option would be to travel north into Switzerland. But this would mean travelling through territory controlled by further German divisions and their Italian colleagues. And once they tried to cross the Swiss border, they might be turned back. It was an agonizing choice.

*

One family which had faced a similar situation was that of Miriam Cividalli Canarutto. Miriam was seven years old when the fascist government enacted the Racial Laws. As a result, her father lost his job as a train engineer in Florence, and she and her sisters had to move to a Jewish-only school. Her uncle had been arrested as an anti-fascist organizer the day after war had been declared, and deported to a camp. They did not see him again. For the next two years, the family moved back and forth between Florence and Ferrara, 120 miles to the north, where Miriam's maternal grandmother Isa lived.

After the Nazis occupied Florence in September 1943, Miriam's father purchased a small estate near Pisa. The farmers who worked on the estate knew the family was Jewish but protected them. Later that autumn, the local German commander asked for a list of all the Jews in the area. Her father's *fattore* told him it was time to hide. Over the next few months, they moved from one house to the next. 'We were very grateful,' Miriam later recalled, 'but I wish they had given us a little more to eat. Some hot milk, perhaps!' At one point Miriam's mother Vanda became ill. In hospital, she was told she had cancer. The doctors said they were obliged to inform the authorities that she was a Jewish patient, but in the end, after pressure from the local community, they did not report her. After a few weeks, Vanda returned home, but she remained frail and in pain.

In March 1944, one of the *contadini* working for Miriam's father told him that the family was in imminent danger. Somehow they had become known to the Germans, probably betrayed by an Italian. They must flee. He took them by car to Santa Maria Novella railway station in Florence. It was a huge risk, as many knew Miriam's father from the time he had worked there before the war, but amazingly nobody reported them. The family – Miriam, her parents, three sisters and grandmother – travelled north by train through Nazi-occupied Italy, arriving a day later at the Swiss border. To cross into Switzerland, the remainder of the journey had to be done on foot. It was an extremely hazardous journey over the cold and foggy mountains, and the family made use of a guide. Vanda was still weak from her cancer and Isa was a slow mover. At one point the guide said that they must split up. He told Vanda and Isa to return to Italy while the rest would push on to Switzerland. Miriam was terrified. 'Don't worry,' her grandmother reassured. 'Please take care of my mother,' Miriam pleaded. 'I will,' Isa replied.

A few hours later, Miriam, her father and sisters made it over the border. As for Isa and Vanda, they decided to ignore the guide's command and continue on towards Switzerland. Not long after, they heard German voices. Vanda hid behind some trees but Isa was spotted by the soldiers. 'Who are you with?' they asked her. 'I am alone,' Miriam's grandmother replied. After a few more minutes, the Germans took Isa away. Remarkably, Vanda went undiscovered and made it by herself across the border. Many years later, they learned that Isa (whose full name was Isa Ascoli, née Magrini) was deported to Auschwitz, where she was murdered.

In the end, Robert and Nina Einstein had made a different choice to Miriam's parents. Rather than trying to escape to Switzerland, they had stayed in the villa; then, when the threat was imminent, Robert had gone into hiding in the woods nearby. Two families, two different situations, two different outcomes.

# 7. Il Focardo, 1944

Nina, Seba and the five girls were still down in the cellar of the villa Il Focardo. The mood was tense. They could hear everything that was going on upstairs through the gaps in the wooden floorboards. First, came the sound of boots going back and forth as the soldiers searched the house. Doors and drawers were being opened and closed. Furniture was being dragged around. After an hour or so, the tempo settled down. There was less moving about. At one point it sounded like some of the Germans were engaged in a prolonged game of ping-pong. At another, an accordion was heard and then the piano. At first, the children had been amused by these strange sounds but, as they had become increasingly hungry and thirsty, they had started to whine.

Later, as the afternoon approached, it sounded like a party was under way above them. Voices grew louder, wild. There was raucous laughter, the smashing of glass and then the shooting of guns in the air. With each shot, the group in the cellar flinched. The adults tried to comfort the children. How long could this go on?

There was now an eerie calm. Occasionally, it was possible

to hear muted voices, a discussion maybe, an order being given. But for the most part, silence. This gave Nina time to think. The more she thought about it, the more she realized that the day's events were unusual. In Florence, Pisa and Rome, the Jews had been rounded up, put on trains and sent away. What was happening here at Il Focardo was different, more personal. They were not being targeted simply because they were Jewish. The soldiers had arrived specifically looking for Robert Einstein.

There was one more thing that was strange. When, earlier that morning, she had walked through the broken doors and into the hallway, the commander had mentioned Albert Einstein. Why was he asking about Robert's cousin, who they hadn't seen for more than a decade, and who was more than 4,000 miles away in the USA?

# 8. Princeton, New Jersey, 1944

By the time the German soldiers burst through the doors of Il Focardo, Albert Einstein had been one of the world's most famous people for more than two decades. He had first come to the attention of his scientific peers in 1905 when, while working as a clerk for the Swiss patent office, he had published his Special Theory of Relativity. Ten years later, he published his General Theory of Relativity. These two theories would revolutionize mathematics and astrophysics, and would lead the way to nuclear energy, the study of black holes, and the development of computer chips and lasers, to name just a few. And yet, at the time, his findings attracted limited academic attention.

It was only in 1919 that Albert Einstein's fame grew to stratospheric proportions. For this was when a British scientist sent a team to an island off the west coast of Africa and another to Brazil to observe a total solar eclipse, in the process confirming Albert's prediction that starlight was indeed deflected by the sun's gravitational field. Albert was now headline news, not only in Europe, but around the world. His celebrity was heightened still further when, in 1922, he won the Nobel Prize for Physics. This time it was for his discovery of the law of the photoelectric effect, which described the impact of electromagnetic radiation, such as light, when it hits a material, and was a contribution to the development of quantum physics.

In the early 1930s, with the rise of Adolf Hitler in Germany, Albert was increasingly targeted in the press by the Nazis and their supporters. They wanted to destroy him. Not only was he the country's most famous Jew, he was also an outspoken pacifist, which was anathema to the so-called Third Reich. In 1933, a booklet was published in Germany entitled *Juden sehen Dich an*, or *Jews Are Watching You*. Sanctioned by Nazi propaganda chief Josef Goebbels, the booklet contained the biographies of some of Germany's well-known Jews, including two pages and two photographs about Albert Einstein. After each name was printed the word *Ungehängt*, or 'Not yet hanged'. This was no idle threat. On 30 August 1933, the German-Jewish philosopher Theodor Lessing, another of those included in the list, was shot dead by two Nazis at his apartment in Marienbad, Czechoslovakia (today Mariánské Lázně in the Czech Republic). This was the first Nazi political assassination to take place beyond Germany's borders. The following day, Lessing's murder was widely reported around the world, including by the *New York Times*, which carried the story on its front page, under the headline 'Lessing, German Refugee, Slain in Prague; Attacks on Others Abroad Are Feared'.

If that was not clear enough, it was widely circulated in the media that Albert Einstein was now an assassination target. The story spread across Europe. In London, for instance, on 7 September 1933, the *Daily Herald* ran the headline 'Price Placed on Einstein's Head' across the entire top of its front page. Then, beneath an advertisement for alcohol ('If you haven't tasted Gordon's Lemon or Orange Gin you don't know what you're missing!'), the paper reported that a 'notorious organisation of Nazi killers' had placed Professor Einstein on its 'death-list' and had 'put a price on his head'. The story said that, in return for the murder of Albert Einstein, the German government was offering £1,000, or around £430,000 in today's money.

At the time of all this news coverage, Albert and his wife Elsa were in Belgium. When a journalist from *Le Soir* asked him for a response, he said, 'I do not fear danger.' However, the paper reported that his 'wife was greatly distressed' and that he 'thought it wise to put his affairs in order'. The next day, 9 September, Albert wrote to a

*Daily Herald*, 7 September 1933.

friend, saying that they would be immediately leaving Belgium because of the threat. Shortly after, he arrived in Norfolk, England, where he was photographed under armed guard. A month later, Albert and his wife took a boat to the USA, landing on 17 October 1933. In the time since Albert left Germany, the Nazi venom towards him had, if anything, grown more intense. They denounced his theories as 'Jewish' and 'un-German', burned his books in the street, seized his bank account, searched his summer residence for arms and stripped him of his German citizenship. He was, according to many accounts, the Nazi regime's enemy number one. His survival, the Nazi regime believed, posed a direct threat to the Third Reich. Put at its simplest, killing Einstein would reinforce the message to the German public that the Nazis' opponents (symbolized by the Jews) were weak and that Hitler and his colleagues were strong.

Eight years later, on 7 December 1941, Albert Einstein was living in Princeton, New Jersey, when Japan bombed Pearl Harbor. Until this point, he had been known as one of the world's leading pacifists, but now he changed his position. He first became a US citizen and then told the *New York Times*, 'We must strike hard and leave the breaking to the other sides,' adding: 'I believe the war will come out well for the democracies, but it will be costly and we'll need big sacrifices.' It was a somewhat convoluted statement but interpreted widely as being pro-war and anti-Nazi.

Albert did not stop at public proclamations. On 24 June 1943, the US Navy announced that the famous scientist had agreed to work for them 'on several mathematical physical problems in ordnance research'. Then, on 2 February 1944, it was reported by the *New York Times* and other papers that Albert Einstein had donated the manuscript of his ground-breaking theory of relativity to the US government's fourth war loan drive. The proceeds of the $6.5 million sale, it was promised, would be used to build weapons against Germany. News of all this extremely public anti-Nazi activity would have made its way back to Berlin.

Albert also engaged with his adopted country's war effort in less public ways. On 2 August 1939, with the help of the physicist Leo Szilard, he wrote a letter to President Roosevelt informing him that he believed a 'nuclear chain reaction in a large mass of uranium' might become possible and consequently 'that extremely power-ful bombs of a new type may thus be constructed'. The letter concluded with him alerting the president to the possibility that Germany was already working on its own version of the bomb. To his friends, Albert would say that it was the existential fear that Hitler might develop such an ultimate weapon that drove him to pursue this technology on America's behalf. A few weeks later, Albert received a response from the president that he had already convened a board 'to thoroughly investigate the possibilities of your suggestion regarding the element of uranium'. This board led directly to the formation of the Manhattan Project and the development of the atomic bomb.

While it is not known how much the German government knew about Albert's war efforts, given that the Manhattan Project was shrouded in the highest secrecy, there were leaks, particularly to the Soviets. And Hitler's regime certainly knew that he was helping the US military. As such, by the summer of 1944, Albert Einstein was, if anything, considered by the Nazi regime to be even more of an enemy than in 1933. They wanted him assassinated. The threat was still very real. But the world's most famous physicist was living in the USA, well beyond their reach.

The same was not true for his cousin, who lived in German-occupied Italy.

# 9. Il Focardo, 1944

When the German commander arrived at Il Focardo on 3 August 1944, he was extremely frustrated not to find Robert at home. One person who knew Robert's location was Nello Dino.

Nello was seventeen years old and worked as a bookkeeper's assistant on the neighbouring estate of Torre a Cona. Many of his friends had joined the partisans, but his father thought him too young to be fighting the Nazis and had insisted that he take this job. Soon after his arrival at Torre a Cona, a German unit had requisitioned the estate, forcing Nello to move into one of the remote farmhouses. It was a small shack, about 200 yards from the villa Il Focardo. Also staying there was the Torre a Cona *fattore*, along with a doctor named Massart. One night, worried that the Germans would begin stealing the livestock, Nello made contact with some partisans who were hiding in the nearby wood and together, under the cover of darkness, they moved all the cattle to safety. In the morning, he informed his boss, who gave his approval, saying, 'If the partisans eat the calves, at least they will have been eaten by Italians.'

It was during this visit to the woods that Nello first encountered Robert Einstein. They met again when Robert visited the *fattore*'s farmhouse. In one of their early conversations, Robert shared how much he missed his family. The following evening, Nello told Dr Massart that he was sorry for Robert and his family. 'I felt again at that moment, like the night before, so much pity for those people,' Nello later recalled. 'I felt ashamed to be Italian because many Italians had in the past persecuted and were still persecuting the Jews.'

Then, on 2 August – the day before the German unit took over the villa Il Focardo – Nello had seen Robert again in the woods. He was with a large group of partisans who, sensing that the Germans would be soon on the run, were readying for battle. The leader of this group was called *Potente*, or 'mighty one'. He happened to know Robert's daughter Luce as they both studied medicine at Florence University. Nello recalled *Potente* counselling Robert, 'Get your women out of the villa because it's too risky to remain there. A few more days and the British will be here.' But Robert said he would stick to his plan. With the fighting so close, where was it safe to go?

From their vantage point on the hill, Nello, Robert and the partisans could see the main road below. News of the British and American approach had reached the valley. Over the next few hours, they observed German forces hurrying north, by truck, car, motorcycle and on foot. Early the following morning, before Nina arrived for her meeting with Robert, the partisans were gone. They had received orders to move out: first up to the hilltop village of San Donato in Collina, then by track through the woods that covered the hill of Montisoni, down to the small town of Antella, where they were to proceed with caution to Bagno a Ripoli and then on to the outskirts of Florence. 'We took shelter in the thickest woods,' Nello later remembered, 'regretting that we were left alone, without the protection of the partisans.'

It was within this context of chaos and diminished security that Robert met Nina at the edge of the woods and then, following the loud sounds of crashing, watched as she ran back towards Il Focardo.

Now, twelve hours later, it was too dark to see what was going on at the villa. It had been agreed with Nina that he would stay hidden, no matter what, but being stuck here was immensely frustrating. What was happening at the villa? he must have wondered. Was everything all right?

# 10. Il Focardo, 1944

An entire working day had gone by since Nina, Seba and the five girls had been forced into the cellar with the *contadini*. From their watches they knew it must be past sunset. There was no sense that their ordeal would be over any time soon. The parents held their children close. The minutes ticked by achingly slowly, permeated with fear.

Then they heard a commotion from above. The metal gate was unlocked and then the door behind was pushed open. Light poured into the cellar. Heavy boots thudded down the stairs.

'*Raus!*' a soldier barked at them. '*Raus! Raus!*' A machine gun was waving at them dangerously. 'Upstairs! Everyone upstairs!'

As soon as they climbed up the cellar stairs, Nina and the other captives were bustled along the corridor and into the front hallway. 'Who are the Einstein family members?' a German soldier shouted. 'Say your names.' One by one they did as they were told. They were now separated into two groups. Nina and her two daughters, along with her sister Seba and the three nieces were jostled upstairs to the first floor. There they were marched along a landing and into a small back bedroom. One of the women asked what the Germans wanted from them. 'You are accused of espionage,' a soldier replied. 'Now we will see.' With a click, a soldier locked the bedroom door behind them. Once again they were being held captive.

Meanwhile, the second group, including Orando and Pipone and their families, were pushed outside and told to leave the villa. As soon as they were in the driveway, Orando told the other *contadini* to hurry home. They moved off, heading towards their anxious families, who had not seen them all day. Orando and Pipone escorted their wives and children to Casa Bella and then, after saying a quick goodbye, hurried along the track towards the woods. They wanted to let Robert know what was happening at the villa.

By now it was 8 p.m. and darkness was falling. In the distance, they could hear the sounds of bombs exploding over Florence and the retort of anti-aircraft fire. The night was crisp and thankfully fresh. After the day's brutal heat, it felt like the temperature was dropping with every step they took.

Ten minutes after leaving Casa Bella, Orando and Pipone found their boss, who was with Nello in the woods. They quickly explained what they had seen at the villa. The Germans had taken over the place, pushed everyone into the cellar, where they had remained all day until Orando, Pipone and the *contadini* had been released just minutes ago. Last they had seen, Nina, Seba and the five young women were being pushed from the hallway up the stairs towards the bedrooms on the first floor. As Orando would later testify, he knew that Robert was 'wanted as a member of the Jewish race', which was why he had 'rushed into the woods to warn his boss of his family's imprisonment'. As to what would happen next, he had no idea, but the Germans' aggressive behaviour up to that point was deeply concerning.

Hearing the news, Robert grew agitated, asking frantic questions. Were his wife and daughters all right? How about Seba and the nieces? As he paced back and forth his voice rose, becoming increasingly desperate. Nello and the others worried that he might give their position away to the Germans. They tried to keep him calm, reassuring him that everything was going to be fine, but he persisted. He had to join his family, he said, he must help them. How could he just stay in the woods while his family was in danger? But Orando, Pipone and Nello told him this would be a grave mistake. As for a rescue effort, there were too many German soldiers at the villa. They had no weapons of their own. It would be futile. There was no guarantee that he could help the others and he would be putting all their lives at risk. Finally, after they went back and forth a few more times, he relented. For now, at least, Robert agreed to remain hidden in the woods.

And all the while, in the direction of Florence, the orange, yellow and gold streaks of artillery fire and aerial bombardment could be seen blistering the night sky. The liberation was in full swing.

Over the previous eleven months, the Allies had made significant headway in their Italian campaign. Having first landed on 9 September 1943 at Salerno, southeast of Naples, they had pushed north up the spine of Italy, taking town after town. Naples had fallen. Then, following a gruelling battle, Monte Cassino. And finally, in June 1944, Rome. The Allied forces were under the command of Lieutenant General Mark Clark, who at forty-eight years of age was the youngest three star general in the US Army. His forces comprised five American divisions and three British divisions. Operating alongside was the British Eighth Army, under Lieutenant General Oliver Leese, including soldiers from New Zealand, India, Canada and South Africa.

In response to these Allied territorial gains in the south, the Germans had made a tactical decision to withdraw. As part of this effort, Field Marshal Albert Kesselring had built a 200-mile long system of fortifications north of Florence, from the Mediterranean Sea in the west to the Adriatic coast in the east. This so-called Gothic Line comprised more than 2,000 machine-gun nests, bunkers and observation posts, which were constructed between the peaks of the Apennine mountains. It was towards this line of defence, in the first week of August 1944, that the Germans were retreating just as the Allies were on the brink of taking Florence and its surrounding area.

Back at the villa, Nina, her sister Seba and the five young women were still being held in the bedroom upstairs. Unlike the dark cellar at least it had a window and, although it was now twilight, it was possible to discern shapes amidst the shadows.

With them in the room was a young German soldier. He was not much older than Anna Maria, Cici, Lorenza and Paola, and was yet to grow into his adult body; he looked little more than a boy. He had short blond hair and blue eyes and stood by the door guarding the exit. He held a machine gun with little confidence and seemed unlikely to use it. Sitting on the single bed with nothing to do but wait, Nina peppered him with questions. When could they get something to drink or eat? Why were they being held? When would they be set free? But he didn't know anything. He had been told to keep watch and not let them out of the room. He spoke quietly, and the women could sense that he felt as uncomfortable as they were, though it was he who was blocking the door.

After about an hour, they heard the sound of approaching steps. The door was opened, the young soldier stood aside, and the commanding officer walked in. Again he asked Nina for her husband's location. Thinking it might ease the situation, Nina showed him her identity documents. These proved, she said, that she was of Italian nationality and Christian. Like him, she was an Aryan. The German officer didn't seem to care. He was looking for the Jew Robert Einstein. A few moments later he left the room.

For several minutes the captives were gripped by an incredible unease, unsure what would happen next. Now that the *contadini* had left, the precariousness of their situation could no longer be denied. Lorenza and one of the other young women started to cry. 'We were worried,' she later said, 'we were scared.' Outside the room there was silence. Then, there was a loud crash, followed by another, and another. 'From the bedroom we could hear a great uproar,' Seba recalled. 'There was a tremendous ruckus of breaking furniture and breaking glasses and plates.' They didn't understand the reason for the German soldiers' wanton destruction.

Paola looked desperately at Nina. Her aunt knew what that meant. Her niece really needed to pee. She gave Paola a questioning glance. 'I can't wait,' the girl said quietly. Nina worked up the courage and asked the young guard if her niece could go to the toilet. She had not been all day. The soldier called for one of his colleagues. This man arrived a few moments later and, pointing a gun at her back, escorted Paola to the bathroom. A few minutes later, she was back.

The rampage did not stop. There was the sound of shattering lamps and mirrors, crystal vases and goblets being smashed one by one, heavy objects being hurled and boots stomping up and down the stairs. The walls shook with the physical impact. Then, there was the low rumbling cacophony of wood and strings being assaulted. 'The piano,' cried Luce. This was followed by an even more terrible sound. Ali, their dog, was yelping horribly. It sounded like someone had kicked him hard. 'They're hurting Ali!' Paola cried, running for the door, but the young soldier barred her way. 'Mama,' said Cici, 'they're hurting Ali.' Tears slid down her face. 'Don't cry,' said Luce kindly. Paola started hitting the guard with her fists. 'Let me out!' she screamed. 'Let me out!'

It was at this point that a lieutenant opened the door. He told them all to come downstairs; the captain wanted to speak with them. As they walked through the vestibule at the bottom of the stairs they noticed its white walls were covered with graffiti. A few steps further forward and they arrived in the Sala Rossa. The power was off but the room was well lit by candles. They were shocked by what they saw. Nina's beloved piano was in pieces. The oil painting of Albert Einstein had been sliced by a knife. The family's radiogram was upended. The girls' toys were scattered all over the floor, mixed with broken pieces of furniture and glass, and books with their covers torn off. A yellow bear had been jammed on to the end of a broomstick and used as a target. One of the Germans was wearing Luce's scarf.

Around the room, half a dozen soldiers lounged on the furniture that was still intact. Among them was the captain, sitting behind a small table to the left of the dismembered piano. He spoke to them first in German, which the children could not understand, and then in French, which they could. He smiled as he spoke, attempting to be reassuring. From a table he lifted a black ball and showed it to them. 'We found this in the cellar,' he said, 'it is dynamite.' He then accused them of giving food to the partisans and sending radio messages to the English. Nina and the others protested that they had never had dynamite in the house and they certainly had not been helping the partisans or sending messages. The captain shouted at them to be quiet. 'So, we have found this dynamite,' he said. 'This is very serious. I will now interrogate each one of you in turn.'

The women were then taken back upstairs to the bedroom. All except Nina.

# 11. Il Focardo, 1944

The German captain insisted that he be told where Robert had gone. Realizing they were in danger of losing their lives, Nina decided to tell him the truth. Robert had kept away from the villa for the past two weeks. Sometimes he spent nights in the woods. Other nights he passed with local farmers. He was nearby, but she did not know where he was at any one time. The captain looked unconvinced. He ordered two of his men to take her and search for Robert.

Nina and the two soldiers walked outside and headed for the woods. They passed Casa Bella, and then climbed the slope towards Il Manco, a small cottage 350 yards to the north-west. The Germans ordered Nina to call out her husband's name. So she did. 'Roberto,' she whispered. They insisted she speak louder. 'Roberto, Roberto,' she called again, this time with more force. Her voice cut through the still summer-night air, but there was no reply. The soldiers urged her on, towards the dark forms of the trees higher up the rocky track.

At this very moment, thirteen-year-old Franco Giorgetti was in his bedroom. He lived with his parents and two sisters at

Il Manco. His father took care of the cows and sheep for the neighbouring Torre a Cona estate. Franco knew the Einstein family, having attended the Sunday mass each week at Il Focardo since he was a little boy. Though he was not friends with the children – they tended to play with those on their own estate – he liked them, particularly the pretty blonde younger daughter, Cici.

'Roberto, Roberto, Roberto,' came a female voice from outside. Franco went to his window and saw in the moonlight Nina Einstein walking up the track with two German soldiers. Franco hoped that Robert was hiding. He knew the stakes. Everyone did. Franco was seriously alarmed. What would happen if they found Robert? And what about his daughters Luce and Cici?

Two hundred yards away, Nello, Orando and Pipone were standing next to Robert in the woods. They could hear Nina calling his name. 'I'm going, I'm going,' said Robert. The *fattore* put a hand over his mouth. 'Didn't you agree that you would not reveal yourself even if your wife called you?' he whispered. Again, they heard Nina's voice: 'Roberto, Roberto, Roberto.' When Robert made a move forward, they held him back. 'They will kill all of us if you go out there,' Orando said urgently.

Away in the distance, they could see a light on at the villa. They wondered what was going on back there. What had they done with Seba and the five young women? The last time Orando and Pipone had seen them they were being pushed out of the hallway and up the stairs.

For another thirty minutes, Nina kept calling Robert's name, all the time walking up and down the track near where they were hiding. Finally, the German escorts gave up. Apparently they had concluded that either Robert was not in the vicinity or he was refusing to reveal himself. They turned around and, with Nina between them, headed back down the track until they were out of view.

Still standing at his window, Franco followed their progress. Nina was now coming back towards him, still calling her husband's name. And then he saw them disappear.

While Nina was out looking for her husband, a soldier came into the back bedroom and said it was Luce's turn to be questioned. She followed him down the poorly lit stairs to the Sala Rossa. What was going to happen? What were they going to do to her? Around her were objects she had known since her early childhood, now destroyed – the piano on which her mother played, the sofas and armchairs where her father liked to sit and listen to the radio, the side table on which her mother set cups of coffee and books of poetry. She was flooded with terror. Having almost completed her medical studies, Luce was accustomed to stressful situations, but this was something entirely new. She was worried about her mother, who by now had been gone for almost an hour. And she didn't know where her father was. It was unlikely that anyone was coming to rescue them.

Still sitting behind the small table, the captain asked Luce for her father's whereabouts. She replied that she did not know. He repeated the question, this time more forcefully. Trembling, Luce repeated that she really did not know. Apparently sensing the young woman's unease, the captain told her not to be concerned. If her father wasn't guilty then nothing would happen to him. He asked if her father helped the partisans. She said he had not. What about giving them food or passing messages? Again she said no. How about her mother or sister or cousins? Once more, Luce said she knew nothing about this. The commander then asked about the dynamite. Thinking that she should protect the others, Luce tried to take the blame, but the Germans didn't seem to care. It would later be revealed that they had planted the dynamite.

After a few more questions, the captain told Luce to fetch her younger sister. Luce walked upstairs and was let back into the bedroom where the other women were waiting. They noticed that her mood had changed significantly. 'Luce tried to console us,' Seba later remembered, 'she embraced me very tightly. I think she understood it was dangerous.' It was now that Luce took off her necklace and tied it around her aunt's neck and said: 'Remember my love.'

Luce then told Cici that the Germans needed them both downstairs and the two sisters left the room. It was not lost on anyone that the only people being interrogated were those with the surname 'Einstein'.

When Luce and Cici reached the Sala Rossa, they found their mother waiting for them. The atmosphere was extremely tense. Nina had been unable to find their father. It was now Cici's turn to be questioned. She was nine years younger than Luce and lacked the confidence of her sister. Despite the fierce questioning, however, she denied any knowledge of the dynamite or of helping the partisans. She also said that she didn't know where her father was.

The mood now changed. The German captain decided he had no further need to be civil. No more efforts were made to win over the cooperation of Nina and her two daughters. A heavy dread descended on the Sala Rossa.

Meanwhile, in the bedroom upstairs, Seba, Paola, Lorenza and Anna Maria were still under armed guard. As the minutes ticked past – five, ten, twenty, thirty – they strained to catch what was going on in the Sala Rossa, but it was impossible to hear more than the murmur of voices.

It was now fourteen hours since the women had been taken hostage. Outside the window they could see the terrace illuminated by the full moon. And from further off came the urgent sounds of war. Perhaps the Allies would arrive in the morning and they would be liberated. But would they all make it?

Seba was petrified. 'Never had my sister worried herself about politics or espionage,' she later said. 'She had always dedicated herself to charity and she was loved by all the *contadini* for her goodness and generosity. Luce was about to take her final exam in medicine. She went about everywhere assisting and comforting sick people.' And as for Cici, she was the 'flower of grace and innocence'.

Seba was also terrified by what might happen to herself and her three nieces. 'We were waiting in mortal anguish.'

Then, to their horror, they heard the sound of gunfire.

'There was a shot and a scream,' Lorenza recalled. 'Then another shot, and another scream. And still another shot.' The women were distraught. Anna Maria fell to the floor. The young soldier who was guarding them was also shocked; there were tears in his eyes. He dropped his gun and held his head in his hands.

Four hundred yards away, Robert Einstein started running.

# 12. Il Focardo, 1944

Seba held her three nieces tight. They were all crowded on the bed. Lorenza, Paola and Anna Maria were crying uncontrollably. Seba was trying to remain calm. To think it through. What had just happened? Who had been shot? Was it Nina, Luce and Cici? The thought was too awful to comprehend, but was there a plausible alternative? Perhaps the soldiers were firing into the air, like they had earlier that day. The young women were exhausted after hours of captivity and terror. Seba was also in shock, but she remained alert and hypervigilant. They were trapped here, in this room, but could they find a way to escape? What would happen if they didn't try?

They heard heavy footsteps on the stairs and then the door was yanked open. It was the lieutenant. Behind him stood two other soldiers. The lieutenant told them they had to leave the villa immediately. The four women were shoved violently downstairs. As they reached the bottom of the stairs, Seba begged her captors to allow her into the Sala Rossa. She was desperate to know what had happened to Nina, Luce and Cici, but the captain refused to let them in. Instead, they were pushed through the front hallway and into the garden.

As they left the villa, they saw the German soldiers pouring petrol on the furniture, window frames and doors. The villa was soon ablaze.

Seized by an instinct of self-preservation for herself and the young women, Seba hurried them through the gates of the villa and up the track towards the woods. They had to find Robert.

The thirteen-year-old Franco Giorgetti was still in his room at Il Manco. Looking out of the window, he now saw four women come towards him. They were walking through the peach orchard that filled the valley between Il Manco and Casa Bella. It was Seba, Lorenza, Paola and Anna Maria. They were moving slowly, heavy with the horror of what they knew without knowing. Seba was slowest of all, given her bad hip. As Franco watched them approach, he wondered: where were Nina, Luce and Cici?

In the distance, he could now see black smoke rising into the sky. He guessed this was coming from Il Focardo. What was going on? He ran downstairs and saw that just as the four women arrived they were joined by Robert, Orando and Pipone, who had come from the woods.

It was chaos. Everyone was speaking at once. Orando said that he had heard gunfire. Lorenza and Paola said that they'd heard the same thing but were locked upstairs so couldn't see what was going on. Someone else said they couldn't be sure if the women had been shot. Robert shouted that he knew – he knew that his wife and daughters were dead. He had to go to the villa. Now. He had to see them. He started to move in that direction. Seba grabbed his shoulder. 'No, you mustn't give satisfaction to those brutes,' she cried. He shrugged her off and took a step forward but the others held him back.

Orando pulled Robert towards Il Manco, but he resisted. He was determined to go to the villa. Robert repeated that he knew that Nina, Luce and Cici were dead and screamed wildly that he had to kill himself. Horrified, the others replied that he mustn't go. Whatever the truth, Robert must not add another tragedy to that day. The discussion went on and on. It was hard to hear what people were saying, they were talking so fast and on top of one another. Finally, Robert relented and was persuaded to go inside the small house. All the while, the black smoke from the villa rose into the night sky blotting out the full moon.

Around 2 a.m., when the others were asleep, Robert quietly wrote a note and left it on the table. It said that as the Germans had now gone from the villa, he intended to head east in order to find other soldiers. He then stepped outside and made for the woods.

'His plan was to find death,' Franco later wrote. 'He hoped to meet members of the German army and when they said "Stop!" he would continue and they would shoot him.'

While Robert was setting off from Il Manco, the last of the German forces remaining in Florence were completing their destruction of the city's infrastructure in preparation for their final withdrawal.

Three days earlier, the German High Command had distributed posters around Florence instructing all residents who lived near the River Arno to leave immediately. More than 4,000 people took refuge in the Palazzo Pitti, the enormous stone compound which had been home to the Medici rulers of Tuscany, while others found shelter in churches or joined friends and family in the countryside. Over the next three days, the Germans laid mines and other explosives on the city's bridges. Their aim was to slow down the Allies' advance.

Ponte alle Grazie was the first bridge to be blown up, at 9.50 p.m. on 3 August – around the time Seba and the young women were fleeing Il Focardo. As the medieval bridge tumbled into the Arno, the blasts reverberated around Florence and into the countryside beyond. The detonations continued throughout the night until dawn. Four more bridges were destroyed: Ponte alla Vittoria, Ponte alla Carraia, Ponte San Niccolò and Ponte Santa Trinita. The only bridge that was left intact was the Ponte Vecchio.

The sun was just edging into the sky on 4 August as the last explosion could be heard across the valley near Il Focardo. It was at this point that the local priest Giuseppe Agnoloni was disturbed by a loud knocking on his front door.

Born less than an hour's drive from Il Focardo, the thirty-year-old Don Giuseppe was in charge of the congregation of Santo Stefano, the small medieval stone church in Le Corti, just 500 yards from Il Focardo. He was extremely fond of the Einsteins and considered them to be friends. Each Sunday morning, he would walk from Santo Stefano, along the main road towards San Donato in Collina, and then up Via Focardo to the top of the hill; there he would be greeted by one of the girls who would cheerfully escort him to the Sala Rossa where Robert and Nina would be waiting. After a short catch-up on the week's news, the priest would excuse himself, don the robes necessary for mass, and then lead the service for the *contadini* at the villa's small chapel.

Three days before the Germans stormed through the doors of Il Focardo, Luce had gone to the priest's home and presented him with a stack of papers. They had spent two hours in deep conversation about whether the Einstein women should remain in the villa. Luce pointed to the documents – a selection of recent antisemitic articles, posters and government announcements – and the priest agreed that there was no doubt that Jews were in danger. By this point, Robert had been in hiding for more than a week, and Luce asked how she and her sister would be treated: would they be considered Jewish or Aryan? The priest urged Luce not to wait to find out the answer. She and her sister and mother should leave Il Focardo immediately. 'Go,' he had entreated the young woman, 'get out of here. Here in the country you are at the mercy of the first rascal that comes along. In Florence no one knows you. You do not have "Einstein" written on your forehead.' He then added, 'If I were as free as you, I would have left long ago.' The priest remembered Luce looking at him seriously and with a terrible sadness in her eyes. She clearly felt trapped. If they left, they might run into German soldiers or get caught up in the fighting. If they stayed, they remained vulnerable to betrayal and discovery. When he and Luce said goodbye, he wasn't sure what she would decide. She shook his hand and walked away.

Now it was 5 a.m. on 4 August and someone was knocking at the priest's door. He looked out of the window and saw two *contadini* standing outside. 'Father,' they called, 'come to the villa at once.' He quickly dressed and then hurried to Il Focardo as fast as he could. When he arrived, he was shocked by what he found. The villa was on fire. There was an acrid smell of burning in the air. The roof was gone and part of the front wall had collapsed. Blackened beams smoked against the lightening sky. In front of the main entrance was gathered a large group of *contadini*. Some were crying, others were cursing. Don Giuseppe sent most of them away, because there were still Germans in the area and they might return at any moment. One of the few to remain was Orando, who accompanied the priest through the broken front doors into the hallway.

He paused at the entrance to the Sala Rossa. Then he pushed open the door and walked inside. 'A dreadful, horrifying spectacle appeared before my eyes,' he later wrote in his memoir:

> Three women lying on the ground, with large wounds on their temples, in the midst of an immense lake of blood, reaching to the opposite wall. I could see that before they had been machine-gunned they must have been embracing and thus fell holding each other: the mother, Nina, in the middle; Luce, the eldest daughter, on the right arm; and Cici, the youngest daughter, on the left. I stood stunned, breathless, unable to say a single word.

Nina, Luce and Cici Einstein were dead.

# PART TWO
# Aftermath

Once the experience of evil has been
endured it is never forgotten.

– Natalia Ginzburg

# 13. Il Focardo, 1944

With Robert nowhere to be found, and the priest having left to make funeral arrangements, Orando Fuschiotti took control of the situation. The first task was to take care of the dead. The bodies needed to be removed from the Sala Rossa and prepared for burial.

Orando and another farmworker carefully picked up Nina from the floor and carried her to the laundry room at the back of the villa. This part of the building had largely escaped the fire and was still usable. They then returned to the Sala Rossa to move Luce and Cici. With the three bodies relocated, Orando went to look for Erenia, his wife. She was shocked to hear the news. Like her husband, she cared deeply for the Einsteins. After giving her a moment to process what she had just heard, Orando asked if she would be willing to prepare the bodies. She said she would take care of it. Thanking her, he set off to find his brother-in-law, a coffin-maker who lived in San Donato in Collina: they needed three caskets as soon as possible.

To make ready the bodies, Erenia would need help, so she brought Giulia, Pipone's wife, along with her own sister. The three women set about their task in respectful silence. First, they removed Nina's, Luce's and Cici's soiled and bloodied garments: shoes, dresses, stockings and underwear. Next came the cleaning. The machine guns had sprayed bullets with little precision. There were extensive wounds to the chest, stomach and legs. The women used rags to gently wipe away the blood and other fluids. They took their time, treating the victims with utmost care. When the bodies were ready, the women wrapped them in white linen sheets.

Soon Orando returned with his brother-in-law. He brought simple wooden caskets from the stock he had made in expectation of intense fighting between the Germans and the Allies, and these were carried inside. The linen-wrapped corpses were now placed in them, ready for burial.

When Orando went back outside, he was amazed to find a small group of British military vehicles parked next to the villa's gates, surrounded by *contadini*. Among those gathered was Nello Dino, the assistant bookkeeper. It was a moment of extreme and conflicting emotions. It was just hours since the beloved estate owner's wife and daughters had been brutally murdered, but now, after four long years of war, Allied troops were here in the driveway of Il Focardo.

A young American climbed out from one of the cars. 'He was wearing plain clothes and had long hair down to his neck,' Nello Dino recalled in later testimony. 'He rushed towards us and shouted, "Where are the Einsteins?"' Orando met the newcomer and explained what had taken place at the villa over the preceding few hours. The long-haired young man looked around bewildered and began to cry. He said that he had been in Italy with the Allied troops for three months and had orders to find the members of Albert Einstein's family.

Orando showed the visitor inside the villa. The timbers were still smoking. The scorched walls were too hot to touch. The air pulsed with heat. They walked past the Sala Rossa to the back of the house and saw the three victims in their matching caskets. The young man asked about Robert Einstein, to which Orando replied that he hadn't seen him since the night before, when he had left Il Manco. He was most likely dead as well.

Devastated, the young man walked back through the house to his car, where he picked up the radio telephone. 'Call Washington,' the young American said in a broken voice. 'Tell the president that the Einstein family has been destroyed.' He then climbed into his vehicle and sped away.

The *contadini* who witnessed the scene looked on in amazement. They knew that just a few miles away the US Army was in the middle of a desperate battle to capture the city of Florence, and yet not only had a local commander sent someone out into the remote countryside to determine the well-being of Robert Einstein, but there appeared to be senior officials in the American government who were interested in his fate. Even within the context of all the tremendous changes that were taking place at that very moment, this was surprising.

Shortly after the departure of the young American, Don Giuseppe returned. He went with Orando to the laundry room, where he examined the bodies. After a few moments, he judged that all was in order and thanked the women for their tender work. Next, and even though the victims were Protestant, he said a Catholic benediction over each body.

Once the prayers were over, the priest went to find Signor Landi, a *contadini* who worked on the estate, who lived nearby and owned a cart and oxen. There had been few formal burials recently, because of the fear that those attending might get caught in crossfire from the fighting, but the priest felt that this situation was exceptional. The murder of the Einstein women was so brutal and the motivation so malicious that the community needed to come together to express their collective grief and outrage.

Don Giuseppe therefore asked Landi if he could transport the bodies to the nearby cemetery, explaining that they should not be left inside the villa for much longer, given the summer heat. Landi readily agreed, and a few minutes later he pulled up in front of the villa's entrance. With the help of some others, he carefully loaded the three caskets on to his cart. Once everything was secure, Landi climbed up to the seat, picked up his whip and with a cry to move off, the oxen started forward. Behind the cart walked the priest, Orando Fuschiotti and his wife, Pipone and his wife and her sister, along with a dozen or so *contadini*.

They were taking a considerable risk. From the alarmingly loud machine-gun and rifle fire, it appeared that German forces were fighting Allied soldiers just up the valley. Every few seconds, the air was punctured by the boom boom of artillery, followed a few moments later by exploding ordnance. Everyone in the funeral party was keenly aware that the war was close by. Yet they marched on, committed to honouring those murdered the day before. After around an hour, the sombre cortège arrived at Badiuzza Cemetery.

Built in the late nineteenth century, the graveyard was a small rectangular plot, thirty yards by forty, bordered by stone walls. It was not only the closest burial ground to the Einstein villa, it was also possible to see Il Focardo from inside the cemetery. There would be no lengthy funeral mass. This was partly because Nina, Luce and Cici were not Catholic, and partly because of expediency given the battle raging nearby.

The *contadini* carefully lifted each coffin off the cart, carried it into the cemetery and placed it beside the freshly dug graves. Once all the coffins were there, they lowered them into the ground as the priest recited a quick prayer. The service took less than half an hour. It was almost midday, the heat from the sun was searing. Nobody felt safe exposed out in the open. They wanted to get home.

Lorenza, Paola, Anne Maria and Seba were not among those who attended the burial. It had been decided that it would be safer for the four women to stay out of view. The Germans might return; besides, they were so traumatized by the events of the previous twenty-four hours that they were in no state to take part in a public ceremony. For now, they remained at Pipone's and Giulia's house. They were all in a state of shock. Nina was dead. So were Luce and Cici. Robert was gone. Parts of the villa were destroyed. Ali the dog was killed. The Allies had arrived. And somehow, through all this, they had survived. What did it all mean? Where would they live? Who would look after them? 'As the hours passed,' Nina and Robert's niece and god-daughter Anna Maria later wrote, 'we began to realize what had happened and the situation we found ourselves in and we wondered, "Now what will we do? What will become of us?"'

Perhaps most confusing of all, life was continuing as usual, as if nothing had happened. The cockerel ushered in the day. The sun rose high in the sky. The peaches needed to be picked or they would rot. How was this possible when their world had been turned upside down? And so, gripped by grief and loss, they huddled close together, trying to give comfort to each other as best they could.

Orando had one more task to complete. He caught a ride to Rignano sull'Arno, the administrative centre for the municipality, and walked into the town hall. There he reported the deaths of Nina, Luce and Cici. He gave the three victims' ages as fifty-nine for Nina, twenty-seven for Luce and eighteen for Cici. Under nationality, the clerk wrote 'Italian Citizens'; and under race, they added *ariana*, or 'Aryan'. For the marital status of the two daughters a single adjective was used – *nubile*, or unmarried. As for Nina, she was listed as being the wife of the engineer Robert Einstein.

But where was the engineer Robert Einstein? It was notable that he had not attended the funeral of his beloved wife and daughters, nor was he the person to report their deaths. Neither the *fattore* or any of the *contadini* had seen him since he had fled in the middle of the previous night. Since he had left that note saying he was looking for German soldiers.

The day after the murder of Nina, Luce and Cici, around 200 German troops took shelter in the Convento dell'Incontro, a Franciscan monastery located on a hilltop three miles northwest from Il Focardo. With its 360 degree outlook over the Arno valley, including the centre of Florence, it was considered a key strategic site that had to be defended come what may. The Germans barricaded the doors and positioned their artillery.

In the afternoon of 5 August, two days after the Einstein murders, long columns of British, Australian and New Zealand infantry – the bulk of them men of the Duke of

Cornwall's Light Infantry – arrived from the direction of the village of Troghi. They passed the road that led to Il Focardo and took up positions further along the valley, from where they began firing towards the monastery. The Germans holed up in Incontro responded in kind. 'The fury of war was unleashed,' wrote the priest Don Giuseppe, who watched the action unfold from the safety of Santo Stefano church. 'The hill was enveloped in smoke. Flames, artillery bursts, and machine-gun fire followed one another without interruption. It was an inferno.' Within minutes, more than thirty British soldiers were killed. Stretcher-bearers scurried around the fields collecting the wounded and carrying them to the waiting ambulances, which immediately sped off towards the rear lines. 'The battle was horrific,' the priest recalled.

Throughout the evening of the 5th and into the next day, the Allied offensive continued. Mustangs and Hurricanes swept through the sky, bombing and strafing the monastery. Sherman and Churchill tanks fired endless shells towards the enemy position, their impact booming across the Arno valley. 'From the church courtyard, with other parishioners, I witnessed those terrible clashes,' recalled the priest. 'We watched the calamitous spectacle through gaps in the walls.'

The valley around Troghi was filled with thousands of Allied soldiers. There were at least 200 tanks, supported by armoured cars, jeeps and supply trucks. The earth was torn up by these vehicles, the air filled with clouds of thick orange dust. Cannons fired from morning to night without interruption. The empty shell cases piled up on the ground in large mounds. Finally, around 6 p.m. on 8 August, the British forces broke through the German defences and captured the monastery. 'Everything was reduced to an immense pile of rubble. Nothing remained of the beautiful sanctuary,' wrote the priest, noting that 'The Germans with their limited resources had resisted with extreme vigour to the last.' Bodies were strewn throughout the monastery. More than 100 Germans were killed and many more injured. Sixty-seven were taken as prisoners of war.

For four long days and nights, the local citizens had hidden from the fighting. They huddled in their homes, surviving on the small amounts of food and drink they had previously stashed. At last, shortly after sunset on 8 August, the thunder and earth-shake of the artillery bombardments stopped. The fighting appeared to be over. When they felt it was safe, they climbed out of their underground chambers and looked around. The sun was low in the sky. The temperature beginning to cool.

'We were finally free,' the priest later wrote. 'There were no more fears. A new world. The joys of life were upon us. The suffering we had endured was a memory.'

If Robert had walked northwest after leaving Il Manco in the middle of the night, he would have found the German soldiers he was seeking in just over an hour, at Incontro. Instead, he headed southeast along the River Arno.

At first, in the early hours, it was dark and cool. Later, after the sun rose, the air quickly warmed and soon it became baking hot. All the while, his mind was gripped by images from the day before: Nina running away from the woods, the sound of machine guns, the villa on fire. At any moment, he expected to encounter some Germans so that he could get himself shot but, to his surprise, he hadn't seen a single one.

That first night he found shelter somewhere near the village of Santa Maria Maddalena, where he fell asleep, exhausted. The next morning, he pushed on and by nightfall he had reached the village of Figline Valdarno. Again, he hadn't spotted a single member of the Wehrmacht, let alone the SS. The following day, and the day after that, he continued his trek south. It was still treacherously hot. Dehydrated and mad with grief, his progress slowed to little more than a shuffle. That evening, he collapsed in the woods near the village of Restone. This was the fourth night since he had left the note for Orando and the others at Il Manco. The day after, he moved off again, still hoping to bump into German soldiers. It was another gruelling day, another day of disappointment. Shortly after sunset, he arrived at the small agricultural town of Montevarchi twenty miles southeast of Il Focardo.

By now, after days of marching and little food, he was wrung out and disorientated. His clothes were dirty and torn. As he entered the town, he saw a group of young partisans ahead of him, blocking his way. Most of them were teenagers. They wore military boots, khaki trousers and an assortment of faded khaki shirts. The eldest of the group stepped forward and asked to see his identity papers. Now that they were close, Robert noticed that the young man had a finger on his holstered gun.

Robert explained that he had a 'delicate matter to discuss'. Seeing that the newcomer was no threat, the partisan leader took him to a quiet place behind a nearby shop. When they were alone, the young man introduced himself as Alberto Mario Droandi and then asked Robert what he wished to talk about. Robert replied that he wanted Alberto to hand over his pistol. Not a little surprised, the partisan asked him why he needed it. Robert said he wanted to kill himself. This shocked Alberto even more. He pressed Robert to tell him why he wanted to do this. After all, the Allies had finally arrived, the war was almost certainly over: wasn't this a time for hope, a time to celebrate? So Robert recounted his terrible story – about having to hide in the woods, about not revealing himself when his wife called for him, about the murder of his wife and two children. 'He was convinced that he was responsible for his family's end,' Alberto later remembered. 'And he said that if he had revealed himself to the Germans, the family would probably have survived. So now he had to follow the same destiny and commit suicide.'

Alberto felt deeply sorry for this man who had suffered so greatly, but he would not help him to end his life. It was against his upbringing: suicide was a sin according to Catholic teachings. Instead, he asked what else he could do. Robert said that if he couldn't kill himself, then perhaps he could speak with the priest at the church of Santa Maria al Giglio. Alberto offered to accompany Robert; it was just a few minutes' walk away.

Arriving at the church, they found that parts of the exterior were in ruins, having been hit by a bomb two weeks earlier. They clambered over a pile of stone and rock and walked inside. There they found the priest, who greeted them warmly; he apparently knew the engineer. Robert explained what had happened to his family and once again said he wished to commit suicide. The priest tried to persuade him that this was the wrong choice, but Robert said he was determined. The conversation continued for some time. Finally, Robert agreed that before making the decision he would take some rest. He was, after all, exhausted. Grateful for this small respite, the priest took his friend to his house, gave him some food and showed him where he could sleep. Worried that Robert might harm himself if left alone, Alberto sent two men to watch over him during the night.

The following morning, Alberto returned to see how Robert was doing. 'From his grim expression I saw that he had not changed his mind,' Alberto recalled. Realizing that Robert was more determined than ever to end his life, the partisan came up with a new argument. 'I suggested that he had a responsibility to take care of the young nieces left at Il Focardo. That if he killed himself now, there might be problems with their inheritance.' This seemed to break through. Robert thought about what Alberto said, about his nieces all alone, and then he agreed.

A few hours later, Robert hitched a ride with Alberto back to Troghi. Before climbing out of the vehicle, Robert promised the young man that he wouldn't think about ending his life without having fulfilled his family duties. 'I was happy because I had secured something positive, even if small, from a terrible situation,' Alberto recalled. 'I thought that maybe time would give him wisdom and that his pain would lessen. And that just maybe, with the nieces to take care of, he would find interest in life again.' After waving goodbye to Alberto and his comrades as they drove on towards Florence, Robert turned and headed in the opposite direction. He walked out of Troghi along the main road towards Il Focardo. It was 9 August 1944.

As he passed through the villa's tall wrought-iron gates, Robert was met by Orando. The *fattore* was relieved to see his *padrone* still alive, but he was also overwhelmed by feelings of compassion and sorrow for his boss, who was clearly in the white heat of grief.

After Robert had explained what he had been doing for the past five days, Orando said that they had been unable to wait to bury Nina, Luce and Cici and that the ceremony had been dignified and correct. He also said that while Robert had been away they had searched the house and come across something peculiar. Among the items they found were a number of small notices, about four inches by five, typed in purple ink. Each bore the same message, in Italian. Orando handed one of the notices to Robert. It read:

Zone of Operations 3.8.44

The German HQ makes it known:

The family Einstein is guilty of espionage.
They have been in constant touch with the enemy.
The family was executed on the third day of August 1944.

The Commanding Officer

The words added salt to an already open wound. They were a clear attempt to justify the cold-blooded murders. But there was something else. A quick comparison of the notices revealed that on each one the first letter of the word 'operations' had initially been typed as a 'p' and then corrected with a heavy 'o'. The notices had clearly been duplicated. Apparently, the Germans had printed them before they arrived at Il Focardo, which in turn meant that the attack on the Einsteins was not a spontaneous act – it was premeditated.

In a broken voice, Robert asked to see where the killings had taken place. Orando led him inside.

In the days that followed his return to Il Focardo, Robert was determined to have the murders investigated, to find someone in authority who could track down the perpetrators and hold them to account. But who should he speak to? The British, Australian and New Zealand soldiers that had taken part in the battle for Incontro had departed, heading north to sweep up the enemy stragglers. Meanwhile, American and other Allied troops were in the process of taking Florence and, once this was achieved, were busy running a city that had suffered from years of war. Whenever Robert saw a passing soldier he asked for help, but nobody had the time or inclination to pay him attention. There were more pressing matters at hand. The murder of a woman and her two daughters was just another sorry episode from this terrible conflict.

Five days after returning to Il Focardo, on 14 August, Robert finally found someone prepared to listen. Maybe the appalling nature of the triple murder moved this stranger. Or perhaps Robert mentioned the name of his famous cousin, which caught the person's attention. Whatever the cause, his statement was now taken down by the unnamed American soldier.

Robert started by providing the background to the crime. The visit by German soldiers in late July asking for his whereabouts. His going into hiding ('I perceived immediately the danger,' he said, 'and succeeded in going far from the villa') and then he moved on to the day of the killings. The women being told to go to the cellar to protect themselves from possible British shelling ('It appears that this advice was given with the aim to have them watched,' Robert reported, 'so that they could easily arrest and murder them'). The destruction of his home ('they systematically broke all my furniture and every little thing in the villa'). Hearing the sound of machine guns ('that made me guess of the tragedy that had just taken place'). And then Il Focardo being set on fire ('I had to be restrained from entering the villa so that I did not suffer the same fate as the rest of my family'). As to the suggestion that he, his wife, daughters or nieces had stored dynamite or participated in espionage, Robert was adamant: 'both of these accusations were absolutely without any basis'. He then made what must have been a truly difficult admission: that if Nina, Luce and Cici 'had been hiding [with him] in the wood [then] all the misery that has been could have been easily avoided'.

The questioner then asked if the engineer had any idea about the perpetrators' identity. Robert stated that the German unit included 'one captain and two lieutenants who acted and looked like they were S.S. men'. Robert concluded his testimony with the following statement: 'I shall be restless until the murderers and their hirings have had the punishment they deserve.'

Immediately after taking the testimony, the unnamed American soldier wrote up the affidavit. In all, it ran to more than a thousand words. Having read what was written, Robert signed it at the bottom, 'Engineer Robert Einstein', and gave his address as 'Villa Il Focardo', to which someone later added helpfully, 'Near Florence'. This single-page statement was then taken to the local US Army headquarters, along with another signed by Robert's sister-in-law Seba. They were read, stamped in bold red capitals with the word SECRET, and then forwarded to a unit that had been established just four days before on 10 August 1944: the US Fifth Army War Crimes Commission.

# 14. Il Focardo, 1944

At 11.30 a.m. on 17 September 1944, a little over six weeks after the Einstein murders, a green Jeep pulled up to the tall metal gates of Il Focardo. On its bonnet was stamped a white five-pointed star inside a white circle, signalling that it belonged to the US Army.

Out of the vehicle climbed Major Milton Wexler in freshly starched military uniform, brown shiny shoes and peaked cap. In his bag he carried a sheaf of papers and some pens. With him were four other members of the newly formed US Fifth Army War Crimes Commission. Wexler was here to investigate a triple murder.

Before the war, Wexler had been a criminal attorney. Born in New York City to Jewish parents, he completed his law degree at the University of Wisconsin. After graduating, he joined the firm of Nathan Belby in Manhattan as a courtroom litigator. He was a man of medium stature, with short-cropped dark hair, a high forehead and a dimpled chin. His eyes were hazel and penetrating.

Following the outbreak of war in Europe in 1939, he

volunteered for the army at the age of twenty-five. Later, after the USA joined the war, he was deployed to Libya for the North African campaign. There he was given the job of assistant to the inspector general of the US Fifth Army, under the command of General Mark Clark. In September 1943, he landed at Salerno along with more than 100,000 men. Three months later, he received orders from General Clark's office 'to investigate any cases of alleged atrocity that you come across'. By the end of the month, Wexler had submitted a report on his first case, the murder of fifty-two civilians in Bellona, a small village outside Naples.

As his unit moved north, he heard about other war crimes committed by the Germans in Italy. In Naples, the forcible deportation and killing of civilians. In Capua, the appalling murder of scores of unarmed civilians. In Rome, 335 people killed by German soldiers as a reprisal for a partisan attack, in what became known as the Ardeatine Caves massacre. As each new atrocity was discovered, Wexler and other lawyers attached to the US Army carried out investigations, gathering witness statements and whatever facts they could determine, to be used for future war crimes trials.

The background to these early war crimes investigations can be traced to the establishment of the United Nations War Crimes Commission (UNWCC) on 20 October 1943. A key part of the UNWCC's work was to gather evidence for the possible future trial of alleged Axis war criminals. The same week that the UNWCC was created, the foreign ministers of Great Britain, the USA and the Soviet Union gathered at the Kremlin in Moscow, along with dozens of generals, diplomats and advisors, for the start of a two-week conference to discuss cooperation. On 30 October, the foreign ministers issued a number of announcements, among them the 'Declaration Regarding Italy', which stated that 'Fascism and all its evil influence and configuration shall be completely destroyed and that the Italian people shall be given every opportunity to establish governmental and other institutions based on democratic principles'. It also included a provision on war crimes: 'Fascist chiefs and army generals known or suspected to be war criminals shall be arrested and handed over to justice.' Another of the so-called Moscow Declarations was the 'Statement of Atrocities' signed by President Franklin D. Roosevelt, the prime minister Winston Churchill and the Soviet premier Josef Stalin, which spoke of 'monstrous crimes' having been committed in Nazi-occupied Europe. It placed a particular emphasis on the Soviet Union, France and Italy, and gave a warning to those guilty that 'the three Allied Powers will pursue them to the uttermost ends of the earth and will deliver them to their accusers in order that justice may be done'.

In early August 1944, Wexler arrived in Florence with the US Fifth Army. The first few days were occupied with stabilizing the city, ensuring that there were no enemy snipers or other holdouts, and that the major access routes were made passable, including the five blown-up bridges. Next they ensured electricity and water systems were functioning, established food and medical supplies and set up a headquarters. Then the Americans turned their attention to war crimes. So it was that, on 10 August, Special Order Number 223 was issued by Major General Alfred Gruenther, chief of staff to General Clark, announcing the formation of a new United States War Crimes Commission for Florence and the surrounding area. Among those appointed to this commission was Major Milton Wexler. His first task was to find out what had happened in the city prior to the arrival of the Allied forces, to speak with community leaders and to become familiar with the lie of the land.

A little over a month later, at ten in the morning of 15 September, Alfredo and Marino Curzi walked into Fifth Army Headquarters in Florence. They said they wanted to report a war crime. They were directed to a room upstairs and told to wait. A few minutes later, Wexler came in to see them. The brothers said that on 12 August – nine days after the Einstein murders – German soldiers had attacked civilians in and around the hilltop village of Sant'Anna di Stazzema, seventy miles northwest of Florence. By the day's end, up to 560 people had been killed. Here is part of what the forty-three-year-old Alfredo Curzi said:

> I saw the Germans rounding up the civilians. On arrival at the square near the church, they put all the civilians together in one corner near the precipice. They took the chairs and benches from the church and put them all around the civilians with straw and wood and they started a fire. Then they started to machine gun the civilians.

Wexler took the brothers' testimony to his superior officer, Lieutenant Colonel H. L. Ostler, who agreed that an investigation was required. If more than 500 civilians had really been killed, this would make it one of the worst atrocities they had come across in Italy. Ostler had an order typed up: 'You are directed to investigate the alleged war crime perpetrated near San Anna [*sic*] Italy.' Wexler was to start immediately.

But this would not be the only crime Ostler asked to be

investigated that day. Before he left, Wexler was given a second, almost identical order: 'You are directed to investigate the alleged war crime perpetrated near Troghi, Italy, about 3 August 1944.' This second order came with a dossier that included the statements collected by the unnamed American soldier a month before. Inside the dossier was a covering note: 'Herewith copies of statements signed by Roberto EINSTEIN and Sera MAZZETTE [*sic*], on an atrocity committed by German troops.' At the bottom of the page was the following comment: 'In case further investigations are found necessary, the addresses of the a/n [above named] Italians have been given.'

This was highly unusual. With just three victims, the Einstein murder case was far smaller than the massacre at Sant'Anna di Stazzema, and yet it was being given the same priority by the American authorities. Why, among all the many instances in which Italian civilians had been tragically killed, was this one chosen? Wexler had, of course, noticed the surname 'Einstein' on the dossier he was given, and, like the majority of American citizens, he had heard of the most famous scientist in the world, Albert Einstein. What he would not have known, because this was a closely held secret, was that the director of the FBI, J. Edgar Hoover, had been keeping a file on Albert Einstein since his arrival in the USA in 1933, and that from time to time he shared his findings with the US Army's chief of staff. Among these documents was an informer's report that the famous scientist was on a Nazi 'Black List' of enemies they wished to kill. Nor would Wexler have been made privy to any informal, private request made by Albert Einstein to his friends in government asking them to keep an eye out for his cousin in Italy. For Wexler, the reasons behind the investigation remained a mystery. What mattered, however, were the results. He had been asked to investigate the murders at Il Focardo and report back, so this was what he would do.

The following day, Wexler was driven to the Fifth Army stockade in Livorno to interview two German prisoners of war who belonged to the unit that had carried out the atrocity at Sant'Anna di Stazzema. The session lasted almost five hours, from 1 p.m. to 5.50 p.m. From these interviews, and those with the Curzi brothers the day before in Florence, it was clear that he would have to visit Sant'Anna di Stazzema itself, inspect the site and collect testimony from more survivors. He would also need a medical expert who could identify victims from jawbones and dental records. He made plans to visit in the coming weeks, but first he had to go to Il Focardo.

On the morning of 17 September, Wexler woke up early and was driven the two hours from Livorno to the villa Il Focardo.

Milton Wexler's initial task was to become familiar with the crime scene. He was taken around the property by Orando. First, he was shown the now-repaired front doors, then the back bedroom where Seba and the young women were kept for most of the day, and finally the Sala Rossa, where the killings had taken place. There he examined the bullet holes above the fireplace and in the wall nearby. In all, he counted thirteen impacts, and assessed they were caused by small-arms fire. This could have been anything from a handgun to an assault rifle or a sub-machine gun.

As he made his way around the villa, Wexler made no effort to collect fingerprints, blood samples, shoe or boot marks, or ballistic or other forensic evidence. His experience back in the USA was as a lawyer, not a homicide detective, and he did not have the training or equipment to gather (let alone process) forensic material. But even if Wexler or his colleagues had attempted to collect such evidence, it would not have been straightforward. The fire had destroyed parts of the villa, while the crime scene itself, the Sala Rossa, had been visited by numerous people since the murders, who had disturbed the evidence.

With the tour of the crime scene complete, it was time to speak with the witnesses. Given it was September and the weather was fine, the interviews took place in the court-yard outside the villa. The three commissioners sat behind a wooden table. Next to them was a clerk, who would type a verbatim record of the proceedings, and an interpreter, who would assist with translation. Both were American. Major Wexler took the lead on the questioning. First to be inter-viewed was Robert Einstein, who sat on a chair in front of the commissioners. After swearing he would tell the truth, he provided his name, age and address, and then the same details for his wife and two daughters.

These basic questions completed, Wexler started by asking about the days running up to the murders.

> Wexler: Did your wife and daughters leave with you, or did they remain behind?
> Robert: I left alone. My wife and two daughters remained in the house.
> Wexler: Why did they remain?
> Robert: Because the Germans were always correct and kind.

Wexler: Then why did you leave?

Robert: Because they had ordered the Goering Division
to arrest me.

Wexler: Was this because you were a Jew?

Robert: Yes.

Wexler: Are your wife and children Jewish?

Robert: No.

Wexler: How do you know they had an order to arrest
you?

Robert: I believe because a round-up patrol from the
Hermann Goering Division asked about me,
so I figured it was to arrest me because I was
a Jew.

Robert's comment that 'the Germans were always correct
and kind' was a reference to a group of soldiers who had
arrived at the villa six weeks before the murders. This unit
were friendly and courteous to the family. Robert had even
played chess with one of the officers. Perhaps, however, he
was also being ironic, given what later happened. Or maybe
he was chastising himself for leaving his family in the house
without him.

Robert also said that his wife and daughters were not
Jewish. The three women would have agreed. Nina was
brought up as a Waldensian. Both Luce and Cici would
have said that they were Waldensians too. They attended
church. They celebrated Christmas and Easter. They said
their prayers before they went to sleep. Some in the local
community knew that Nina, Luce and Cici were Christian.
This was certainly true of the priest, Don Giuseppe, and
the *fattore* and his deputy, Pipone. But most of those who

lived nearby believed that the entire Einstein family was Jewish.

How about the German soldiers who invaded Il Focardo, would they have considered the three women to be Jewish? The treatment of those with mixed religious heritage was complicated in Germany. The Nazis were obsessed with lineage, particularly when it came to Aryan ancestry. Since they came to power in 1933, they had issued numerous policy statements on the subject and, as the years went on, they took an increasingly hard-line approach. For the Nazis, Judaism was a question of race, not religion, and was therefore inherited, no matter a person's personal beliefs or practice.

Following the so-called Nuremberg Laws enacted in September 1935 and their clarification in November of that same year, a Jew was defined as someone who had at least three Jewish grandparents. If a person had two grandparents who were Jewish, then they were *Mischlinge* ('mixlings') in the first degree, or half Jews. This was true even if they were baptized, regularly attended church, were not married to a Jew, eschewed all things to do with Judaism and, critically, even if their mother was not Jewish (which is, for Orthodox Jews, the key determinant). As the years progressed, many senior Nazi leaders argued that half Jews should be treated the same as full Jews, calling for their sterilization and deportation. By 1944, first-degree *Mischlinge* faced increasing restrictions: they were forbidden from holding positions of authority, attending university, marrying or having sex with Aryans, and serving in the Wehrmacht. They were also required to take part in forced labour. While in Germany the rules were inconsistently applied, and some care was taken towards *Mischlinge* for fear of upsetting their Aryan relatives, this was less true in other countries. As such, across German-occupied Europe – in Poland, Denmark, France, Belgium, the Netherlands, Luxembourg and Italy – *Mischlinge* were frequently forced to identify as Jews. As a result, thousands of them were killed in the Holocaust. This meant that when the German soldiers took over Il Focardo on 3 August 1944, it was not only Robert Einstein who they would have considered to be non-Aryan. They would have also seen Luce and Cici to be of an inferior race: *Untermenschen*, or 'subhumans'.

As for Nina, her marriage to Robert would have been considered a 'blood disgrace'. Hitler said that a woman found guilty of race defilement should have her hair cropped and be sent to a concentration camp. Others, such as the Nazi propagandist Julius Streicher, believed that race traitors should be sentenced to death. Such views had been widely disseminated in the German newspapers and radio and consumed by the general population, including troops now active in Italy. As such, the German soldiers who broke into Il Focardo on 3 August 1944 would have seen Luce and Cici as subhuman and Nina as a race traitor.

It is also worth noting that Robert stated without qualification that he was a Jew. This was in line with his being an atheist – plenty of people who identify as Jewish do not believe in God or take part in Jewish rituals – and it put to bed claims that Robert converted to Catholicism when he was younger.

With the questions about the period prior to 3 August now complete, Wexler moved on to the day of the murders.

Wexler: Where were you when you heard the shots?

Robert: Three hundred metres away.

Wexler: Did you see the shooting?

Robert: No, I just heard it.

Wexler: Then you did not know at the time who had been shot?

Robert: I didn't know, but I thought it must have been my wife and daughters.

Wexler: When you returned to the villa [on 9 August] had the Germans left?

Robert: Yes, the Germans left the house the same night – August 3rd.

Wexler: At what time of day on August 3rd did you hear the shooting?

Robert: I don't know exactly, but I believe it was about nine o'clock p.m.

Wexler: Did either of your nieces see the shooting?

Robert: No.

Wexler: Do you know of anyone in the community who actually saw the shooting?

Robert: No.

Wexler: Tell me what you discovered when you returned to the villa.

Robert: I discovered the holes in the wall and the house was set on fire, but the fire had stopped.

Wexler: Where were the bodies of your wife and children?

Robert: They had been buried already.

Wexler then asked Robert about the men who committed the crime.

Wexler: Do you believe that the soldiers or officers who did the shooting were members of the Hermann Goering Division?

Robert: No, I believe they were S.S. men, about 50 [*sic*], with an order to do something in my house. I believe the order was to take everything in my house and abuse my wife and daughters.

Wexler: Did you see the uniforms of any of these soldiers who you believe were S.S.?

Robert: No, they didn't have insignia.


Wexler was being intense and relentlessly specific in the questioning. Mindful that this case had been given the highest priority, he was not holding back even if it meant upsetting his interviewee.

For his part, Robert appeared confused at times and lacking focus. When Wexler queried why he left the villa on 16 July, for instance, Robert said 'because they wanted to set fire to the house', which did not happen until after the killings on 3 August. Then, when he was asked, 'Do you have any belief as to why your wife and children were murdered?' he gave a rambling 200-word answer about his four-day hike to Montevarchi. This was by far his longest response and bore no relation to the question. Similarly, when asked whether Orando Fuschiotti had told him about the clothes the German soldiers were wearing, Robert replied: 'Everybody was in the same uniform – khaki.' But it was not apparent if he was speaking about the Germans who arrived on 3 August or those who came before.

Why were so many of Robert's answers unfocused and incoherent? He was born in Germany and spent his adult life in Italy, therefore there was little reason for him to be a fluent English speaker. And even though the American interpreter was there to help with translation, perhaps his Italian was not always proficient. Maybe, also, Robert was finding the conversation emotionally challenging and struggled to keep track of the questions and provide concise answers. After all, this conversation was taking place just six weeks after the murder of his wife and two daughters. By all accounts, he was still in shock.

Robert's answers became clearer, however, when Wexler moved on to discussing more practical matters. 'When you returned to the villa,' Wexler asked, 'was any of your property missing?' Robert said that he had incurred losses including 80,000 lire (equivalent to about £69,000 today), watches, rings, bracelets, various important papers, clothing and shoes. His answer as to whether he had helped the partisans was similarly lucid: he had provided them with fruit, eggs, olive oil and wine, but never weapons or dynamite. As for his wife and daughters, he said, they had never engaged with partisan activities.

Finally, Wexler deployed a tactic which investigators sometimes use when they run out of ideas: they ask an open-ended question. While such a line sometimes generates useful results, often a witness can give an answer that becomes problematic, contradicting a previous statement or undermining their credibility. In this case the gamble paid off:

Wexler: Do you have anything else to state that would be of importance?
Robert: I heard from a priest at the Incontro [monastery] that among 50 German prisoners were

included men who participated in the tragedy in my house.

Wexler: Were they captured by the Americans or British?

Robert: By the British. They were captured near here.

Wexler: Where is the [monastery] located?

Robert: Six kilometres from here.

This could be useful. If the investigators could determine who was held at the Incontro monastery, then perhaps they could track down the men who had murdered Nina, Luce and Cici Einstein. With that final detail, the interview was finished. Robert was excused.

Next to be interviewed was Nina's sister, Seba. As with Robert, Wexler began by asking for her basic information.

Seba said she was fifty-six years old, unmarried, and for the past few years she had helped raise her five nieces: Luce, Cici, Anna Maria, Lorenza and Paola. When asked where she had been on the day of the murders, she said that she had been inside the villa. Unlike Robert, who had been hiding in the woods, Seba would be able to provide a first-hand account of the perpetrators. This type of evidence could potentially be more useful to the investigators.

Next, Wexler asked Seba to describe the officers. She said there were six or seven of them. He pressed her for more details. 'We knew only a captain and a lieutenant,' Seba replied, 'and the lieutenant shut us in the room.'

Wexler: Did you hear the soldiers call the lieutenant by name?

Seba: No.

Wexler: Did you hear the lieutenant call the captain by name?

Seba: No.

Wexler: Were they wearing any particular type of uniform?

Seba: I didn't notice. The farmer's wife [Orando's wife Erenia] told us they were S.S., but I can't confirm that.

Wexler: Do you know what a death's head – a skeleton – is?

Seba: Yes, but I wouldn't say they were wearing that.

Wexler would have found these answers interesting for a number of reasons. First, Seba was not overstating her personal knowledge. Her precision would have given the investigator confidence in her answers. In addition, Seba, like Robert, had heard that the Germans belonged to the SS.

Seba was now asked about the moment that the crime took place.

Wexler: After you heard the shooting, what happened?

Seba: We all screamed and cried because we knew what it was and they opened the door.

Wexler: Who opened the door?

Seba: The lieutenant.

Wexler: Was he alone?

Seba: No, some soldiers were with him.

Wexler: Then what happened?

Seba: He said, 'Justice has been done and the traitors are punished. You can leave the villa, because we will burn it as soon as you are away.'

Wexler: Where did you go?

Seba: To the country.

Wexler: This all happened on August 3rd?

Seba: Yes.

Wexler: What time did you say the shooting happened?

Seba: I think it was 9 o'clock in the evening.

Wexler: When did you first return to the villa?

Seba: We were in the peasants' house and the farmer came and told me my sister and the children were in the villa and were not burned and I immediately went to see them and found my sister in the middle with her one arm on the eldest daughter and in the other she had her spectacles and on the other side was the youngest daughter.

Wexler: Was this the day after the shooting?

Seba: Yes, in the morning.

Wexler: All were dead?

Seba: Yes.

Wexler: Was there any writing or notes by the Germans near the bodies?

Seba: I can't say because the farmer [Orando] gave me this paper. I don't know where it was. There were several notes but I can't say where they were because I have not seen them. He gave them to me.

Wexler: Do you have the notes with you?

Seba: Yes.

Wexler asked her to hand over one of the notices which she did, passing an original to the commissioners. With the document secured, Wexler moved on with the interview.

Wexler: Do you believe that the Germans had violated either of the daughters or the mother?

Seba: I don't know what you mean.

Wexler: Do you believe that the Germans raped or abused them before the shooting?

Seba: No.

Wexler: Did you go to the funeral?

Seba: No.

Wexler: Where were they buried?

Seba: They call it Badiuzza.

Wexler: Did your sister or the children engage in espionage work?

Seba: No, never.

Wexler: Why do you believe that these three were chosen to be murdered?

Seba: I think they wanted my brother-in-law and they didn't find him and it was the cruellest thing they could do, so they killed the wife and the children.

Wexler: Was Einstein himself known as active in partisan work here?

Seba: No.

Wexler: What reason do you believe they had for wanting him?

Seba: I think because he was a Jew.

One of the other commissioners, Major Edwin Booth, now jumped in. He asked for details about the Sala Rossa and the position in which the bodies were found. 'They were almost in the middle of the room,' Seba said, 'my sister in the middle and one daughter on each side.' Booth had two further questions. He asked if she could think of anyone who might know the names of the captain or the lieutenant. She said she did not. How about the unit they belonged to? Seba replied that she had heard that the priest of the Incontro might know. She then offered to point them in the direction of the monastery. The witness was excused.

It was now the turn of seventeen-year-old Paola Mazzetti. The questions were the same. Was she in the villa on the day of the murders? Yes. Was this a new group of Germans? Yes. Did she know the captain's name. No. How did she know he was a captain? 'Because everyone called him captain.' Who was upstairs with her? Her mother, aunt, sister and three cousins. Was the shooting a machine gun or a pistol? 'A sub-machine gun.' Did she know anyone who would be able to identify the Germans who did the shooting? No. After less than five minutes the interview was over.

Next to be interviewed was Lorenza. She was asked only two questions.

Wexler: You have heard the testimony of your sister, is there anything that you wish to add or anything you disagree with?

Lorenza: No.

Wexler: Do you know of any way to identify the German captain, lieutenant or enlisted men who did the shooting?

Lorenza: I believe the manager can, because he told me he remembered the faces, and a few farmers who were in the basement with us.

Finally, it was the turn of Robert's god-daughter and niece Anna Maria. Did she disagree with anything her cousins had stated? She did not. That was it. She was asked no further questions, and was excused. That was the end of the War Crimes Commission's interviews.

The five members of the Einstein family had provided consistent answers. The timing and events matched up, as did the description of the perpetrators (though there was disagreement about their numbers). Without more information about uniforms, rank or insignia, however, it would be challenging to track down the culprits, especially given that so many German units had recently been active in the area and had now withdrawn as the Italian front had moved north, or been redeployed even further afield, to France or East Prussia. And if someone from the local population had betrayed the Einsteins to the Germans, then Wexler was also struggling to identify who that might be. Neither the family nor the *contadini* had provided a name, and without hard evidence it would be challenging to apportion blame.

Most remarkable was the family's explanation for the crime. Both Robert and Seba said the Germans had wanted Robert because he was a Jew; that this was neither a random killing by rogue German soldiers, nor a reprisal against civilians who helped the partisans. Later, the family members would go further: they would say that Robert was specifically targeted because his cousin was Albert Einstein, the most famous Jew in the world, and that the order to kill must have been issued from above, possibly at the very highest level. If this was the truth, it might help explain the US military's extraordinary interest in the case. For if the Nazi regime considered the killing of Albert Einstein's family in Italy to be vitally important then, inevitably, the Americans would think the same. All of which would make the crime not only more significant, it also would make it that much harder to solve.

# 15. Il Focardo, 1944

By 3 p.m., Milton Wexler had all that he needed. He had toured the crime scene, interviewed five witnesses and gathered a general sense of the background to the case. He was just about to leave when Robert asked him for a favour. Would he please write to his cousin in the USA and let him know what had happened. The major said he would and, having taken down Albert Einstein's address, said goodbye. The visit had lasted three and a half hours.

Back in his office in Florence, Wexler placed a piece of Fifth Army Headquarters letterhead into his typewriter and began to tap the keys. A few minutes later, he was finished. Satisfied with what he had written, he walked over to the mailroom and asked that his communication be sent as soon as possible to America.

In the summer of 1944, Albert was taking a vacation on Saranac Lake, in New York State, not far from the Canadian border. One day in August, he and some associates took an eighteen-foot sailing boat out on the water. Everything was going well until it struck a rock, cracking a hole in the hull.

Within minutes, the yacht filled with water and capsized. As the boat turned over, Albert became trapped under a sail, with a rope tangled around his leg. Despite not being able to swim, he somehow managed to free himself and find his way to the surface. Not long after, he and the others were rescued by a passing motorboat.

The accident was reported by the *Lethbridge Herald* on 23 August, under the headline 'Einstein Rescued in Lake'. 'Neither Einstein nor his companions,' the newspaper stated, 'suffered ill effects.' A few days later, Albert described the accident to a friend, saying it had come at a bad time since he'd already been feeling anxious about his sister Maja, who was suffering from a serious illness. He then said that of course his boat accident was nothing compared to what was going on in Europe, and that he was 'grateful' to hear of the recent military successes in France and Belgium.

A few weeks after the accident, Albert returned to Princeton. Arriving home, he went through his mail. Among the pile of papers was an envelope covered with US military stamps. It was the letter from Milton Wexler:

Doctor Albert Einstein
Princeton University
Princeton, New Jersey

17 September 1944

My dear Doctor Einstein,

I take this occasion to communicate with you by personal letter at the request of your cousin, Roberto Einstein, of the Villa del Foscardo [sic], Troghi, a small village approximately ten miles east of the City of Florence. I had occasion to visit in this community and interview Roberto Einstein in connection with a severe tragedy that has overtaken him. Roberto has requested that I inform you that his wife and two daughters suffered death on August 3 at the hands of the Nazi enemies. Roberto, himself, escaped unharmed and is presently living at the villa where he is being carefully attended by his sister-in-law and nieces.

I regret that censorship does not permit me to dwell upon the tragedy which is well known to me. I sincerely regret the nature of this letter and trust that, before long, the war and its terrible consequences will have come to an end with the complete and final defeat of the German armies.

Very sincerely yours
Milton R. Wexler
Major, I.G.D. [Inspector General's Department]

Given his affection for Robert and the horrific nature of the crime, Albert was devastated by the news. Indeed, it was so shocking that Albert kept it to himself because he was worried that Maja's already fragile condition might worsen once she learned about the massacre at Il Focardo.

As it happens, however, Maja had already heard from two other sources that Nina, Luce and Cici had been murdered (though it is not clear why she didn't tell her brother). She later described her reaction in a letter to a close friend:

I received the news of the tragedy of Il Focardo from my cousin and from an American person just after it happened. But my brother gave me the news a month later because he didn't want to upset or frighten me, because from summer to Christmas [1944] I was very ill and I couldn't tell you how much it [the murders] shook me.

For some weeks I was broken [*sfatta*]. I was plagued by terrible hallucinations and they would not leave me. And even now waking up my thoughts always return to that place [Il Focardo].

Meanwhile, back in Italy, Robert was determined to find out who had murdered his wife and daughters. Perhaps sensing that the American War Crimes Commission had run out of steam, he sent a letter to his cousin Albert on 27 November 1944. Despite his occasionally shaky grasp of the language, he wrote in English, presumably not to fall foul of the censors. In his letter, Robert mentioned 'Lori', a nickname for Lorenza, and 'Margot', who was Albert's step-daughter and also lived in Princeton.

Dear Albert;

I don't know if you have heard the terrible tragedy that happened at the 'Focardo': on the third of August, the last day of their permanence here, the Germans killed Nina, Luce and Cici, while I was hidden not far away in the wood. After that crime they burned the villa and sent away in the night Seba, the two twins Paola and Lori and another of my nieces.

The american Inquiry Commission for atrocities has already been here and I trust, that you will help me obtain the identification and punishment of the murders.

For the great difficulties of communications and for the state in which I am, I was not yet able to go and see the house of Maja; but a young lady, friend of us, has been there: the house is in good condition but furnitures have been damaged, as you will understand, by the evaqudees, who occupe it. The library is safe.

I send you my best greetings for yourself, Maja and Margot and I would be very glad to receive your news.

Yours affectionate
Robert

Albert must have been struck by the understatement of his cousin's letter. Robert gave as much space to the condition of Maja's house in Florence as his own tragedy. It was easy to imagine a man so crippled by grief, a mind so shocked, that he was struggling to place a value on things.

How, then, did Albert respond to his cousin's plea for help to 'obtain the identification and punishment' of the perpetrators? The historical record remains unclear, but presumably, given his affection for Robert, he took some form of action. Possibly he contacted people he knew in the Roosevelt administration asking for help. After years of working with various government departments – including his support for the atomic bomb programme – Albert knew people at the very highest level. Even if he was not acquainted with exactly the right official in the Justice Department or the Pentagon, he knew people who knew people. Assistance could have been in the form of a letter or a telephone call or perhaps even a meeting. At the very least, Robert hoped that important folk back in Washington might become more interested in the case, and that this would help the ongoing investigation.

In the meantime, Maja and Albert wrote directly to Robert and his nieces to extend their condolences and support. An article in *Il Nuovo Corriere*, a Florentine newspaper, described the content of some of these letters. Apparently, in the weeks after the murders, Paola and Lorenza had written to their American cousins and somehow managed to present an upbeat tone, sending them a song 'in honour of the liberating Allies'. By return, Albert and Maja replied that not only did they appreciate the song but had shared it with their friends. 'And Lorenza and Paola, with eyes red with weeping, try to smile,' the paper reported. 'And they wonder how that little thing of theirs [the song], born in the countryside on such sad days, ever made it all the way across the ocean.'

Maja also wrote to her husband Paul Winteler, who was living in Switzerland. She first sent a postcard in which she explained what had happened at Il Focardo. Later, she wrote a letter which briefly touched on the same subject:

> I wrote you a card to tell you the terrible news from my cousin's family Robert Einstein. He lives in Florence with Seba and the twins after the death of his wife and his two daughters who were so tragically murdered by the Germans as they retreated through Italy.

Maja and Albert had fled the Nazis. They were 4,000 miles away when Nina, Luce and Cici were brutally murdered. Maja and Albert had survived, their relatives had not. Later, some would describe the emotions associated with this complex situation as 'survivor's guilt'. Back in 1944, Maja put it more simply. She said she was *sfatta* – broken.

A few days after Wexler sent his letter to Albert Einstein, the statements gathered from Robert, Seba, Paola, Lorenza and Anna Maria were typed up at Fifth Army Headquarters in Florence, along with a summary of the case signed by Wexler and the other two commissioners.

Five days later, Wexler's report made its way in triplicate to the desk of the commander of the Fifth Army, at the headquarters in Florence. The following day, 28 September 1944, the commander's assistant adjutant general reviewed the documents, approved them, and despatched them up the chain of command. His covering letter to the commanding general of the North African theatre of operations concluded with the line 'forwarded for such action as may be deemed appropriate'.

In the first week of November, the dossier arrived on the desk of a clerk working for Operations Branch at the Pentagon in Washington DC (section 2b-939), which handled highly classified material including signals intelligence. The dossier was given a file number and then, on 7 November, it was sent on to the office of the judge advocate general, who, in addition to supervising court martials, was responsible for investigating war crimes for the US Army.

On the twenty-fifth of the same month, a new memorandum was added to the folder from someone using the initials 'CAB'. At the top of the page was stamped the word SECRET in bold red letters. Below this was typed the memo's subject: 'German massacre of the Einstein family at Villa al [*sic*] Focardo, Troghi, Italy'. Then, under the heading

'Facts', it stated that 'The war crime consisting of the shooting of the wife and two daughters of R. Einstein. Excuses for the machine-gunning was espionage and storing of dynamite within the villa which charge is contended as baseless', adding that the crime had been carried out by 'unidentified Germans'. Later, someone used a red pencil to underline Robert Einstein's name, along with the words 'unidentified Germans'. The memo then concluded that the case would be 'held pending determination of what agency will take cognizance of German atrocities against Italian nationals'.

As the wheels of American military bureaucracy continued to turn, the Einstein murders were moved from one desk to the next. On a worksheet, a clerk entered the location for the crime, the victims' names, their nationality ('three female Italian civilians') and information on the accused ('unknown German officers and soldiers, perhaps members of SS'). They then gave the names of the three witnesses who had provided statements: Seba, Robert and Paola. Lorenza and Anna Maria were not listed; presumably the value of their testimony was deemed insufficient to merit mention.

A summary of the offence was given at the bottom of the page. It included a motive: 'Likely reason is that [Nina's] husband is a Jew.' This conclusion was significant. By this point, the Allies had come across hundreds of war crimes carried out by German soldiers assisted by Italian collaborators. The murder of the Einsteins, though, was highly unusual. Thousands of Jews had been rounded up and deported from Italy, but it was extremely rare for them to be killed in Italy. More than this, if it was true that the Einsteins had been specifically targeted because of their last name, as the family and many of their neighbours believed (rather than because of

any support for the partisans or because of some spontaneous brutality), it did not take a great leap of imagination to
conclude that there was a political dimension to the murders.
Nor was it hard to sympathize with Robert whose entire
family had been taken from him in one terrible moment.

# 16. Il Focardo, 1944

In the days and weeks following Wexler's visit to Il Focardo, Robert remained in shock. Most days he spent sitting in a chair, by himself, staring out of the window. He found it difficult to concentrate and was easily startled by loud noises and sudden movements. He felt profoundly anxious and thought constantly about suicide. He struggled to eat and was withdrawn and lethargic. He didn't sleep much, didn't go out, didn't see friends, didn't read books or play chess. He was also uninterested in the affairs of the estate, which was a problem for at this time of year there was much that needed to be done: the peach trees had to be pruned, the olive trees had to be harvested and the oil pressed, and the farm equipment had to be repaired and readied for the following year. These matters were left entirely to the *fattore* and his deputy.

At one point the priest Don Giuseppe walked over from Santo Stefano in Le Corti to see how Robert was doing. Like many people who interact with those who are suffering from profound grief, particularly those who have lost children, the priest was uncertain and a little nervous. Should he mention the tragedy? Should he speak about Nina, Luce and Cici? Should he say that Luce had come to see him just days before the murders? Or that, because he did not know what else to do, he had said a Catholic benediction over their bodies, despite their being Protestant? 'I was very puzzled,' Don Giuseppe later recalled, 'because I really did not know what to say to him.'

The priest found Robert sitting by himself in an arm-chair. He wasn't reading a book or a newspaper. Neither was he asleep. He was just sitting there, staring into space. Don Giuseppe offered his hand, which Robert took and gently shook. 'But I was dumbfounded when I observed him,' the priest said. 'I looked at his face. He was covered as if with *squame* [scales]. I can't find another word to describe it prop-erly. I have never seen anything like it'.

The priest sat down close to Robert but felt that he could not say a word. He stayed like that, in silence, for almost an hour. Then he shook Robert's hand again and left 'with great dismay in my heart'. When he spoke to Orando and Pipone, the priest learned that this was now Robert's normal behaviour.

Over the next few weeks, Don Giuseppe returned again and again to see Robert. But always it was the same. They sat together in silence. It was clear to the priest that, in addition to his grief, Robert was suffering a strong sense of guilt: guilt that he should have done more to save his loved ones, that he was somehow responsible for their deaths. 'Never, however, was I able to say a word of comfort to him. I did not have the courage. But what could I say to him after that dreadful tragedy?' And so they remained, sitting next to each other in silence, minute after minute, without uttering a syllable. Then, with a touch on his friend's hand, the priest would leave.

Robert's teenage nieces Lorenza and Paola were also struggling. At birth they had lost their mother, and a few years later were abandoned by their father. Now they had suffered the brutal murder of their two cousins and their adoptive mother. The loss was overwhelming. 'I could not face the memory of that horrific scene and the unbearable void of their absence,' Lorenza later wrote. 'The emptiness is so terrifying that it prevents me from breathing. I feel my heart no longer beating. But then every so often it comes back.'

Lorenza was tormented by nightmares. In one dream, she recalled, 'The partisans are coming, through the window I can see people moving between the bushes and bayonets shining. And I say: "Here they come to save us, here they come." But they never arrive. "Here they come, they are coming, they are just a few steps away, here they are!" The door opens, it's not the partisans, it's the SS. I wake up.' In another dream, she saw her eldest cousin: 'I turn around, from the top of the staircase I see Luce covered in blood. She advances, her face punctured, she looks at me, smiles, comes towards me, but the soldiers' shouts are louder than her voice.' And then, in a third dream: 'Ali, our dog, climbed on top of me and placed his paw on my chest. I told him to leave because he was soiling my dress, but he wouldn't leave. I got really frightened, because Ali had become a wolf that wanted to devour me.'

Lorenza would later describe her emotional state following the murders as dissociated: 'Lying in the dark, I find myself with fragments of a thought. Bits of memory, a firefly, a Beethoven sonata and the Wehrmacht in my bed.' The stress and shock impacted her behaviour: she couldn't 'accept being calm, serene, to eat, drink or sleep,' she wrote, 'because something tells me I'm not allowed this serenity.' She also began to question her religion. 'I know it is sad to no longer believe in God for someone who believed in Him as much as I did.' Where previously she had gone to church and appreciated the comfort that it had given, now she would 'look at that crucified Jesus and the red blood coming out of his ribs, feet and hands. And then I think of them, the blood on their faces and on their clothes'.

Paola was also shattered by what had happened on 3 August. 'It was terrifying,' she later said, 'it was the end of the world, the end of the world.' More analytical than her twin sister, Paola spent a lot of time thinking about the details, trying to figure things out. She remembered certain moments more sharply than others. While she had little memory of their time in the cellar, the images from when they were locked in the bedroom were clearer. When Luce returned after being questioned downstairs, for instance, she remembered that she had removed her necklace and given it to Seba. For Paola, this meant that Luce guessed what was about to happen. Paola also remembered the shots being fired. And a female scream. After thinking about it some more, she concluded that it probably came from Cici, who was the youngest of the three who were killed and would not have suspected anything.

Robert's god-daughter and niece Anna Maria, was also profoundly affected by the murders. She described their previous life at Il Focardo as 'paradise'. The killings ended all that. She would later say that what happened on 3 August 1944 was by far the most painful event of her life. Unlike her cousins, however, she didn't want to talk about it, preferring to keep her thoughts and emotions to herself. And with her parents still in Pisa, Robert unavailable, and Seba and her cousins dealing with their own grief, it was a lonely time. To occupy herself, she helped the *contadini* with their tasks on the estate.

Beyond the sudden loss of Nina, Luce and Cici, the three cousins had also suffered individual trauma. They had been held captive for more than twelve hours fearing for their own lives, they had heard their aunt and cousins being murdered, and now Robert was overwhelmed by heartache and depression. Socializing came with its own challenges and triggers. When the young women spent time with others – the children they had grown up with on the estate, the *fattore*, the local priest – they found it difficult to be normal. As Lorenza wrote: 'I pretend to laugh and joke, while others genuinely laugh. But why can't I? Others can and I cannot. Rather, I am not allowed. Why can't I? The others can and I can't. It's not even that I can't. I'm not allowed to.'

Robert's despondency was made worse by the unusually cold and gloomy winter. From the terrace of Il Focardo it was possible to see the peach and olive trees draped in white frost. And despite the fires in the villa that were kept going throughout the day by the *contadini*, it was impossible to keep warm: the ceilings were high, there was no insulation in the walls and the old doors and windows were draughty.

As the calendar turned from November to December and into 1945, life remained grim. For all of them – Lorenza, Paola, Anna Maria and their uncle Robert – certain days were particularly hard. Christmas and New Year's Eve were dismal, with nobody wanting to celebrate. Then came the birthdays which, as it happened, fell early in the year: first Cici's on 23 February. Next Nina's on 24 March. Then Luce's on 19 April. Each a reminder of the person who they had loved, who had been lost. With Robert lacking the capacity to guide the young women, the anniversaries came and went without commemoration. At the end of each day, Robert took himself upstairs. Sometimes, rather than turning right to go to his and Nina's bedroom, he turned left, and went to Luce's bedroom. Somehow in sleeping in his eldest daughter's narrow bed he found comfort.

During their school's term time, the young women lived with Seba at the family's apartment in Florence at Corso dei Tintori 21. The twins slept in one room while Seba and Anna Maria were in another. Every now and then, Robert came to see them. 'It was very hard,' Anna Maria later recalled. 'My uncle was deeply depressed. He said very little but it was clear he felt racked by guilt for what had happened.'

There was one time when Robert spoke to Anna Maria with feeling. By this point, she had still not heard from her parents and was unsure of their situation. In a serious tone, Robert said that he had thought carefully about her future. She was a good student, he said, she worked hard and clearly had an appetite for learning. He therefore thought that she should attend university and he would pay for her tuition fees. Anna Maria was both grateful and deeply moved by this. As for Robert, he was making good on his promise to the partisan Alberto Droandi that he would assure his nieces' future.

On another occasion, when Robert, Seba and their nieces were all together in the apartment on Corso dei Tintori, they were visited by a young journalist who wrote for *Il Nuovo*

*Corriere.* This man had heard that the twins were fine painters and wanted to see their work. Arriving at the door, he was welcomed inside and they all sat in the living room. 'They were very friendly,' he recalled. 'I almost didn't notice the mourning that surrounded me.' It was just before he was about to leave, as one of his hosts was responding to a remark about the poor state of Italy, that 'they sighed in a particularly sad way' and then recounted what had happened to their family. Over the next few weeks, the journalist returned to the apartment and formed a clear impression of them. The young women were full of 'terror, pain, youth, intelligence, love and art'. As for Robert, he was 'serious, calm and noble'.

Though in the past Florence had been a place of fun and distraction for the Einsteins, the city was now in chaos. Much of Renaissance Florence had been destroyed by the Nazis. There was little left of Via de' Bardi near the Ponte Vecchio, which had previously been lined with palaces, churches and other notable buildings. The part of the city that stretched along the river near Ponte Santa Trinita was in ruins, while many historic houses were also destroyed, including that of Machiavelli. 'The Florence that we and successive generations of men since the days of the Medici knew and loved is no more,' the American foreign correspondent Herbert Matthews wrote in *Harper's Magazine*. 'Of all the world's artistic losses in the war, this is one of the saddest.'

With the arrival of spring, the days lengthened, the weather warmed and the skies cleared. But inside the villa Il Focardo, the mood remained gloomy and desolate, haunted by the torments of traumatic grief. For the most part, the house was filled by silence. The young women retreated to their bedrooms, Robert to his chair by the window. 'He seemed to have become numb to everything,' recalled Don Giuseppe. 'Nothing interested him any more; he was now a stranger to everything.'

All the while, the survivors living at Il Focardo were reminded of those who a few months before had lived with them at the villa. In the clothes left hanging in the closets, the pictures on the walls, the sheets of music resting on the shelf ready to be played. 'How is it possible that our dead never show up?' Lorenza wrote. 'That they stay in the ground when their shoes are still in the entrance hall?'

With Robert withdrawing more and more into himself, the chances of solving the case declined. Not only had he seen the events unfold and was therefore a key witness, but of those living in Italy he had the closest relationship with Albert Einstein, and was therefore potentially best placed to understand the motivations behind the assault. Perhaps even more importantly, it had been Robert who had instigated the inquiry. Without him, Milton Wexler would never have started the investigation, and without him pushing and cajoling the authorities, there was a good chance the case would languish, especially given the competing demands on the US military as it attempted to take over the reins of war-torn Italy.

If this case went unsolved, it could have repercussions far beyond the family's personal tragedy. It would mean that authoritarian regimes could assassinate not only their political enemies but also the families of their enemies with impunity, making it more likely to happen again in the future. Or, to put it most simply: if the murder of Albert Einstein's family went unpunished, who was safe?

# 17. Il Focardo, 1945

At the start of April 1945, after months of being held up by the Nazi forces who had expertly dug into their fortified positions in the mountains north of Florence – and with frustration growing among Churchill, Stalin and Roosevelt – the Allies were finally ready to launch their spring offensive. The aim was to seize Bologna, Milan, Verona and the other northern cities and, in the process, bring an end to the war in Italy.

Under the command of General Mark Clark, the Allies now had over 1.5 million women and men active in the Italian theatre of operations (including American, British, Brazilian, New Zealand, South African, Polish, Indian and Australian troops). Helping them were tens of thousands of Italian resistance fighters (including communists, Jews and other partisans) who more than made up for their lack of training with their local knowledge and passion for victory. Meanwhile, the Axis powers had nearly 500,000 personnel – mainly German soldiers and Italian forces loyal to Mussolini's Italian Social Republic – under the command of General Heinrich von Vietinghoff.

Having launched a diversionary attack to pull Axis forces

away from the main assault, the Allies pushed north towards Bologna. After overcoming stiff resistance with the help of significant partisan belligerents, they were able to capture key locations, including Ferrara and Parma. Bologna experienced desperate street-to-street combat before it was taken on 21 April. And then finally, four days later, partisans entered Milan – Italy's largest northern city and its industrial powerhouse.

That evening, Benito Mussolini, who had been based in Milan for the last week, fled the city. The following day, he and his mistress Clara Petacci tried to cross into Switzerland but failed. On 27 April, they tried again. In a last desperate effort, Mussolini and Petacci, along with fifty other leading Italian fascists, took refuge in a convoy of Luftwaffe troops who were trying to make their way north towards Germany. The convoy was attacked by a small group of partisans near the village of Dongo near Lake Como and, shortly after, Mussolini was discovered cowering in one of the trucks. He and Petacci were taken to a farm near Dongo, where they were held pending further orders. The next day, 28 April, Mussolini and Petacci were driven fifteen miles to the south, to a quiet, narrow lane near the village of Giulino di Mezzegra. Here the truck stopped, the pair were walked to a stone wall outside the entrance of a villa and, at 4.10 p.m., shot with a sub-machine gun. The bodies were then loaded back into the truck and, early the following morning, dumped on the ground in Piazzale Loreto in Milan. Over the next few hours, the bodies were kicked, urinated upon, shot at by numerous guns and then strung up by their feet in front of a nearby petrol station.

The following day, 29 April, the German High Command in Italy agreed to lay down its arms. Nine days later, on 8 May,

*Top Left:* Albert's father, Hermann Einstein.
*Top Right:* Albert's mother, Pauline Einstein (née Koch).
*Bottom Left*: Albert and Maja Einstein.
*Bottom Right:* Jakob and Hermann Einstein's business in Italy.

*Top left:* Robert and Nina Einstein.
*Above:* Nina with Luce, Cici and twin babies,
Paola and Lorenza.
*Left:* Robert Einstein.

*Top:* Nina Einstein with her two young
daughters, Luce (*left*) and Cici (*right*).
*Left:* Cici Einstein when older (circa 1940s).
*Right:* Luce Einstein when older (circa 1940s).

*Top:* Paola, Robert, Anna Maria, Lorenza, Eugenio (Anna Maria's brother) and Seba in front of the entrance to Il Focardo.
*Bottom:* Nina, Lorenza, Paola, Cici, Seba and Luce in Perugia.

*Above:* A postcard of Il Focardo.
*Left:* The front entrance to
Il Focardo.

*Top:* 'Pipone' Galante, deputy estate manager, with Paola, Lorenza and others.
*Left:* Alberto Droandi, the partisan who helped Robert Einstein.
*Right:* Orando Fuschiotti, the *fattore* (estate manager).

*Top:* Albert Einstein under armed guard in the UK, 1933.
*Bottom:* Albert Einstein and his sister Maja Einstein, New York, USA, 1939.

*Above:* Hitler and Mussolini meeting in Florence in 1938.
*Left*: Hitler and Mussolini's parade in Florence in 1938.

the Allies accepted the unconditional surrender of Germany's military forces in every operational theatre. Around the world, newspapers were covered in towering headlines: 'Germans Proclaim Surrender', announced the *Sydney Morning Herald*; 'Germany Quits', proclaimed the *Sacramento Bee* and many other local papers in the USA; 'Peace in Europe', declared the *Daily Mail* in England; 'Victoire!' the *Liberation Soir* succinctly stated in France. Meanwhile, in Italy, *Il Giornale* announced, 'The Germans Have Capitulated'.

Robert Einstein and his nieces were relieved to hear the news. But unlike September 1943, when the *contadini* had run outside in celebration of the premature armistice, there was little commotion or fanfare on the Il Focardo estate. The war had come at such a great cost. Nearly 4 million Italians had served in the military, with around 320,000 killed and at least the same number wounded. Some 600,000 Italians had been deported to Germany as forced labour, having refused to join the Wehrmacht. About 200,000 volunteers took part in the resistance, including those who fought with the British Army; nearly 22,000 were killed, including both partisans and civilians, by German forces in response. In addition, 8,564 Jews had been deported from Italy and the territory it controlled to the concentration camps – most of them never to return. Many of Italy's cities were badly damaged, as was the country's infrastructure: railways, bridges, factories, roads. In short, Italy had been crushed. And, of course, the family had suffered its own devastating losses.

One of the few visitors to see Robert during this time was Enrico Bürgisser, the former owner of Il Focardo. He brought along his sixteen-year-old son Giancarlo, who had been born in the villa and lived there till 1937, when Robert purchased the property. Enrico had heard about the murders and wished to convey his condolences. According to Giancarlo, this visit took place 'under very sad circumstances'. Robert was in a 'tragic state', unresponsive, a shrunken man. The encounter was brief. Enrico and Giancarlo said their goodbyes and soon left.

And then, in the weeks of late May, something began to shift. Perhaps it was the better weather, which had turned warmer and drier. Or maybe it was the sweet smells of spring: flowering jasmine, fresh-cut grass, and the strawberry scent of the magnolia trees. Or it could just have been the passing of time, allowing the pain and heartache somewhat to ease. Whatever it was, with each day Robert gradually spent more time walking around the estate.

The *padrone*'s perambulations gave hope to the *contadini* that perhaps the worst of his depression was over. Certainly, with so many of the men absent after years of war, Il Focardo could really do with its owner's attention. There was much to be done. The peach trees needed to be thinned out, the animals required constant care, and the equipment needed to be readied for the harvest.

Over the next few weeks, further major developments were announced on the radio and reported in the newspapers. On 2 June, Pope Pius XII gave a speech warning of 'revolution and disorder' in Europe. Three weeks later, Italy's prime minister Ivanoe Bonomi resigned. The following day, the Battle of Okinawa concluded in victory for the Allies, a prerequisite for the ground invasion of the Japanese home islands. Then, on 5 July, General Douglas MacArthur, commander of US forces in the southwest Pacific, declared that the Philippines had been liberated from Japanese rule. And five days after

that, on 10 July, in a more positive sign that post-war nor-
mality was returning to Europe, it was announced that the
Louvre Museum in Paris would reopen its doors.

That same day, the *contadini* at Il Focardo were out in the
orchard picking peaches. It was swelteringly hot; there had
been no rain for weeks and the ground was brittle and brown.
Up on their wooden ladders, with their reed baskets dangling
from their arms, the workers collected the peaches hanging
ripe and juicy from the bowed silver-brown branches. It was
slow, careful work. To earn the best price at market, the fruit
needed to arrive unbruised and unblemished. The pickers
were therefore on the lookout for dark spots left by mould
or any trace of insect damage. Such fruit were put to one
side to be enjoyed by their own families, or, if too ruined,
tossed to the ground for the rodents and the deer to enjoy.
From time to time, the pickers washed their hands, for if
left too long, the hairs from the peaches produced an itchy
rash on the skin. Nevertheless, the labour was not unpleasant. The sun shone kindly from the bleached blue sky, the
peaches' sweet aroma hung in the air, and all the while the
*contadini* were conscious that their labour stood in delightful
contrast to the recent armed conflict during which so many
had lost so much.

It was at this moment, while the *contadini* were busy picking peaches, that Robert stepped out of the villa's front door,
walked through the garden, and headed up the track to see
his friend Pipone. Robert first stopped at Casa Bella, but the
deputy *fattore* was not there, so he kept walking. A few minutes
later, he found him in the orchard, watering the peach trees.

'Is it all right if I take a peach?' the *padrone* asked as he
walked up. Pipone smiled. 'Of course,' he said, 'you can take

any that you like.' Then he gestured to the orchard. 'After all, it's all yours.'

Pipone was pleased to see Robert in the orchard, taking exercise, out in the fresh air. But he was also cautious. Robert had been despondent for months. And while he had been reluctant to confide in Don Giuseppe and the girls, he had opened up to his friend, the deputy *fattore*. They had spoken often with Robert going over and over whether he should have remained hidden in the woods and Pipone reassuring him that he had done the best he could in an impossible situation. Even if Robert had returned to the villa, both he and his family would probably all have been murdered. Despite his friend's calm words, however, Robert couldn't find solace. Which was why it was good to see him asking for a piece of fruit today. Now, standing with a hosepipe in his hand, Pipone again invited Robert to take any peach that he liked. But still Robert hesitated. 'You choose,' he said to the deputy *fattore*. 'Choose the best one, as if it was the last I ever ate.'

And so Pipone walked over to a tree, assessed several peaches with his expert eye, touching each carefully before plucking one, large and juicy and golden warm in the summer sun. He handed it to Robert, who held the peach in his hand for a moment, grateful, before taking a bite. The sweetness of the fruit overwhelmed his senses. He smiled and took another bite. And smiled again. He then thanked his friend, said goodbye and walked away back towards the villa, still taking bites from the peach.

# 18. Il Focardo, 1945

Around 8.30 in the morning on 11 July, Orando walked into the villa looking for Robert Einstein. He and his wife had been expecting him to come over for breakfast, but the *padrone* had not shown up. The air inside the villa was warm and close as the previous night the temperature had remained in the low twenties. The ground floor was quiet, which was strange, as the estate owner was an early riser. So Orando went upstairs and found the door to the *padrone*'s bedroom was closed. He knocked. When there was no reply, he opened the door and stepped inside. Robert was lying on his bed, gasping. The *fattore* looked around and saw an empty veronal bottle on the ground. Later, it was determined that he had taken as many as twenty-three sleeping pills.

Realizing what had happened, Orando rushed over to Casa Bella and asked Pipone to keep an eye on the *padrone*. He then ran to Adolfo Caldini's house and knocked loudly on the door. 'Adolfo!' Orando said urgently. 'We have to drive the engineer to the hospital.' Adolfo knew immediately who Orando was talking about. For many years he had been the Einsteins' driver. Taking Robert and Nina into Florence, driving Luce and Cici to school and back, collecting friends from the railway station.

A few minutes later, Adolfo's black Fiat Balilla crunched up the narrow gravel driveway and pulled up outside the villa's front door. Orando and Adolfo hurried inside. They found Robert slouched in a chair in the front hallway, semi-conscious. Pipone was holding his head so that it did not flop over. As they approached, Robert let out a weak moan. The three men carried Robert's limp body through the front door and placed him in the car. The *fattore* sat next to Adolfo in the front. Robert was in the back with Pipone. Adolfo sped towards Florence. The journey was challenging. With all of Florence's usual vehicular bridges across the Arno destroyed by the Nazis, there was a massive line of cars and trucks trying to cross the temporary Bailey bridge that had been built on top of the wreckage of Ponte Santa Trinita. As they drove on, Robert was still making small noises, but his breathing was slow and shallow.

After more than an hour's drive, they arrived at Careggi University Hospital in the north of Florence; considered the best medical centre in the region, it was where Luce had completed part of her training. Pulling up at the emergency doors, the *fattore* ran inside for help. A few moments later, orderlies were carrying the barely breathing Robert Einstein inside. Soon after, he was transported upstairs to an intensive care ward, lifted gently on to a metal cot and covered with a thin sheet. The doctors and nurses worked quickly to pump his stomach. By the day's end, he was stabilized but unresponsive. His prognosis was not good.

*

The sleeping pill veronal had first come on the market in 1904. The first commercially available barbiturate, it had been created by the German chemists Emil Fischer and Josef von Mering, who named it after the city of Verona. In the USA it was known as 'barbital' and in the UK as 'barbitone'. Around the world, veronal and its various offshoots were prescribed for the treatment of a variety of complaints, including mania, insomnia, schizophrenia and epilepsy. It was also widely used as a sedative. The use of these barbiturates peaked during the inter-war period. In the USA, for instance, the production of barbiturates increased by more than 400 per cent from 1933 to 1936.

By 1945, it was well known that veronal was being widely used to assist suicide. Indeed, by this point there had been many famous cases reported in the newspapers, including the Austrian writer Stefan Zweig in 1942 and the Greek musician Attik in 1944. Meanwhile, authors such as Agatha Christie, Dorothy Parker and D. H. Lawrence had included characters in their books who killed themselves taking veronal. In 1945, however, the actual numbers of barbiturate-related deaths remained relatively uncommon. It would be another five years before this would change. In England and Wales, for instance, there were fifty reported cases of barbiturate-related deaths in 1945. This would rise to 300 in 1950 and then 650 by 1965. Perhaps the most famous case took place when Marilyn Monroe died of an overdose in 1962. The American Pharmaceutical Association was so worried about this issue that at the very moment Robert was in hospital in Florence they were organizing a conference on the topic of suicidal use of veronal and similar substances. It would take place in Washington DC later that year.

*

The day after Robert was admitted to hospital, Thursday 12 July, Anna Maria hurried over to Santo Stefano in Le Corti to look for the priest. She found Don Giuseppe in the chapel, preparing for the weekend service. In tears, she explained that her uncle had tried to kill himself and asked the priest if he could do something to help. Shocked by the news, Don Giuseppe agreed to go to the hospital with Anna Maria.

When they arrived, they were directed to the room where Robert was being kept. He was in a coma and barely breathing. The priest did his best to provide comfort to the young woman. They knelt by Robert's bedside and prayed together. Afterwards, Anna Maria reminded the priest that she had been baptized and asked that he bless her uncle. 'Between tears, she insisted that I give him the comforts of our faith,' he later recalled. This was a difficult choice for the priest since Robert was not baptized. But seeing it meant so much to the young woman, and concluding it could only benefit the soul of his friend, he made a decision. With one hand on the cross hanging around his neck and the other hovering over Robert, Don Giuseppe gave the blessing and absolution *in articulo mortis*: 'By the faculty given to me by the Apostolic See,' he softly recited, 'I grant thee a plenary indulgence and remission of all sins. In the name of the Father, and of the Son, and of the Holy Ghost. Amen.' After completing the prayer, the priest looked over at Anna Maria. 'She was greatly pleased,' he said, 'and somewhat relieved.'

For the rest of the day and through the night, Robert remained in a coma. It is not known who else visited him during this period. It is also not recorded who was present, if anyone, when at 3.50 p.m. the following day, 13 July 1945, Robert Einstein was declared dead at Careggi Hospital.

He was sixty-one years old. Like so many others who committed suicide before, during and after the Second World War, Robert would not be counted as a victim of the Holocaust. Yet, many consider him to be the fourth victim of the Il Focardo crime. He was driven to take his life out of grief and guilt, his pain made worse by the failure of the authorities to bring those responsible to justice.

'The poor engineer!' Don Giuseppe later recalled. 'He was a very fine person, a truly superior man in terms of intelligence and culture. He had interests not only in the sciences, but also in art and literature. For the terrible suffering [Robert] endured, I firmly hope that God in His infinite mercy has welcomed him into His blessed kingdom, to enjoy the infinite happiness of Paradise for ever with his loved ones.'

The priest ended his account with the following words: 'Thus ended the drama of that family, totally annihilated by Nazi ferocity. All this is proof that war is the most heinous thing that human wickedness has ever devised!'

# 19. Il Focardo, 1945

In the hours following Robert's death, Orando was going through his boss's personal effects when he came across a bundle of letters addressed to those close to him. The first had been written on 16 June. Apparently Robert had known he would kill himself for at least four weeks.

Among the letters, Orando found one to himself, dated 30 June:

My Dear Orando

I'm sorry that with my death I must bring you not only grief but also much aggravation. But I prefer to die at Il Focardo, where my relatives suffered martyrdom, and I wish to be buried as close to them as possible. Please provide a zinc casket so that the transfer of all four bodies to the cemetery in Rome will be possible without too much difficulty.

I leave Il Focardo to Paola and Lori [Lorenza], certain that you will do your best to administer the property in their interest.

Give my regards to Mrs Erenia, to who I'm grateful
for all the attention on me, your mother, your brother
and sister-in-law with their little girls, who have been a
great comfort to me in my brief exile; kiss Marinella and
Antonello [Orando's children]!

I apologize if I have sometimes been a little rude; please
say hello to all the *contadini* who have been my friends, and
I hug you affectionately.

Roberto Einstein

Another of the letters found among Robert's posses-
sions was to his god-daughter and niece Anna Maria. Dated
16 June, it was the first of the farewells that he wrote.

Dear Picchia [Little One]

You especially, given your faith, will be pained by my
taking my life, but I no longer have the courage to go on
living in my current condition. Forgive me! On the other
hand, you will soon return to live with your family and
will no longer need my assistance.

I ask that you be good to others, especially to your
mother, on who life has not always lavished gifts! Try
always to be tolerant of other people's ideas, to broaden
your horizons, for your own good and that of those you
must not only teach but also educate; 'educate' according
to the etymology of the word, meaning leading them out
of childhood towards youth and life. Then you will not
lack the limited happiness that this earthly existence of
ours can offer, nor the inner satisfaction that comes from
knowing we have done everything possible for the good

of those who love us. I kiss you and hug you with all my affection.

I love you
Uncle Roberto

Anna Maria was profoundly moved when she read this letter. Though she was not as close to Robert as Lorenza and Paola – she had arrived at the house aged seventeen and lived with him for less than two years – she greatly respected him. As such, she considered the letter an extraordinary gift.

Not long after Robert killed himself, Anna Maria packed her bags and said goodbye to her cousins and aunt Seba. After the terrible events of the last year, she was glad to leave Florence and return to her parents in Pisa. There she enrolled in university. For the rest of her life, she would remain grateful to Robert for paying for her university fees.

Meanwhile, Orando Fuschiotti began putting Robert's wishes into action. He spoke with his wife's brother, the coffin-maker, and asked him to provide a casket. He contacted Nina's brother Corrado in Rome and informed him that his daughters Lorenza and Paola were now without guardians and he needed to take care of them. He also conveyed the news that the twins were going to be the new owners of Il Focardo. There was, however, one instruction that was not followed. After some discussion with the priest, it was agreed that Robert should be buried in Badiuzza Cemetery next to his wife and daughters.

This decision was notable for a number of reasons. In his letter to Orando, Robert had clearly asked that his wife and daughters be disinterred so that they could be buried with him in Rome. In addition, it was highly unusual for a Jewish person to be buried in a Catholic graveyard, especially given that Robert had committed suicide, an act that typically precluded a Catholic burial. Perhaps the *fattore* and the priest believed that it was doubtful that a cemetery could be found in Rome that would agree to take all four bodies. Perhaps they felt it was ghoulish to disturb the three women so soon after their tragic end. Or perhaps they considered the Einstein tragedy was in some way theirs: to have the bodies removed would be one loss too many for the community to endure.

Whatever the reason, a week or so after Robert died, his body was taken from the hospital morgue in Florence, loaded into a small van and then carried south, across the River Arno, through the town of Bagno a Ripoli, over the hilltop village of San Donato in Collina to the modest stone-walled Badiuzza Cemetery. There a sombre ceremony was held. Seba, Anna Maria, Lorenza and Paola were in attendance, along with a group of *contadini* including Orando and Pipone and their wives. The priest, Don Giuseppe, presided over the ritual. Once the body was lowered into the ground and the prayers were over, two gravediggers shovelled dirt into the hole. Robert Einstein was reunited with his wife and two daughters, overlooking his beloved Il Focardo.

Though Robert Einstein's suicide was just one of countless heartbreaking stories that had occurred in Italy over the past six years, there was something about it that caught the press's attention. So much so, that in the days following his death, numerous newspapers published articles about Robert and his family.

On 28 July, the Florentine paper *Il Nuovo Corriere* ran a long piece under the headline 'The Germans Keep Killing'. The article started with a short biography: 'Robert Einstein, electrical engineer, born in Munich about sixty years ago, was a victim of Nazi persecution because, like his cousin still an exile in America, and all his relatives, the Einsteins are Jews.' Then, after recounting the details of the murders at Il Focardo and Robert's subsequent death, it did something perhaps surprising, particularly in a conservative Catholic country such as Italy whose traditions strictly shunned suicide. It praised Robert for somehow remaining alive as long as he did – it had been 344 days since his entire nuclear family had been murdered – and it commended him for his fortitude. 'Robert Einstein demonstrated true heroism in choosing to continue to live following a cruel tragedy that, in just one hour, eliminated his entire family.' The article then moved on to a more general theme, pointing out that Italians were still dying months after the end of hostilities. 'The tragedy of war,' it said, 'has infinite offshoots.'

Another Florentine paper, *La Nazione del Popolo*, also devoted an article to the Einsteins. Its author was a professor of German language and literature called Rodolfo Paoli, who was also a friend of Robert and Nina. He began by saying that there had been little coverage of the murders of Nina, Luce and Cici Einstein when they happened because the 'tragedy was lost in the din of cannon, tanks, aeroplanes, and the jubilation of the arrival of the Allies'. For his part, he wanted to focus on Robert's elder daughter, Luce, who, as it happened, he knew. He had met her in the woods near Il Focardo in the summer of 1944. 'Among the university students massacred by the Germans,' Paoli wrote, 'I don't think I've heard

anyone mention how much Luce Einstein deserves attention.' There was one episode in particular he wanted to relay.
On 3 August 1944, when the soldiers accused Nina and the
others of storing dynamite in the villa on behalf of the partisans, Luce 'sensed the gravity of the situation, and with a
heroic impulse took the blame, saying the family knew nothing about it'. The Germans were stunned as they knew this
to be untrue. It was they, the Germans, who had planted the
dynamite. In addition to Robert losing his dear wife that day,
he had lost his two daughters, the 'flower of youth taken by
a senseless hate'. This is what had driven him to take his life.

Throughout these newspaper accounts, all published
just weeks after the war's end in Italy, there emerged some
common threads: profound horror at what had happened
to Nina, Luce and Cici, deep sympathy for Robert and the
choices he had made, and total outrage against those responsible for the family tragedy.

There was one aspect of the story that was not covered by
the Italian press. The idea that the Einsteins were betrayed by
a local person or persons is prevalent among many of those
close to the events. This was certainly the belief of Anna
Maria Boldrini, Nina and Robert's niece and god-daughter. It
was also the view of the *fattore* Orando Fuschiotti and his wife
Erenia, as well as others such as Nello Carrara and his wife
Gaetanina Gattai who lived near Il Focardo. One theory was
that a woman who worked at the Einstein villa had a boyfriend
who supported the fascist administration and he had given the
family away.

Another of those who felt the family were betrayed was
Beniamino Morandi, who was around the same age as Cici,
Lorenza and Paola, and had played with them as a child at

Il Focardo. 'Someone must have betrayed the Einsteins,' he later recalled. 'The Germans would never have found them if an Italian hadn't showed them the way.' As he shared this, tears ran down Beniamino's face.

In late July 1945, around a fortnight after Robert took his life, the former partisan Alberto Droandi was sleeping on the terrace outside his mother's home in Arezzo. It was Alberto who, a year earlier, Robert had met in Montevarchi after walking for four days in the woods and asked for his gun. In the time since, Alberto had received an award for his wartime service and was now trying to restart his life.

After his many nights in the woods, Alberto was used to sleeping outside; in any case, it was pleasant to be out on the terrace during these hot summer nights. He was still asleep when his mother opened the window above his head and woke him up. She handed him a cup of coffee and a newspaper. It took him a few moments for his eyes to focus, and then he saw the story: the engineer Robert Einstein had killed himself. There was also a picture of the engineer. He looked far healthier in this photograph than the man he remembered approaching him that night in Montevarchi a year before.

Despite his hopes for Robert, Alberto Droandi realized that 'time had not healed his wound or lessened the pain'. Later, the former partisan decided to send a summary of his encounter with Robert to Albert Einstein in the United States. Perhaps the famous scientist would appreciate knowing the details; maybe he might even find them comforting. 'I wanted to do this but I didn't get around to it,' Alberto Droandi later admitted. 'I knew that the physicist would one day visit the grave of Robert Einstein in Italy, so I decided to wait and talk to Albert till then.'

Decades later, Alberto Droandi was finally persuaded to record his memories. 'Up to this point, only a few of my relatives and friends were aware of this story,' he said. 'But now I will pay homage to the memory of the deeply wretched [*disgraziatissimo*] engineer Robert Einstein.'

Among the items Orando found in Robert's personal effects was another letter, this one to Paola and Lorenza. It was shorter than those he wrote to Anna Maria and Orando. He encouraged them not to wear black in mourning and said that he had left them all his assets. 'Forgive me, if I was a bit annoying and grouchy,' he wrote. 'Remember me, Cici, Luce and Nina and what we taught you'.

Lorenza and Paola were overwhelmed by Robert's suicide. They had lived with him for more than half their lives, he had played the role of father and uncle, provider and carer. For them, it was another appalling loss.

On the first Sunday after Robert's burial, the twins walked to Badiuzza Cemetery, where they placed flowers on the four graves. 'A wall of water tumbles over me like a wave,' Lorenza would later write. 'Us above the ground, us below the ground. The girls with dirt in their eyes, Uncle with dirt in his eyes sails underground because he is Jewish.' Paola comforted her sister, telling her not to cry, and gave her a kiss. They then returned home.

Not long after Robert's death, Paola and Lorenza's father Corrado arrived in Florence to be with his daughters. It had been eleven years since they had lived together under one roof. It must have been a challenging adjustment. Their mood may have been lifted somewhat by the changes they began to see around them. The streets were starting to be cleared of rubble and work had begun on rebuilding the bridges across the Arno. The markets reopened, and lipstick, stockings and chocolate were now widely available. *Gelato* was even being sold again next to the Ponte Vecchio and across the city. There was also positive news in the art world. Just a few days before, a trainful of predominantly Renaissance works of art, including oil paintings, sculptures and frescoes arrived in Florence. Then, to the great joy of thousands of onlookers, they were paraded through the streets on a convoy of trucks draped with flags, one of which declared, 'The Florentine treasures, stolen by the Germans, are returned by the Americans'.

At the end of this eventful summer, the twins started back at Michelangelo High School to complete their final year. Each day, they walked to school, attended their assigned classes – history, mathematics, literature, art – returned to the apartment for lunch and then spent the afternoon doing their homework. It was a new routine, a scaffolding on which to try and build a new life.

A few weeks into the new term, Paola and Lorenza made their way to the University of Florence in Piazza San Marco. There they followed the signs to a lecture hall, where they found more than a hundred people already in their seats. They were the parents, grandparents and siblings of students who had died during the war. Also in the auditorium were staff members, and friends who had now graduated. Looking around the room, they spotted their father Corrado and went to sit next to him.

The ceremony started with the rector of the university, Piero Calamandrei, standing in front of a podium and welcoming the audience. He then declared the event to be a 'day of mourning' for the fallen students and that they 'must not forget' the young men and women who had been killed while still studying at the university. Then, in a more upbeat tone, he spoke about the changes since the war's end.

> If we compare Italy as it was a year ago and as it is today, and try to calmly assess the miracle of its people, who already in just one year have been able to live, to get up and begin again, to look about without despair, not only can we commemorate our fallen with sadness, but also we can feel that, inspired by their example, we should not close ourselves off with regret for the past but move bravely towards the future.

The rector paused for a moment and looked at the audience before continuing. 'The day has come for us all to cease hating,' he said. 'This is what the dead who we commemorate today would have wanted. And now we remember their names.'

He started with Robert and Nina's eldest daughter. 'Luce Einstein was born in Munich on 19 April 1917. She studied here as a medical student,' Piero Calamandrei said. 'She was slaughtered for her surname by the German SS, along with her mother and sister, in Rignano sull'Arno on 3 August 1944.' He then paused again and looked over to Lorenza and Paola; this was a signal. The twins stood up and walked towards the stage. Two weeks earlier, Corrado had written to the rector suggesting that his daughters represent the family. They had grown up with Luce, he said, she was their *compianta*, their much-missed loved one. Now, standing on stage, the twins shook the rector's hand and received Luce's posthumous diploma. The audience clapped loudly. Many had tears in their eyes.

After the ceremony, Corrado walked home with his two daughters. It was a moment of survival, a moment of family togetherness.

Not long after, disaster struck again. The fifty-three-year-old Corrado was cycling down a street when he was hit by a motor vehicle. A death notice paid for by the family was published in the local newspaper *La Nazione del Popolo*; it recorded simply that he had 'died suddenly, torn from the affection of his loved ones'. Two days later, Corrado was buried in the Cimitero Evangelico agli Allori, the city's Protestant burial ground, just south of the River Arno. Afterwards, a small gathering was held at the family's apartment at Corso dei Tintori 21. Paola and Lorenza had now lost both parents, both adopted parents and the two cousins they had grown up with. They were only eighteen years old.

Following Corrado's death, it was decided by Seba and other close relatives that it would be best if Lorenza and Paola lived away from all the tragedy that had taken place in Tuscany. The sisters were collected by Tullio Vinay, a thirty-five-year-old Protestant minister and family friend, who removed them to a Waldensian community in the Alps. 'We were saved by people who understood what had happened,' Paola later recalled. 'Everyday they preached love, not revenge. Through the love we were given, we were able to regain the joy of living.'

With her nieces gone, it was time for Seba also to leave. Having tidied up the apartment, she locked the door and moved back to Rome. With that, the last remaining member of the Einstein family departed Florence. They had first arrived in the region in 1921, when Maja had rented a home with her husband Paul. Later, Robert and Nina would purchase the villa at Il Focardo nearby, and the girls would attend the local schools. Over the course of a quarter of a century, the Einsteins had experienced the ascent of Mussolini's fascist regime, Hitler's visit to Florence, the enactment of the Racial Laws, the German occupation of Tuscany, the rounding-up of Jews, the murder of Nina, Luce and Cici on 3 August 1944, the liberation of Europe by Allied forces and Robert's suicide.

It had been a tumultuous period, at times filled with great joy and happiness, at others profound pain and despair. For those who had perished, the struggle was over. For those who had survived – Lorenza, Paola, Anna Maria, Seba, Maja, Albert – there was still plenty with which to contend.

# 20. Princeton, New Jersey, 1945

After years of aerial bombardment, artillery fire and street-to-street fighting, Italy's administrative infrastructure was in disarray. Government departments were understaffed and under-resourced. Their buildings were either in ruins or, if still standing, ill-equipped and poorly maintained. The transportation they relied on, such as rail, shipping and air, was barely functioning. All of which had a devastating impact on reliability. One of those most affected was the Poste Italiane, the country's postal service, which had a monopoly on the delivery of letters. The news of Robert's tragic suicide, therefore, took longer than usual to reach his cousins in America. Perhaps as much as six or eight weeks. And when it did arrive, Albert Einstein was consumed with other matters.

In the summer of 1945, the famous scientist was sixty-six years old and was back at Saranac Lake in New York for a vacation. It was here that he heard the extraordinary news on 6 August that the United States had dropped an atomic bomb on the Japanese city of Hiroshima. Three days later, a second bomb was detonated, this time over the city of Nagasaki. Six days after that, on 15 August, Emperor Hirohito announced on national radio that Japan would capitulate.

Though Albert was relieved the war was finally over, he was deeply shaken by the news coming out of Japan. On 8 August, the *New York Times* ran a large headline on its front page declaring: 'Atomic Bomb Wiped Out 60% of Hiroshima'. A little over two weeks later, on 23 August, the same paper stated that the toll of the two bombs was 190,000 people killed and injured. Other papers were giving even higher figures. The casualties were appalling in their own right, but Albert had a personal connection to the devastation: six years earlier, he had written to President Roosevelt encouraging him to start an atomic bomb programme. Albert later told *Newsweek* that he regretted his early support for what had become the Manhattan Project. 'Had I known that the Germans would not succeed in developing an atomic bomb, I would have done nothing for the bomb.'

This was Albert's state of mind when he received the news about the death of Robert Einstein. By this point, Albert had experienced his fair share of grief: the death of his parents; the death of two of his grandsons; the death of his second wife, Elsa. Over the years, he had acknowledged these losses in his correspondence. Here, for instance, is what he said after his mother Pauline died in February 1920, aged sixty-two, following a long and difficult fight with cancer. 'My mother died a week ago today in terrible agony,' he wrote to a friend. 'We are all completely exhausted just from witnessing it. One feels in one's bones the significance of blood ties.' And here is what he wrote to his son and daughter-in-law two days after the death of their six-year-old son Klaus in January 1939: 'Although I saw him for such a brief time, he was just as close to me as if he had grown up under my eyes. Thus, this blow has hit me terribly hard, after all the difficulties and bitterness that the past years have brought.'

So how did Albert respond when he learned that his cousin had killed himself? After all, they were close. For more than eleven years, they had grown up in the same house in Germany and then Italy. Their fathers had been in business together. Robert's father, Jakob, taught Albert algebra. As adults, Albert's sister had spent time with Robert's family in Florence, and Albert and Robert had kept in touch by mail. But there is, unfortunately, no record of how Albert responded to his cousin's suicide besides a letter written by Maja.

On 17 September 1945, nine weeks after Robert's death, Maja wrote to her close friend Bice Besso Rusconi, who lived in Geneva. Writing in Italian, she started by saying that she was 'homesick for Italy and that place that I think is my real home', and added that 'my brother says hello to you'. She next turned her attention to Robert's family. She asked if 'Seba Mazzetti and the twins are still in Florence? I want to see them; it would make me very happy.' Then she wrote: 'The nightmare of Roberto's death will never leave me. That poor man must have suffered desperately during that year to make him kill himself. God will forgive him.'

After hearing that Robert's wife Nina and their two daughters Luce and Cici had been brutally murdered, Maja had said that she was *sfatta*, or 'broken'. The news of Robert's death can only have deepened her desolation. Her brother Albert was also likely to have been deeply affected, though no evidence has been left behind to confirm this. What is also not confirmed is whether the great scientist, in addition to feeling shock and grief, connected the three murders and the suicide to the Nazi regime's desire to kill him. After all, many in Italy believed that the murder of Nina, Luce and Cici Einstein was an act of revenge for the words and actions of Albert Einstein.

Over the next decade, Albert continued to lose close members of his family. In 1948, his first wife, Mileva, died in Zurich. Three years later, his sister Maja died in Princeton. The year after that, Maja's husband Paul died, also in Switzerland. Then his long-time friend Michele Besso died. 'Now he has again preceded me a little in parting from this strange world. That signifies nothing,' Albert wrote to Besso's sister and Besso's son. 'For people like us who believe in physics, the separation between past, present and future has only the importance of an admittedly tenacious illusion.'

During this time, there were numerous stories in the press that the famous scientist would be coming to Italy to pay respects to his cousin Robert. On 16 April 1953, for example, *L'Unità* – a newspaper based in Milan that served as the official organ of the Communist Party – announced that '[Albert] Einstein will visit the tomb in Troghi where Robert Einstein, his first cousin, is buried, together with his wife and two daughters'. Eight months later, on 29 December 1953, the Israeli newspaper *Yedioth Ahronoth* reported (under the headline 'Einstein to Pray at the Grave of His Murdered Family'): 'Professor Albert Einstein is going to pay a visit next spring to Il Focarno [*sic*].' This second article was filed by Elie Wiesel from Paris, the same Elie Wiesel who went on to write various books about the Holocaust and won the Nobel Peace Prize. It is highly questionable, however, that such a visit ever took place given there is no record of Albert Einstein returning to Europe after his departure in 1933. The rumours appeared to reflect a widely held need to complete the narrative.

In the early 1950s, Albert began to 'develop a peaceful sense of his own mortality', according to his biographer Walter Isaacson. At the funeral for his friend the physicist Rudolf Ladenburg in 1952, for instance, Albert stated that 'Brief is this existence, as a fleeting visit in a strange house . . . the path to be pursued is poorly lit by a flickering consciousness'.

On Sunday 11 April 1955 – ten years after Robert's death – Albert suffered severe abdominal pain. He was taken to Princeton Hospital on 15 April, where he refused surgery for his aortic aneurism. The following day, he was visited by his son Hans Albert, his stepdaughter Margot and his close friend Otto Nathan. At one point Albert told Otto that he was concerned that the country of his birth might rearm. Right to the very end, he was expressing his apprehension of renewed German violence. Albert died at 1 a.m. on Monday 18 April. He was seventy-six years old.

In the years after the war's end, the murder of the Einstein family in Italy was just one of the countless atrocities that attracted public attention around the world. The newspapers reported that more than 6 million Jews had been killed in the concentration camps. Hundreds of thousands of others, including Roma, gay men and women, priests, Jehovah's Witnesses, disabled people and political prisoners had also been murdered, while millions of prisoners of war had died from maltreatment, and millions of civilians had been deported and exploited as forced labour.

Meanwhile, the victors made good on their promises to organize a series of war crimes trials. The most important was the International Military Tribunal in Nuremberg in 1945–6, where the twenty-four most prominent Nazis were put in the dock, along with the collective leadership of six German organizations, including the General Staff and High Command of the Wehrmacht. But there were other trials as well, in Belsen, Dachau, Minsk, Tokyo and Krakow, to name a few. For years, the newspapers and radio covered these proceedings with great diligence. By the mid-1950s, however, the world was exhausted by the horror. Moreover, the governments of the USA, UK and France were increasingly concerned about the Soviet Union, and were rapidly moving their resources to combat what they perceived as a growing threat. Quietly, and with little fanfare, the majority of war crimes investigations were put on the back burner.

One of the crimes to be forgotten was the murder of three members of the Einstein family that had taken place in a villa outside Florence. The war was now over. The Nazis no longer posed a threat. A memo was written by an unnamed member of the US Army judge advocate general's office in Europe. Under the case reference number 16-71, the clerk wrote that the Einstein murders file had been closed. The reason given was: 'Forwarded to Italian government since all victims are Italian nationals.' Not long after, the file was sent to the Italian government. But with their attention focused on rebuilding their country, the Italian officials simply placed the file in a drawer. And that – at least for now – was the end of the matter.

For the Einstein family, however, as for so many throughout Italy and beyond, the violence, pain and heartache of war could not be forgotten. They still wanted answers to what happened on 3 August 1944. They still wanted the perpetrators to be identified. And they still wanted them brought to justice.

# PART THREE
# Justice

The important thing is not to stop questioning.

– Albert Einstein

# 21. Rome, 1994

In the years following the Second World War, the Italian authorities showed little interest or enthusiasm in investigating the war crimes that took place during the fascist period. Indeed, on 22 June 1946, Italy's government of national unity passed the so-called 'Togliatti Amnesty' (named after the minister of justice and head of the Communist Party Palmiro Togliatti), which pardoned or reduced the sentences of Italian soldiers who took part in atrocities in Greece and Yugoslavia and Ethiopia, Italian partisans who carried out extrajudicial killings, and Italian fascists who helped the Nazis conduct attacks against civilians.

The Italian government was more willing to support British and American efforts to go after German war criminals who were officers in the Wehrmacht and SS. In 1946, Eberhard von Mackensen and Kurt Mälzer were given life sentences for their role in overseeing the massacre of 335 Italian citizens at the Ardeatine Caves in Rome. In May 1947, Albert Kesselring was sentenced to life in prison for the same atrocity. That year, Eduard Crasemann was sentenced to ten years in prison for his role in the brutal massacre of

174 civilians in the Fucecchio Marshes, west of Florence. The Allies also sentenced Max Simon to life imprisonment for his part in the masacre of around 770 civilians in Marzabotto, south of Bologna.

From 1948, the Italian government took over the prosecution of German war criminals, which resulted in a series of trials in the late 1940s and 1950s. The vast majority of these collapsed because of insufficient evidence, legal technicalities and prosecutorial incompetence. Other individuals evaded justice, including Erich Priebke and Herbert Kappler, who were both implicated in the Ardeatine Caves massacre. The first absconded to Argentina; the second spent thirty years in prison then escaped by being carried out of a military hospital by his wife in a large suitcase. By the mid-1950s, only thirteen Germans had been found guilty of committing war crimes in Italy. Of these, four were executed, two died in prison, five were released early and two remained incarcerated. These figures were meagre when compared to the scale of the crimes. During the period of German occupation, close to 22,000 Italian civilians – more than 8,000 Jews and 14,000 non-Jews – were killed as a result of persecutions, war crimes and deportations. This was in addition to the 600,000 Italians who were deported to Germany after refusing to serve in the Wehrmacht.

By the 1960s, a narrative had entered the Italian national psyche that it was the Germans who were responsible for the appalling things that happened during the war and the Italians had nothing to do with it. On the one hand, there were the Evil Germans: the bloodthirsty occupiers, the perpetrators of massacres against civilians, the masterminds of the round-ups, deportations and death camps. On the other hand, there were the Good Italians: the partisans hiding up in the hills, the men who refused to fight for the German Army, the police officers and government officials who would not enforce Nazi orders, and all those who helped the Jews escape persecution.

The myth of the Evil Germans and Good Italians could be seen in various cultural productions of the post-war period which celebrated the heroics of Italian resistance fighters. Also, within this Good Italian group – and this is where the narrative became creative – were the Italian soldiers, government officials and police officers who assisted the Germans but did so, according to the legend, without malice or bad intention. These archetypes featured in numerous memoirs, academic treatises, novels and also films. A good example of the last is Roberto Rossellini's *Roma città aperta* (*Rome, Open City*), which won the prestigious Palme d'Or at the Cannes Film Festival in 1946. In an iconic scene at the film's end, a firing squad made up of Italian soldiers takes aim at a partisan priest, but they all intentionally miss their target. He is killed instead by a German officer.

The myth of the Good Italians, however, ran counter to reality. The Italians who rounded up and then sent more than 100,000 Slovenians, Croats, Serbs, Montenegrins and others to Italian-run concentration camps, where several thousand of them died. The Italians who, on 12 July 1942, killed 100 civilians in the Croatian village of Podhum. Or those who, on 16 February 1943, murdered 175 civilians in the Greek village of Domeniko before burning down their houses. The Italians who passed the anti-Jewish Racial Laws in 1938, and who on 1 December 1943 issued Police Order

Number 5, requiring that all Italian Jews be arrested and put in 'special concentration camps'. The Italians who, on that same day, deported twenty-six Jews from the Carmelite convent on Piazza del Carmine in Florence and sent them to Auschwitz. The Italians who, on 3 August 1944, helped the Germans find the members of the Einstein family at the villa Il Focardo.

This darker history was rarely talked about. That was, until the mid-1990s.

Late one evening in 1994, magistrate Antonino Intelisano was working in the military prosecutor's offices in the Palazzo Cesi-Gaddi on Via degli Acquasparta in Rome. Appointed just a year before, Antonino was one of the newer members of the team. Needing to find some documents for his investigation into the SS officer Erich Priebke, Antonino walked to the storage room. When he entered, his attention was drawn to a large, six-foot-high wooden cupboard. Curiously, it had been positioned so that its doors faced the wall. He found a janitor and, when he asked about the cupboard, the janitor explained that it had been like this for years and, as far as he knew, it just contained some old files.

His interest now piqued, Antonino turned the cupboard around and opened the doors. Inside, he found stacks of documents dating from the mid-1940s. When he looked more closely, he discovered they were investigation files relating to war crimes that had taken place in Italy during the time of its fascist regime. In all, there were 695 files, along with a general register listing 2,274 crimes.

The discovery of the cupboard in Rome and the long-lost war crimes investigation files it contained was picked up by the national media. In an article about the story for *L'Espresso* magazine, the journalist Franco Giustolisi described the cupboard as the *Armadio della Vergogna*, or 'Wardrobe of Shame'. The name stuck, becoming a metaphor for Italy's general amnesia about the fascist period.

One of those to follow the extensive media coverage about the Wardrobe of Shame was Carlo Carli, a member of the Italian Chamber of Deputies. He was born in Pietrasanta, a village close to Sant'Anna di Stazzema, where the Germans had killed up to 560 people in August 1944. The families of many of his school friends were victims, and his mother had also lost a close friend. Whenever he visited Sant'Anna di Stazzema, he saw the blackened ruins of the houses and the churchyard where the bodies of the victims had been set on fire. All this made him angry. And curious. Why had the Germans killed all those old people, pregnant women and babies? They were clearly not partisans. And why had nobody faced trial? When he asked people in the community, there were no answers.

As soon as Deputy Carli heard about the Wardrobe of Shame, he realized that something must be done. 'I was told by many people that it was too late to investigate,' he remembers, 'but I would not be stopped.' He worked tirelessly to persuade his colleagues in the Chamber of Deputies to set up a commission of inquiry. And once it was established, he spent two years listening to witnesses, reading archival documents and visiting the sites where the crimes took place. When the commissioners came to write the report, however, they could not agree on its conclusions. As a result, there was both a majority report and a minority one, reflecting the country's divided history. According to those in the majority, led by the businessman Enzo Raisi who had been appointed by Silvio Berlusconi's right-wing government, the failure to prosecute war crimes in Italy was a result of bureaucratic errors in the justice department. Nothing more.

Those in the minority, led by Deputy Carli, were more critical. They said that the files had been buried following political intervention in the 1950s for three reasons. First, the then government did not want to alienate Germany, the country's economic partner. Second, it did not want to open up investigations into Italy's own war crimes, including those carried out by its soldiers in Yugoslavia, Greece and Libya. And third, there were individuals occupying senior positions in politics, the military and the security services who still remained sympathetic to the former fascist regime.

'It would have been better if there was one unified report,' Deputy Carli says, 'but it was important that this history was written.' He continues, 'People don't properly know about this fascist period of history. It is vital to know about Mussolini and his crimes.' He adds, 'Germany has closely examined its history. Italy has not.'

There were 695 files in the Wardrobe of Shame. These covered some of the worst atrocities suffered by Italian civilians during the Second World War. Their stories were pored over by journalists and historians, and over the next weeks and months were endlessly discussed on talk shows and in newspaper columns. This sent shock waves through a population that had been shielded from this information for decades.

Among the files in the Wardrobe of Shame, however,

there was nothing about the murder of Nina, Luce and Cici Einstein. It seems that even though the Pentagon had sent a copy of the US War Crimes Commission file to Rome in 1946 so that the Italian authorities could take over the case, it had for some unknown reason disappeared along the way. It would take another five years for someone to pick up the trail. That someone would be an Italian, but they wouldn't be living in Italy.

# 22. Cologne, 2002

Carlo Gentile was born in 1960 in the coastal town of Imperia, close to the Italian border with France. 'I grew up in an area of Italy where the memory of the occupation and of the war was still very present,' he says. Though his family did not personally suffer persecution during the war, he heard stories about what happened from his elderly relatives. 'There were many winter evenings spent listening to grown-ups talking about all the terrible things that happened in the war.'

In elementary school, Carlo was shown pictures from the concentration camps, which made a big impression on him. 'That must have informed my basic curiosity,' he states, 'a desire to find out who the perpetrators were.' After obtaining a PhD in history and Jewish studies, he moved to Cologne, where he became a university lecturer with a focus on Italy and the Nazi period. 'There was, at the core of my interest, an intuition that this topic was important in a broader context, both for Italy and Germany. A sense of justice to be served after decades of impunity.'

In the late 1990s, Carlo was reading a book about war crimes in Italy when he came across a passage that mentioned the Einstein murders. This was the first time he'd heard of this crime. His focus was on other matters, but he made a note and hoped to look into it later. Over the next few years, he checked in with his contacts in the relevant criminal justice divisions in Italy and Germany and was surprised to learn that neither country had ever investigated the killings at the villa Il Focardo.

In 2002, Carlo Gentile was in the United States visiting the National Archives in College Park, Maryland, near Washington DC. One day, with a little time on his hands, he asked if they had anything on the Einstein case. Around thirty minutes later, he was called to the issue desk and handed a thin manila folder. Carlo took it back to his table and set about reading its contents. Inside the file, he found the report compiled by Milton Wexler and the War Crimes Commission. In this were Robert's and Seba's statements which, he noted, both said that the perpetrators belonged to the SS. He also saw the comment by an American official that the crime was committed by 'unknown German officers and soldiers, perhaps members of SS'. Would it be possible, Carlo wondered, to identify the war criminals after all these years? He made a copy of the file and brought it back home to Cologne.

A few weeks later, Carlo travelled to the military archives in Berlin. There he asked to see the troop-movement and casualty reports for Tuscany in the summer of 1944. His plan was to determine which German units were active in the area at the time of the crime and from this generate a longlist of possible suspects. After days of painstaking research, he determined that there were no SS units stationed near Il Focardo in late July or early August 1944. The one

exception was an SS officer called Dr Alexander Langsdorff, who was in Florence with orders to protect valuable
art. Carlo noted that Langsdorff was known not to wear SS
uniform and so could not have been the person spotted by
Robert or Seba. If not the SS, the historian concluded, the
perpetrators must have belonged to the Wehrmacht, the
German armed forces.

Carlo continued with his search. After methodically
looking through hundreds of pages, he discovered that the
territory south of Florence was controlled by the German
Tenth Army during the week the crime took place. A little
later, he was able to narrow this down to a single division of
the Tenth Army: the 715th Infantry Division, which was stationed near the front southeast of Florence. Zeroing in still
further, the historian established that the 715th had a small
number of units active in the area close to villa Il Focardo on
3 August 1944: units from the 735th Grenadier Regiment and
the 104th Panzergrenadier Regiment. He had his longlist.

The historian next used an old military map to plot the
movement of these troops. For the 104th he recorded
the following positions near the River Arno: Pontassieve,
Troghi, San Donato in Collina, Incontro. That last name
sounded familiar. Carlo Gentile went back to the US War
Crimes Commission report he had copied at the Washington
archives. After a few seconds, he found what he was looking
for: a question and answer from Robert Einstein's testimony
on 17 September 1944:

Wexler: Do you have anything else to state that would
be of importance?

Robert: I heard from a priest at the Incontro [monastery] that among 50 German prisoners were included men who participated in the tragedy in my house.

According to Robert's statement, after carrying out the murders at the villa Il Focardo, the German soldiers had moved on to the Incontro monastery, where they were later captured by the British. From the troop movement reports, Carlo knew that the German forces at Incontro belonged to the 104th Panzergrenadier Regiment. This suggested it was the 104th, not the 735th, who may have committed the crime. He looked again at the map. Incontro was just three miles from Il Focardo; it worked.

This was the link for which the historian had been looking. He next searched for the name of the commander of the 104th Panzergrenadier Regiment. He soon found it. The commander's name was Captain Clemens Josef Theis. His rank was the one mentioned by various eyewitnesses. With a beat of excitement, Carlo Gentile wondered if he had just identified the person responsible for the murder of Nina, Luce and Cici Einstein.

In March 2005, after checking and rechecking his work, Carlo decided it was time to share the results of his research with the appropriate authorities. He typed up his findings, made copies of the relevant archival documents and submitted a dossier to the Central Office of the State Justice Administrations for the Investigation of National Socialist Crimes in Ludwigsburg, Germany. A little over sixty years since the crime was committed, the Italian historian hoped that his research might be enough to have the Einstein case reopened.

# 23. Ludwigsburg, 2005

After the Allied governments' commitment to the prosecution of Nazi war crimes faltered in the 1950s, the mantle was taken up by other parties. One of those to step into the arena was the State of Israel. Most famously when, on 11 May 1960, members of its intelligence service Mossad travelled incognito to Argentina, captured Adolf Eichmann (one of the architects of the Holocaust) and brought him back to Jerusalem for trial. Later, frustrated by what they saw as inaction on the part of governments, private citizens became active in the Nazi-hunting business. They included Simon Wiesenthal, the Jewish-Austrian survivor of the Holocaust, who spent a career tracking down Nazi war criminals, such as Franz Stangl (the commandant of the Treblinka death camp). Almost as famous were Serge and Beate Klarsfeld in France, who dedicated their lives to locating Nazis and bringing them to trial, including the 'Butcher of Lyons' Klaus Barbie, head of the city's Gestapo.

Such was the public interest in bringing war criminals to justice that Nazi hunters became a source of fascination. Numerous thrillers were published on the subject, including

Frederick Forsyth's *The Odessa File* in 1972 and Alistair MacLean's *River of Death* in 1981. Journalists were similarly obsessed. Perhaps the most notorious instance was a series of articles written by Hannah Arendt in 1963 for the *New Yorker* magazine about the trial of Adolf Eichmann. Television was also captivated, with episodes of both *Wonder Woman* and *The Twilight Zone* building narratives around Nazi hunting. Similarly, dozens of movies focused on the topic, from *The Stranger* with Orson Welles in 1946 to *The Boys from Brazil* with Laurence Olivier in 1978 and *Hell Hunters* with Maud Adams and George Lazenby in 1987. Comics also explored this theme, including Marvel's *Captain America*, which had Cap slugging Adolf Hitler on the front cover of its very first edition in March 1941, and often returned to this subject, including an edition in 1980 entitled *Night of the Nazi Hunter*.

In Germany, the task of tracking down former Nazis belonged to the Central Office of the State Justice Administrations for the Investigation of National Socialist Crimes, known for short as the 'Central Office'. Established in 1958 in Ludwigsburg, thirty miles north of Stuttgart, its objective was to identify, investigate and track down Nazi war criminals. For years, it was known as a place of inaction and passivity, where little time or energy was spent in finding former war criminals. Journalists and commentators explained the Central Office's reluctance to act by pointing to the former Nazis who still held positions of power in the government, business and security services. Changes took place at the Central Office in 2000, when Kurt Schrimm became director. Schrimm had spent the previous thirty years prosecuting Nazi war criminals in Stuttgart and relished the chance to work at a national level. Soon after his arrival, he initiated a new approach, encouraging his colleagues to accelerate the pace of their investigations, no matter where such inquiries led.

In 2005, Carlo Gentile's dossier about the Einstein murders arrived on the desk of Director Schrimm. After reviewing its contents, he sent it over to one of his best investigators, Judge Thomas Will.

Thomas Will spent most of his childhood in Nuremberg. He was not yet born when the city hosted the most famous of war crimes trials in 1945 and 1946, but the legacy had a big impact on him. 'For me the history was always present,' he told a journalist in 2023. 'Fascinating, not in an admiring way, but in a way that made me want to understand what happened and why it happened.'

After graduating from law school, Thomas Will began his legal career in 1994 in the state of Saxony-Anhalt before working as a judge in Dessau. Then in 2003, at the age of forty-three, he applied to join the Central Office. Upon his arrival, he was assigned several cases involving those that took place in Italy during the war. Given the many decades since the crimes were committed, Judge Will realized that he didn't have much time to bring the perpetrators to justice. To educate himself, he travelled to Italy and spoke with partisan groups, victims and historians. He also visited archives in Rome and met with military prosecutors in La Spezia, near Pisa, who were in the middle of a major war crimes investigation.

As a core member of the Central Office, Judge Will soon attracted media attention. 'Murder is not subject to a statute of limitations,' he said to one member of the press.

'So long as perpetrators are still alive, we will pursue the cases.' To another correspondent, he acknowledged that at times his work could be frustrating. 'After we have found [the perpetrators] alive, after we have forwarded their cases to prosecutors . . . people die while they are on trial,' he said. 'It has become normal in our work. It is our work.'

Judge Will was a tall, thick-set man with wispy black hair that barely covered his ears and a pair of black glasses behind which shone piercing brown eyes. He typically wore a dark suit, white shirt and tie to the office, though sometimes he opted for a blazer and pressed trousers. As one feature writer observed, Will wore a silver watch on his wrist, which he occasionally shook, a reminder of the importance of time in his work. And when he visited the cafeteria around the corner from the office, his preference was for comfort food, such as *Käsespätzle* (cheese noodles).

Now two years into his job, Judge Will opened Carlo Gentile's dossier on the Einstein murders for the first time. After reading the documents, he officially started an investigation, giving it a unique file number: 518 AR 257/05. It was sixty-one years since the murders had taken place, and fifty-nine since the case had last been officially investigated. In his first note on the case, dated 5 April 2005, Judge Will wrote that the crime was 'racially motivated' and – following Gentile's line of thinking – that 'everything points' towards the 104th Panzergrenadier Regiment and, in particular, the battalion commander Captain Clemens Theis.

Judge Will's task was not to charge or prosecute. As with a murder investigation detective in the UK or USA, his responsibility was to investigate the crime, collect testimony from witnesses, gather any possible forensic material, establish a narrative that explained the crime and, if possible, identify potential suspects. Then, and only if he believed that there was sufficient evidence, he would hand the case over to a prosecutor. It would be their job to assess the findings and, if they also agreed that there was sufficient evidence, it would be they, the prosecutor, who would file charges and take the case to trial.

And so Judge Will launched his investigation. He assembled a team and together they wrote to scores of military archives requesting information. They assembled the names of the men who belonged to Clemens Theis's unit and tried to track down their whereabouts; they visited town halls seeking birth certificates, marriage licences and other public documents; and they contacted police departments asking for criminal records and background checks. This was slow, hard work. Real shoe-leather work. But Judge Will knew that it was the only way to conduct an investigation like this. There was a lot of ground to cover; it took time and it required patience.

In December 2005, Judge Will travelled to London to visit the National Archives in Kew. There he found numerous files relating to the activity of British forces in the Florence region in the summer of 1944. Among these was a detailed summary of the battle at Incontro, the monastery just three miles from Il Focardo. These documents confirmed that, at the battle's end, sixty members of the 2nd Battalion of the 104th Panzergrenadier Regiment were captured, corroborating the priest's story that the British had taken dozens of prisoners of war at the monastery (the other part of his story, that they had come directly from Il Focardo, remained unconfirmed). There were two other entries that were particularly noteworthy. The first reported that a Captain Theis was at the monastery on the 4 and 5 August. The second stated that in addition to taking German soldiers prisoner at Incontro, the British had captured Theis's dog, named 'Stolg'. These reports appeared to confirm that Clemens Theis was just three miles from Il Focardo in the days immediately after the murder.

Over the next nine months, Judge Will's team continued to track down members of the 2nd Battalion of the 104th Panzergrenadier Regiment. They discovered that the vast majority had remained in Germany after the war and were surprised to learn, given the veterans' age, that at least twenty of them were alive. Perhaps most significantly, the team established that the prime suspect, Clemens Theis, was also still living. He was eighty-nine years old and residing in Speyer, less than fifty miles from their office in Ludwigsburg.

Judge Will was ready. In his view, there was more than enough evidence to take the case forward. In late 2006, therefore, he began drafting his final report on the Einstein murders. After summarizing the background and detailing the actions taken during his investigation, he moved to his conclusions. To start with, and perhaps most importantly, he stated that the murder of Nina, Luce and Cici Einstein near Florence on 3 August 1944 had been carried out by German soldiers. This was the first official recognition that the crime had been perpetrated by individuals working for the German state. Next, the motivation was likely to be racial: the German soldiers killed the three women because Robert Einstein was Jewish.

By this stage, the case had passed two important checkpoints. First, the historian Carlo Gentile had prepared his dossier mounting a case against Clemens Theis. Then, after a thorough investigation taking more than twenty months, Judge Will had established that there was sufficient evidence to take the case forward. It was time now to hand it over to a prosecutor. According to German law, the office assigned to prosecute a criminal case had to be located in the same district as the accused lived. So it was that, on 29 January 2007, Judge Will wrote to Hubert Ströber, the head of the prosecutor's office in Frankenthal, some fifteen miles north of Speyer. 'I am sending you the file and ask that you take over this investigation,' Judge Will stated, 'the main suspect is Clemens Josef Theis'.

To mark the end of the investigation, Judge Will gave an interview on 10 February 2007 to *Il Secolo XIX* newspaper in Genoa. In keeping with the press's fascination with Nazi hunters, the journalist began by exploring the judge's appearance – 'He has the casual appearance of a dishevelled intellectual' – before providing some background to the case. But while the headline that ran above the article was conclusive, 'Einstein's Executioner Discovered', Judge Will was far more circumspect. 'I have identified a possible culprit, a captain in the Wehrmacht,' he stated carefully. 'The problem will be proving the case, based on hard evidence, evidence that can show that this precise officer ordered the shooting of the three women.' He then added, 'For now, it's just a hypothesis that needs to be verified.'

# 24. Frankenthal, 2011

'Now to one of the most unusual crimes which *XY* has ever dealt with,' the presenter declared, looking straight at the camera. He was dressed in a tight-fitting grey suit, white shirt and pink tie. 'Today, we want to clear up a crime on Albert Einstein's family with your help, namely a triple murder, committed almost seventy years ago. Don't worry right now about how young or old you are or whether the information is significant. It may well be that you have the key piece of the puzzle for which the police have long been looking.'

The television show was called *Aktenzeichen XY . . . ungelöst* ('File Number XY . . . Unsolved'). It was a crime programme in which police officers were invited to speak about their unsolved cases and encourage the audience to call in with information. Almost always these were recently committed crimes. Launched in 1967, *Aktenzeichen XY* was made by the public broadcaster ZDF and was one of the most popular shows on German television, regularly attracting 6 million viewers. Its format had been copied around the world, including *Crimewatch* in the UK and *America's Most*

*Wanted* in the USA. The programme date was 23 February 2011, and it was being broadcast live.

After explaining the background to the case, the presenter introduced the man standing next to him, also wearing a grey suit, white shirt and tie, but looking a good deal less comfortable. This was Hubert Ströber, the head of the prosecutor's office in Frankenthal. The man to who the investigator Judge Thomas Will had sent the Einstein murders file in 2007.

Hubert Ströber was born in West Germany in 1959 and grew up in an old forester's house in the woods thirty miles from Bayreuth in Bavaria. When he was a small boy, the German newspapers were full of stories about Nazis who had escaped to South America and about the trial in Frankfurt of guards, doctors and other personnel who had worked in Auschwitz. At school, he and his classmates were shown speeches given by Adolf Hitler and television programmes about the Holocaust. When he was nine years old, student protests broke out across the country, which were dominated by a question posed to parents and grandparents: What did you do during the war?

As a teenager, Ströber had initially wanted to be a dentist, but after being introduced to economic law in high school, he decided to become a lawyer. He then spent two years in the army, working as a military policeman, and, after studying law at university, became a public prosecutor. For his first post, in 1989, he was assigned to the small town of Hof in northern Bavaria. Over the next twenty years, he worked for both the Federal Prosecutor General and the regional prosecuting office of Rhineland-Palatinate. By 2007, he was deputy head of the Frankenthal prosecutor's office, managing a team of more than forty people. His was a generalist portfolio with cases ranging from knife attacks, murders and terrorism to sexual assault, rape, human trafficking, and kidnapping. Investigating a crime committed by the Nazis in the 1940s was not his usual focus.

Hubert Ströber was therefore a little surprised when he received the Einstein file from Judge Thomas Will along with the official request to prosecute Clemens Theis for possible war crimes. He carefully reviewed the documents that the judge had sent over. Among these was the report compiled by Milton Wexler in 1944. In a note inserted in the file on 26 February 2007, Ströber wrote down various points of interest, including key sections of Robert Einstein's and Seba Mazzetti's testimony. He was, however, a little disappointed. 'The American investigations were very superficial,' he later said. 'I am not criticizing them, they had different operation interests, they had to win the war. But the investigation was not as precise as it should have been.'

Having finished reading the files, the prosecutor launched his own investigation. He contacted the state criminal police in Baden-Württemberg, twenty-five miles south of Stuttgart, and asked them to assign officers to look into Clemens Theis. But when they tried to arrange a visit with the former captain, they were told by his lawyer that he was too frail to speak. To support this assertion, Theis's lawyer provided a medical certificate attesting to his client's poor health. The lawyer added that Theis adamantly denied having anything to do with the Einstein murders.

Not to be deterred, Ströber pursued other lines of inquiry. His team went to the military archives and pulled Clemens Theis's war record, but they found little of interest. They tracked down members of his unit, but none could remember being at villa Il Focardo, let alone the murders. Widening the scope, Ströber told his team to review anything they could find in the media about the case. This was when they came across the German TV documentary *Der Fall Rignano – Die Mörder der Letzten Tage* (*The Rignano Case: The Murder in the Final Days*), made in 2001 by the journalist Tilman Spengler. In this programme, Robert Einstein's niece Lorenza and a former partisan called Vasco Caldini, who claimed to be an eyewitness, both stated that the captain in charge of the German soldiers had worn glasses. Prosecutor Ströber asked the police to contact the local drivers' licensing authority to find out about the suspect's eyesight. After conducting a search, the authority found Clemens Theis's current driving licence. The picture showed a man in his eighties, with receding hair, droopy eyes and ears that stuck out from his ample face. He was not wearing glasses. They went further back, and the earliest licence they could find in their records was from 1995, and this too had him without spectacles. In Ströber's view, this evidence lessened the chances that Theis was the murderer.

In early July 2007, Ströber sent two police officers to visit the villa Il Focardo. This was the first time that the German authorities had visited the scene of the crime. The two police officers, one in a brown suit, the other in grey, arrived at the villa on a pleasantly warm, though overcast, morning. They were met at the gates by representatives of the Italian military prosecutor's office from La Spezia, who would provide them with a tour. First, they walked around the grounds, photographing and videoing the wrought-iron gates, the cypress-lined avenue, the chapel, and the villa's large wooden front doors. Next they went inside and were shown the front hall where the German soldiers had first confronted Nina

Einstein. Then they went to look at the bedroom where the women were held and the Sala Rossa where the shootings occurred. Here they noted patched-up holes in the wall above the fireplace and next to a window; these were probably where the bullets had struck. The Italians also pointed to the place on the floor where the bodies had fallen. The group then visited Badiuzza Cemetery where Nina, Luce, Cici and Robert were buried, and the Incontro monastery, where Clemens Theis and his unit were taken prisoner.

While in Italy, the German police officers drove to Verona to meet a key witness who had never been properly interviewed. There, at Via Francesco Anzani 5, they were welcomed by the eighty-one-year-old niece and god-daughter of Nina and Robert Einstein, Anna Maria Boldrini.

In the more than six decades since the murders, Anna Maria had led a quiet, low-profile existence. She married a man who worked on the railways, had three sons and a daughter, and for thirty years taught Italian at a middle school. She was now retired and lived with her husband in this modest apartment. Since that brief interview with Milton Wexler in September 1944, she hadn't spoken to anyone about the events at Il Focardo, besides her children. She hadn't wanted to talk about what happened, not to investigators and certainly never to journalists. She preferred not to think about it. And yet, after all she had gone through and after all these years, here she was, sitting across from two German police officers who intended to ask her questions about the murders. She was afraid what they might ask and she was afraid that she might say the wrong thing. But they were there, so what choice did she have?

According to the transcript, the interview began at 10.30

a.m. The police officers started by asking her name, age, address and national identity number. They then turned to the day of the murders.

Police: How old were you at the time of the crime?
Anna Maria: 18.
Police: What was your relationship [to the Einstein family]?
Anna Maria: Nina was my maternal aunt.
Police: Regarding the specific facts, are you able to remember and reconstruct what happened on the day of 3 August 1944?
Anna Maria: I remember that a soldier was placed to guard us from the early stages of our imprisonment in the room. At a certain point I heard shots and screams of pain at the same time, they were female screams, so I guessed it was the killing of my aunt and my cousins. It was over in a few seconds. At that point I was completely terrified and collapsed in front of the soldier who was guarding us. Unfortunately afterwards my memories become very vague and I can no longer say whether we were taken down and then out of the villa by the soldiers or whether this happened on our own initiative. What I remember with certainty is that we could not ascertain the fate of my cousins and my aunt.

The police officers moved on to what they were really interested in: information that might help identify the German soldiers.

Police: Are you aware of the name of the German unit responsible for the massacre?

Anna Maria: No, I'm not aware of it.

Police: Can you describe the uniforms, ranks and badges of the German soldiers who came in the previous months or on the day of the massacre? How about their weapons or vehicles?

Anna Maria: No, unfortunately I am unable to provide any description.

Police: Do you remember that the soldiers mentioned ranks, like *Sturmbannführer, Sturmführer, Untersturmführer, Hauptsturmführer*, or other similar words?

Anna Maria: I don't remember anything of the sort.

Police: Are you able to provide a physical description of the German commander or anyone who had direct contact with you?

Anna Maria: I only vaguely remember the German soldier who guarded us and then helped me get up. He was young, he could have been around twenty to twenty-two years old, he had blue eyes. I do not remember other details.

Police: Before being released, did the German military inform you of what had happened and the reasons that led to the killings?

Anna Maria: To the best of my knowledge, no German soldier justified himself in this regard. I think that everything occurred exclusively due to the Jewish origins of my uncle and that his cousin was famous. I do not believe the cause can be attributed to the fact that my uncle and his family were considered collaborators of the partisans. My uncle was a noble and generous person and helped everyone.

The police officers then presented her with a series of black-and-white photographs. Each one was of a man in German military uniform. Some were smiling, others were purse-lipped. Almost all were officers and wore an iron cross around their neck. There were thirty-two in all. The policemen wanted to know if she recognized anyone. It was a form of identity parade. The twelfth picture was of Clemens Theis in his early twenties. His appearance was memorable: a thin smile, droopy eyes, dark receding hair, and ears that stuck out sharply. Anna Maria remembered the man who was in charge of the German soldiers that day. She believed that she would be able to pick out his face from a million others. But, after taking her time to examine each photograph carefully, she said she could not identify any of the men. Subsequently, on separate occasions, the police officers showed these same photographs to Robert and Nina's nieces Lorenza and Paola Mazzetti and to the former partisan Vasco Caldini, but none of them recognized the picture of Clemens Theis either.

After the police officers left, Anna Maria called her son Andrea. She told him that the interview had upset her. It was too personal, she said, too intimate. And it had brought back unpleasant memories. She was glad it was over.

With their investigation complete, the police officers returned to Germany. They arranged for the witness statements to be translated, typed up their notes, and passed the documents, photographs and video evidence to the prosecutor's office in Frankenthal.

Hubert Ströber's doubts about Clemens Theis only grew upon reading the police officers' report. He went back to Carlo Gentile's dossier and realized that it was built around one crucial piece of evidence: Robert Einstein's testimony that he had heard that the unit whose soldiers had killed his family was also at the Incontro monastery. The problem, the prosecutor realized, was that Robert's assertion was based on information gleaned from an unnamed priest. Such second-hand testimony was considered to be hearsay and therefore inadmissible by the German courts. It should therefore be given no weight. Without Robert's testimony, Carlo Gentile's theory was severely weakened.

The last remaining argument in favour of Clemens Theis was that he was proximate to the crime. But was this sufficient? Hubert Ströber did not think so. There were tens of thousands of German soldiers active in the vicinity of Il Focardo around the time of the murders. The situation was chaotic. As such, archival reports that identified the locations of German troops at the time of the murders should not be over-relied upon. The historian Carlo Gentile and Judge Thomas Will had both identified Clemens Theis as the chief suspect in the Einstein murders. Hubert Ströber now came to a different conclusion. In late 2007, after just a few months of his own inquiries, he ruled out Clemens Theis as a suspect.

If it was not Clemens Theis, the prosecutor wondered, then who might be responsible? And given the decades since the crime had been committed, what chance was there of finding them? After all, most of the witnesses, let alone the culprits, were probably dead. The evidence, such as it was, had already been gone over by Carlo Gentile and Judge Will. Was it possible that they had missed something? Probably not. As for the crime scene itself, there was no chance of obtaining new evidence. The villa was burned by the German soldiers. The Sala Rossa had since been renovated multiple times. And, as far as the prosecutor knew, no other physical evidence remained, making forensic examination impossible.

Over the next three years, the prosecutor continued to work the case. His investigators contacted more archives, pored through countless documents and interviewed additional witnesses, but they were unable to generate any significant new leads. He could have left it there. Perhaps many other prosecutors would have. But, for Ströber, this was a special case. 'I was aware of the historic dimension,' he recalled, 'and there was considerable public interest in knowing what happened. I wanted to use every possible tool to investigate the case.' That's when he had the idea. Perhaps someone out there in the general public might know something. Which was why Hubert Ströber contacted the producers of *Aktenzeichen XY . . . ungelöst*.

Calling for witnesses on national television, for a crime committed by Nazis that took place decades earlier, was so unusual that it was picked up by the national media ahead of the broadcast. One of those to run a story in the days leading up to the transmission date was *Bild*, the country's largest selling newspaper, under the headline 'Police Hunt Murderers of Einstein's Family'. The story was also reported on by *Der Spiegel*, whose article began 'Police are looking for witnesses to the murder of Einstein relatives', and then anticipated that the programme would reveal 'new clues about the perpetrators'. Both papers provided the date and time for when the programme would be broadcast and encouraged their readers to contact the authorities if they had any information on the crime.

The programme was aired live on 23 February 2011. After outlining the background to the case, the presenter, Rudi Cerne, introduced the man standing next to him. 'Mr Ströber,' purred the presenter, 'it has been sixty-six years now. Most of the soldiers who were involved, as everyone will realize, are probably already dead. Nevertheless, it is being investigated very intensively. What drives you?'

'We only do our duty,' replied Ströber. 'This is a serious crime, a murder of three innocent civilians. So we as government officials are obliged to pursue these acts.' The presenter then asked his guest to explain what he was asking the audience to help with. The prosecutor said that they were taking an unusual approach. They were not looking for the soldiers who killed the Einstein family, but instead they were hoping to find the young man, maybe eighteen, nineteen or twenty years old, who had guarded Nina, Seba and the five girls in the back bedroom and who broke down when he heard the shots being fired. They did not consider him to be a perpetrator. Wanting to emphasize this point, Ströber added, 'This young soldier is not guilty, he is a witness, so he will not suffer any punishment.' And again, so the point was absolutely clear, 'That is very important.'

To demonstrate that the show had the support of the victims' family, the presenter explained that Lorenza Mazzetti had written to them saying, 'I am glad that you are concerned with investigating the Einstein family tragedy', and that she would 'like to meet the young German soldier again' if he was still alive. The presenter now gave out a telephone number and encouraged viewers to call in with information. 'We are crossing our fingers,' he said, 'in the hope that we can help solve this case.' He also stated that there was a reward of up to 5,000 euros available. 'Okay,' he acknowledged, 'maybe that's also an incentive, but it shouldn't just be the incentive.' With that, the segment ended.

And then the phones started ringing.

In the hours following the *Aktenzeichen XY* show, the broadcaster ZDF received more than seventy calls. This information was handed over to the prosecutor's office, which passed it to the police. Within a short while, they concluded that only two of the leads were helpful.

The first of these came from a certain Helmut Seither, who explained that his neighbour Josef Ripp had told him, before he died, that he was part of the Hermann Göring Division and that he had been present at the shooting of the Einstein family. The information was compelling, particularly because it was known from eyewitnesses that members of the Hermann Göring Division had visited Il Focardo in July 1944. When police officers pursued it further, however, they concluded that neither Ripp nor anyone else from the Hermann Göring Division could have been at the scene of the

Zona operazioni, 3.8.44.

IL COMANDO TEDESCO rende noto:

La famiglia Einstein si é resa colpevole di spionaggio.

Essa mantiene costantemente contatto con gli alleati nemici.

La famiglia é stata passata alla fucilazione il giorno 3 Agosto 44.

Exhibit "I"

Il Comandante

16-71-29

*Top:* One of the notices left by Germans at the crime scene, August 1944.
*Bottom:* Remains of the Ponte Alle Grazie in Florence after the Germans blew up the bridges, August 1944.

HEADQUARTERS FIFTH ARMY
OFFICE OF THE INSPECTOR GENERAL
A.P.O. 464, U. S. ARMY

17 September 1944

Doctor Albert Einstein
Princeton University
Princeton, New Jersey

My dear Doctor Einstein,

I take this occasion to communicate with you by personal letter at the request of your cousin, Roberto Einstein, of the Villa del Foscardo, Troghi, a small village approximately ten miles east of the City of Florence. I had occasion to visit in this community and interview Roberto Einstein in connection with a severe tragedy which has overtaken him. Roberto has requested that I inform you that his wife and two daughters, Anna and Luche, suffered death on August 3rd at the hands of the Nazi enemies. Roberto, himself, escaped unharmed and is presently living at his villa where he is carefully being attended by his sister-in-law and nieces.

I regret that censorship does not permit me to dwell upon the tragedy which is well known to me. I sincerely regret the nature of this letter and trust that before long the war and its terrible consequences will have come to an end with the complete and final defeat of the German armies.

Very sincerely yours,

MILTON R. WEXLER,
Major, I. G. D.

*Above:* Letter to Albert Einstein from Milton Wexler, September 1944.

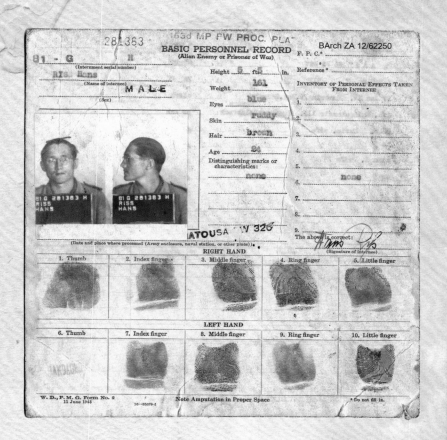

*Top:* Johann Riss's military card as US prisoner of war.
*Bottom left:* August Schmitz.
*Bottom right:* Clemens Theis as a young soldier.

RETURNED DOCUMENTS

**CRIMINI DI GUERRA**

# Scoperto il carnefice degli Einstein

## In Italia il giudice tedesco cacciatore di nazisti. Indaga anche sull'eccidio di Badalucco

dal nostro inviato
**RENZO PARODI**

LA SPEZIA. Il giudice Thomas Will è giovane, ha l'aspetto disinvolto di un intellettuale scapigliato, ma ricopre una carica di responsabilità. Lavora a Ludwigsburg, nell'hinterland di Stoccarda, presso la procura che indaga in prima battuta sui crimini nazisti. Il suo ufficio è un imbuto nel quale confluiscono le segnalazioni sui crimini commessi all'esteroda cittadini tedeschi in uniforme. Piatto forte, le stragi di civili, le rappresaglie, le operazioni "militari" che Wehrmacht ed SS realizzarono durante l'occupazione dei territori sottomessi al III° Reich. Will lavora per rintracciare i presunti responsabili dei più gravi fatti di sangue (gli altri episodi sono caduti in prescrizione) avvenuti in Italia, e trasmette gli atti alla procura competente. Un ruolo cruciale.

L'attività investigativa svolta ai suoi ordini di recente ha permesso di identificare uno degli ufficiali che comandò l'esecuzione del generale Antonio Gandin, comandante della Divisione Acqui a Cefalonia. La procura di Monaco ha archiviato il procedimento nei confronti dell'ex sottotenente Muelhauser, non rilevando elementi certi dell'esistenza dell'omicidio doloso aggravato, unico reato imprescrittibile in Germania. Una delle parti civili, la signora Marcella De Negri, ha presentato appello. Il caso insomma non è chiuso. Si è letto pazientemente tutti i 703 fascicoli spuntati nel 1994 dall'armadio della vergogna. Ora Stoccarda indaga su Sant'Anna di Stazzema (560 morti), Monaco su Marzabotto (850 morti), Bardine San Terenzo (52 vittime), Vinca e Valla (173 civili uccisi), Bergiola Foscalina (71 morti) Fosse del Frigido (147 uccisi). I procuratori tedeschi indagano ma i processi restano lontani. A gennaio Will ha smistato alla procura di Frankenthal gli atti sull'eccidio della famiglia Einstein, moglie e due giovani figlie di Roberti Einstein, cugino primo del fisico Premio Nobel, massacrate nella Villa Il Focardo, in Comune di Rignano sull'Arno (Firenze), il 4 agosto 1944. «Ho individuato un possibile colpevole, un capitano della Wehrmacht - dice Will - È solo un'ipotesi, andrà verificata. Il problema sarà dimostrare, in base a testimonianze, che fu proprio quell'ufficiale ad ordinare di aprire il fuoco sulle tre donne». Nina Mazzetti,

**Lo storico Lutz Klinkhammer**

58 anni e le figlie Luce, 27 e Annamaria detta Cicci, 18, furono abbattute nel salone della villa che le ospitava. Il marito e padre, Albert, viveva nei boschi, temendo, come ebreo, di essere catturato e ucciso dai tedeschi. È verosimile che l'ufficiale appartenesse a uno dei due battaglioni del 104esimo Panzergrenadier Regiment della XV° Divisione, aggregati alla 715esima Divisione di Fanteria stanziata in zona. Lorenza Mazzetti, una bimba all'epoca, cugina delle due giovani vittime, ricorda un giovane tenente biondo che parlava francese. E l'ufficiale scoperto da Will? Difficile dirlo. «Negli archivi del Public Record Office di Londra ho scoperto la testimonianza di alcuni soldati inglesi - aggiunge Will - Sopravvissuti al Focardo poche ore dopo la mattanza, riferirono che il parroco del paese aveva detto di aver raccolto da soldati tedeschi in ritirata la confessione del delitto». Alla procura di Monaco di Baviera è passato anche il fascicolo sulla strage di Sant'Agata (Chieti) 42 civili dilaniati dalle bombe e bruciati, il 21 gennaio 1944. Will ha trascorso alcuni giorni a Pisa, ospite del professor Pezzino, docente di storia e consulente nei processi italiani per crimini nazisti. Alla Spezia ha incontrato il collega Marco De Paolis, con il quale collabora da anni. A Ludwigsburg lo attendono 57 fascicoli, uno riguarda la Liguria: la strage del Monte Faudo (Badalucco), nell'imperiese. Il 17 agosto 1944 due sacerdoti (all'A quasanta) e una ventina di contadini inermi (nell'abitato di Montalto) furono passati per le armi da reparti Alpenjaeger (alpini tedeschi, sguinzagliati in montagna per vendicare un'azione partigiana.

Lo storico Lutz Klinkhammer è un'autorità in fatto di crimini nazisti. E' a Genova, relatore nel convegno sul salvataggio del porto, che continua oggi a palazzo San Giorgio. «La prescrizione ha impedito finora di celebrare in Germania molti processi per crimini di guerra a carico di ex nazisti. Perché il codice penale tedesco soltanto l'omicidio aggravato - e solo dal 1979 - non mai soggetto a prescrizione. Una pronuncia della Corte di Cassazione ha ingarbugliato ancor più le cose, di fatto creando un precedente al quale diverse procure si sono appigliate per archiviare i procedimenti. Eppure nell'opinione pubblica c'è grande interesse per queste vicende». Klinkhammer spiega che l'archiviazione della procura di Monaco per i fatti di Cefalonia non risponde alla domanda-chiave.

«Se anche si considerasse l'ufficiale a eseguito la fucilazione di Gandin e degli altri ufficiali ritenendo di obbedire ad un ordine legittimamente impartito, nulla è stato accertato su quegli ufficiali e sottufficiali che passarono per le armi migliaia di soldati italiani. Si erano arresi e avevano diritto, persino in quella sporca guerra, al trattamento previsto dalla Convenzione di Ginevra».

*Top left:* Milton R. Wexler.
*Top right:* Carlo Gentile.
*Bottom:* 'Einstein's Executioner Discovered', from *Il Secolo XIX*, 10 February, 2007.

( photo nr.32 )
Interno della villa. Piano terra. sala dove furono fucilate le vittime
16

000322

( Foto nr.33 )
Camino della sala. Nelle immediate vicinanze furono fucilate le vittime

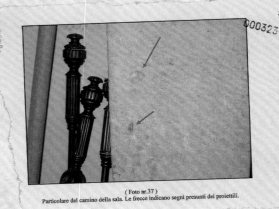

000323

( Foto nr.37 )
Particolare del camino della sala. Le frecce indicano segni presunti dei proiettili.

*Top:* German police investigators in the Sala Rossa, Il Focardo, with redacted faces.
*Middle:* Fireplace near where the victims were shot.
*Bottom:* Bullet holes in the wall of the Sala Rossa.

*Top left:* Judge Thomas Will.
*Top right:* Hubert Ströeber.
*Bottom left:* Barbara Schepanek.
*Bottom right:* Marco De Paolis.

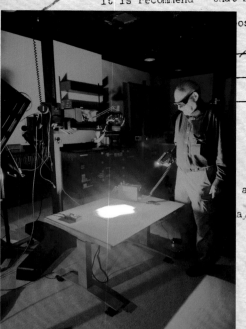

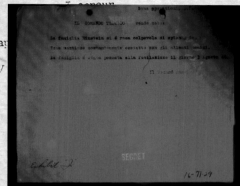

*Top Left:* Brian Dalrymple looks for fingerprints at NARA, near Washington DC, USA.
*Top Right:* Notice left by the Germans examined using laser technology.
*Bottom:* Anna Maria Boldrini with her sons, 2024.

NINA EINSTEIN MAZZETTI N. 24-III-1886
LUCE EINSTEIN N. 19-IV-1917
CICI EINSTEIN N. 23-II-1926
TRUCIDATE DAI TEDESCHI IL 3-VIII-1944

ROBERTO EINSTEIN
IL 13 LUGLIO 1945
HA RAGGIUNTO I SUOI CARI

*Top:* The gravestone of Nina, Luce and Cici at Badiuzza Cemetery, reads: 'Slaughtered by the Germans'.
*Bottom:* The gravestone of Robert Einstein at Badiuzza Cemetery, reads: 'Reunited with his loved ones'.

crime on 3 August 1944 as the entire unit had been posted to East Prussia in mid-July, well before the murders took place.

The second lead was more promising. A viewer named Ulrike Bay had phoned to say that her father, Ernst Otto Stehle, had frequently spoken about a 'terrible crime' from the war. Before he died in 2001, Ulrike's father had said he'd witnessed the murder of a wife and her two daughters at their house in Italy. This memory weighed heavily on him and he wished he could have prevented the killings. Ulrike said that everyone spoke of her father as a warm-hearted and good man. With mounting excitement, Prosecutor Ströber realized that Ernst Stehle sounded extremely similar to the kind young soldier who had guarded Nina, Seba and the five girls in the villa's upstairs bedroom. If he was a match, then it should be fairly simple to identify his commanding officer and then, with luck, they would have the person responsible for the murder of Nina, Luce and Cici Einstein.

The police officers visited Ulrike and formally interviewed her. They also picked up various items of her father's. These included his military service book, which noted that at the time of the murder he was stationed near Florence and belonged to a *Fallschirm-Sturmgeschütz Brigade* (Parachute Assault Gun Brigade). It also recorded that on 2 August 1944, the day before the murders took place, the whole brigade received grey-green uniforms, which tied in with a detail remembered by various witnesses that the soldiers at Il Focardo wore new grey-green uniforms. Most persuasively, Stehle's service book stated that he was of medium height, blond and blue-eyed, all of which matched the description of the young man who guarded Nina, Seba and the five girls.

Ströber now sent his team to the archives to determine the name of the man who led the unit to which Ernst Stehle belonged. The results were soon obtained. The commander of the Parachute Assault Gun Brigade was August Schmitz, born on 22 October 1907 in Krefeld in southwest Germany. At the time of the Einstein murders, his rank was major, but, crucially, his men called him 'Il Capitano' – again matching the memory of various witnesses.

After more time spent in the archives, the police officers were able to track down twenty-six members of Schmitz's Parachute Assault Gun Brigade who were still alive. Most could remember that they passed through the region of Florence when they were retreating in the summer of 1944. Some recognized Stehle as belonging to their unit, but none of them admitted taking part in the crime. One of them, a former private called Schietke, believed that he recognized a photo of the villa Il Focardo and remembered hearing shooting as he walked by the house. He could not give any more details. Another member of the brigade, a motorcycle communication officer, recalled a building near Florence which resembled a *schloss*, or manor house, with a tree-lined driveway, whose owner had a vineyard, and who may have had a moustache and spoke German. Though Robert Einstein had a beard not a moustache, the police officers believed this account was close enough to fit Il Focardo and the estate owner.

To obtain a positive identification of Stehle, the investigators flew to Italy to speak with the eyewitnesses. First, they travelled to Verona to meet once again with Anna Maria Boldrini, but while she said that the photograph of Stehle 'could be' the person who had guarded them in the upstairs room, she could not be certain. Next they drove to Rome to see Lorenza and Paola, but the twins also failed to recognize the photograph presented by the investigators. While Lorenza was with them, however, she drew a sketch of the captain in charge on the day of the murders.

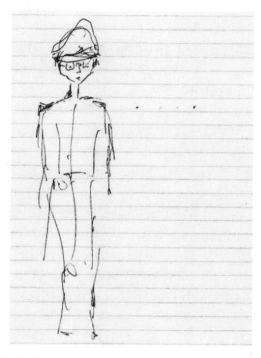

Sketch of German commander by Lorenza Mazzetti, 2011.

'Although I only saw him for a few minutes, he impressed himself on me,' she told them. Despite this contribution, it was not what the investigators had been hoping for. None of the three Italian nieces had been able to identify Ernst Stehle.

205

Prosecutor Ströber continued to search for evidence that would allow him to name the people responsible for the Einstein murders. Finally, after more than eighteen months, he felt he had enough. Seven years after first receiving the case, the prosecutor submitted his final report to Judge Will at the Central Office in Ludwigsburg. 'It seems an obvious conclusion,' he wrote, 'that the killing was carried out by members of the Schmitz Parachute Assault Gun Brigade.' In legal parlance, the word 'obvious', or *naheliegend*, reflected a high degree of confidence. Ströber had therefore not only ruled out Clemens Theis, he had produced his own prime suspect. In his opinion, the most likely person responsible for the murder of the Einstein family was August Schmitz.

Prosecutor Ströber would not, however, be filing charges. This was because, according to his military records, August Schmitz died in San Martino Buon Albergo, near Verona, on 26 April 1945, three days before German forces surrendered in Italy. As for the twenty-six men from the Schmitz Brigade who were still alive, they were all cleared of suspicion because none of them were officers and therefore, the prosecutor said, could not be held responsible as they were too far down the chain of command.

Nevertheless, in his letter to Judge Will, Prosecutor Ströber appeared upbeat. He made it clear that, even though Schmitz was dead, they had found their man. He would now be closing the case. It was, as far as the prosecutor was concerned, a positive result.

According to observers of the case, however, there were several potential issues with the prosecutor's conclusion. To start with, if he was so confident that the Schmitz Brigade was responsible, why did the prosecutor not file charges against the men who were still alive? Surely their rank did not preclude their responsibility as accessories to the crime. There were a number of recent cases in Germany in which bookkeepers, guards and other secondary figures had been prosecuted for war crimes, demonstrating that the German authorities were taking a wider view of responsibility when it came to the Holocaust.

There were other concerns. The Italian historian Carlo Gentile pointed out that while several members of the Schmitz Brigade remembered being in the Florence region around the time of the German retreat, this was a months-long period. None had confirmed that they were close to Il Focardo at the time of the murders. This was in contrast to Clemens Theis and his unit, which could be placed within three miles of the crime scene a day after the murders.

Lorenza Mazzetti was another who had her doubts. Neither she nor her sister recognized August Schmitz. How then could he be responsible? And while she had supported Hubert Ströber's efforts to go on German national television to raise attention to the case, she was disappointed that more had not come from his seven-year-long investigation.

For his part, Judge Will was more circumspect about sharing his opinion on Ströber's findings. It was his job to investigate a case, not to press charges and certainly not to pass judgement. Yes, back in 2007 he had believed that there was sufficient evidence on Clemens Theis to pass the file to the prosecution officer. Indeed, the name of the file contained Clemens Theis's name. But he would not comment further.

Others pointed out that none of the surviving members of the Schmitz Brigade remembered being involved with the killings. This might be because they wished to avoid self-incrimination, but even this was not certain. Though rare, there were instances of Nazis confessing to their sins, starting with the testimony given at the Nuremberg Trials by Rudolf Höss, the commandant of Auschwitz, and Hans Frank, the leader of Nazi-occupied Poland. More recently, in 2014, Reinhold Hanning, a ninety-two-year-old retired dairy farmer, admitted during questioning after his arrest that he had worked as a guard in Auschwitz.

Perhaps most difficult for Ströber's theory, was a piece of evidence found at the National Archives in Kew. A classified intelligence report submitted in August 1944 to British Army headquarters by the Duke of Cornwall's Light Infantry (who had been involved in the assault on the Incontro monastery) mentioned that a German prisoner of war taken on 4 August was a member of 'Assault Gun Bty. [Battery] Schmitz' and that this unit was 'located north of Bologna'. This placed Schmitz and his men more than 100 miles from Il Focardo a day after the Einstein murders.

When put together, this all made it far less likely that August Schmitz or his brigade was responsible for the killing of Nina, Luce and Cici. Which in turn meant that the question of who murdered the Einsteins in 1944 still remained unanswered. A question which would soon be examined by Italy's leading war crimes investigator, Marco De Paolis.

# 25. Rome, 2016

Marco De Paolis was a legend in Italy, the country's most famous Nazi hunter. Between 2003 and 2013, he carried out more than 515 investigations, resulting in seventeen trials and fifty-seven life sentences.

When he began working as a military prosecutor in 1988, no one had been convicted of war crimes that had taken place in Italy for more than forty years. In 2002, De Paolis was promoted to chief military prosecutor in La Spezia and, within three years, he had successfully prosecuted ten members of the Waffen-SS for the massacre of up to 560 civilians at Sant'Anna di Stazzema on 12 August 1944. (Each was given a life sentence *in absentia*, though none would face jail time as Germany refused to extradite them to Italy.) The trial was widely covered around the world. The *Guardian*'s headline was typical, announcing: '10 Former Nazis Convicted of Tuscan Massacre'. Likewise, Deutsche Welle declared: 'Italian Court Convicts Ex-Nazis'. While the local newspaper in Tuscany, *Il Tirreno*, trumpeted: 'Justice after 60 Years!'

The verdict at the end of the Sant'Anna di Stazzema trial had a profound effect on the relatives of victims in Italy.

One of these was Adele Pardini who had been a little girl living in Sant'Anna di Stazzema when she witnessed her mother, sixteen-year-old sister and twenty-day-old baby sister being murdered in front of her. 'For years I was unable to speak about what happened,' Adele shared in 2022. 'At the time, the German soldiers said that the killings were a reprisal for the actions of the partisans. We felt somehow responsible. Guilty for what happened.' She added that the sentencing of the perpetrators changed her family's view. For the first time, they understood that the atrocity had not been a reprisal but an act of terrorism. They began to speak about the crime. 'An enormous burden was lifted from us,' recalled Adele. 'After all those years I did not feel guilty.'

It was around the time of the Sant'Anna di Stazzema trial that De Paolis had first learned of the Einstein murders from Valdo Spini, who represented Florence in the Chamber of Deputies and was also a member of the Waldensian community. Busy with the court case, De Paolis was able to do little more than open a file but, not long after, he began actively to investigate various lines of inquiry, including collecting testimony from local residents and gathering material from the archives. He also provided assistance to the German prosecutor Hubert Ströber, arranging the visit of his police officers to the crime scene in 2007 and setting up interviews with various witnesses.

Meanwhile, De Paolis pursued other war crimes cases. In 2011, he was victorious again, this time successfully prosecuting four German soldiers who had taken part in the massacre of 174 civilians in the Fucecchio Marshes thirty miles west of Florence on 23 August 1944. Once more the newspapers praised the prosecutor for his skill and tenacity.

Once again the relatives of the families expressed profound thanks for his efforts.

As the years progressed, De Paolis and his team continued to investigate the Einstein case. They reviewed documents sent in by concerned citizens. They kept track of developments in Germany. They monitored the occasional newspaper article that was published on the story. But as one witness died after another, there appeared to be less and less fertile ground to cover. The prosecutor became unsure how to advance the investigation any further.

There was one person, however, who never gave up, who remained convinced that the perpetrators would be caught. Like so many others, she had been inspired by the work of Marco De Paolis and she believed those responsible for the murder of her family members would be found guilty, just as had happened with Sant'Anna di Stazzema, just as had happened with the Fucecchio Marshes.

On 24 February 2016, two years after Hubert Ströber closed his case in Germany, the now eighty-nine-year-old Lorenza Mazzetti sent a letter to Marco De Paolis. She said that she had stumbled on something which might be of great interest. 'I want to be interviewed about the political assassination of the Einstein family,' she said, 'because I think I recognize the perpetrator in a photograph I have seen on the internet.'

In the decades since the terrible events at Il Focardo, Lorenza Mazzetti had shown remarkable resilience. After spending a few years in the Waldensian community in the Alps, she moved in her twenties to London, where she attended the Slade School of Fine Art and made a name for herself as a pioneering young film-maker. One of her films, *Together*, told the story of two deaf men walking around the ruined streets of east London (battered by German bombing during the Blitz) which went on to win a prize at the Cannes Film Festival. After returning to Rome in the mid-1950s, Lorenza experienced a mental collapse. Deciding that she must face up to the events of her childhood, she started to write. The outcome, in 1962, was *The Sky Falls*, an autobiographical novel told from a young child's point of view, based on her experiences at Il Focardo. The book was both commercially successful and won a prestigious Italian literary award. In the following years, Lorenza wrote more books, made several further films and ran a marionette theatre for children. She was also well known for her parties. People described these gatherings as rich in both conviviality and the exchange of ideas, where you were likely to bump into some of the most famous people in Europe, including politicians, actors and novelists. Lorenza married twice, first a journalist (Bruno Grieco), who she divorced, and then a surgeon (Luigi Galletti), who died in 1999. Neither marriage produced children. And all the while, Lorenza was unable to let go of the murder of her aunt and two cousins. Some even called her 'obsessed'.

So it was that, on 19 October 2016, Lorenza Mazzetti arrived for interview at the Ministry of Defence, on Viale delle Milizie in Rome. Questioning her were Francesco Trivelli and Michela Sinatra, two investigators from De Paolis's team. They began by asking why Lorenza had contacted their boss, Marco De Paolis. She said that while she had been searching on the website of the Simon Wiesenthal Center – leaders in the search for Nazi war criminals – a photograph of a German soldier had caught her attention. 'The face of

this military officer seemed familiar to me,' she said. 'I recognized him as the commander that entered into the villa
where I was living with my uncle Robert and aunt Nina. My
sister recognized him too.' Eleven years after Carlo Gentile
had named Clemens Theis as the chief suspect in the Einstein murders, and two years after the German prosecutor
Hubert Ströber had identified August Schmitz as a possible
alternative, Lorenza Mazzetti had picked out a third possible
culprit: his name was Johann Riss.

One of the investigators pulled two photographs from a
folder and slid them across the table. They had obtained the
images from the Bundesarchiv in Berlin. In the first picture,
a young soldier stared at the camera full-faced. He was clean-
shaven with lips pursed, his round metal glasses glinting in
the light. In the second picture, the soldier turned his gaunt
face and thick neck and looked to the side. In his hands, he
held a card on which was printed a name: 'Hans Riss', short
for Johann Riss.

Was this the same man she had seen online? 'Yes, I recognize him,' Lorenza confirmed. 'I am very sure that he was
the commander of the group of soldiers that entered the
villa. If I imagine a hat on his head, I seem to see him again
in front of my eyes.' She then added, 'The thing that is fixed
in my mind is the glasses that he wore.' The photograph was
not entirely dissimilar to the sketch that Lorenza had provided to the German police officers five years earlier, after
the *Aktenzeichen XY . . . ungelöst* TV programme had been
broadcast, when they had been asking about Ulrike Bay's
father, Ernst Stehle.

The investigator now wanted to see if they could narrow
down the unit to which Johann Riss belonged. They showed

Lorenza photographs and artists' impressions of various uniforms, caps and types of military vehicle. Lorenza apologized. Though she had seen the German military vehicle that came to the villa on the day of the murders, and had observed what the soldiers were wearing, she could not positively identify any of the pictures she was shown with any degree of confidence. And that was that. After thanking Lorenza for her time, the prosecutors ended the interview at 2 p.m. and escorted her out of the building.

In the years since the murders, Lorenza's twin sister Paola had also displayed astonishing resilience. Not long after the war, she was at a church camp when she met a man from Ulm in Germany. They married, and in 1956 had a daughter called Eva. Their relationship, however, did not last. They divorced and he moved to the USA, where he remarried. Paola was now a single mother and provided for herself and her daughter. She studied psychotherapy under two Jungian specialists and became a qualified practitioner. Over the next few years, she continued to hone her skills, mastering the expressive method known as 'sand play', along with hypnosis and transactional analysis. For some time, she worked with the women's centre at the psychiatric hospital in Trieste. Away from her clients, Paola painted watercolours, which were exhibited in Rome and Paris. In Florence, she co-founded and directed the Gallery of Contemporary Art, where several renowned American artists had their first showings in Italy. She also published several non-fiction books, including one on the signs of the zodiac and another which was a light-hearted exploration of the Bach flower remedies.

Once, when asked how she coped with the tragedies of her

childhood, Paola said, 'I don't know how we managed to over-come it. You can never overcome it. It can't be overcome. One wonders, "Why do you live? To hate or to love?" You real-ize that the only response to cruelty is to live differently. The meaning of life cannot be this. The meaning of life is to take a path where you don't accept evil.' She then said, 'Revenge is not enough, it doesn't help, it worsens the situation.'

Two days after her sister was interviewed in the Ministry of Defence, Paola was questioned by the same police officers at her home on Via del Monte della Farina, close to Campo de' Fiori, in the centre of Rome. Starting at 11.20 a.m., they began by showing Paola a copy of Lorenza's signed testi-mony and asked if she agreed with what her twin had stated. 'I think that what my sister said is complete,' Paola replied, 'and I can't add any useful details.' They then asked her about the man in charge on the day of the murders. 'He was young, thin, of medium height and wore glasses,' Paola said. She also mentioned that he wore a dark uniform, maybe dark blue; the others wore lighter clothes. And that unlike the other soldiers, he did not carry a machine gun. Only a pistol.

The investigators next showed her the two photographs of Johann Riss. 'In the photos you show me, I recognize the physiognomy of the military man we identified as com-mander during the heinous murder of our cousins and aunt, inside the villa Il Focardo,' she said carefully. 'I can say this since I had the opportunity to see his face up close when he told us that we would be interrogated.' Paola was referring to the moment during their captivity when the captain had called Nina, Seba and the five girls down into the Sala Rossa and accused them of espionage. The investigators then asked her to sign and date the photograph of Riss, which she did.

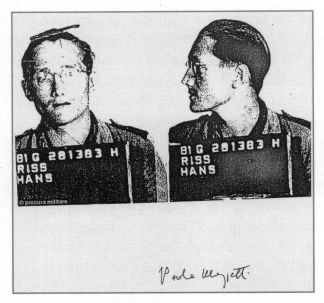

Photograph of Johann Riss, signed by Paola Mazzetti, 2016.

After being shown various artists' impressions of caps, uniforms and military vehicles – none of which she could positively identify – Paola was asked about the notices that the Germans had left at the crime scene, the ones typed in Italian which accused the Einstein family of helping the partisans. She said that she had brought a photocopy with her which, after signing and dating, she gave to them. She then commented that she thought it interesting that the notice had been 'left voluntarily' and that the officer responsible had given his rank. The interview, which had been a little shorter than her sister's, concluded at 1 p.m.

At first, Lorenza and Paola were pleased by the response from the military prosecutor's office. Marco De Paolis's team had clearly conducted research before the interviews, as shown by the photographs which they had obtained from the archives in Berlin. In a follow-up letter to the prosecutor a few weeks after her interview, Lorenza described the man and woman who had interviewed her as 'so kind'. In the months after, she wrote further letters, sharing newspaper articles, photographs and other material that she found during her own research, and asking for updates on the case. But as time went on, Lorenza became increasingly frustrated at the prosecutor's lack of progress. Worse, she felt stonewalled. A typical response from Marco De Paolis read as follows: 'As you know, we are investigating [the Einstein case] but we have not had a positive result. If we have any news in the future, I will keep you informed.'

As the months turned to years, and as Lorenza herself moved into her nineties – raising the prospect that the case would not be resolved before she died – her missives became increasingly fraught. On 7 April 2017, for instance, she sent a letter to De Paolis about the investigation. After thanking him for 'spending so much time on this case', she wrote:

> I showed you the *Daily Mail* article about Riss . . . but that
> was not enough for you. I will send you [another letter] that
> better explains my thoughts. I hope you arrive at the truth of
> the Einstein massacre at Focardo. If I am alive it's because
> the SS commander received orders to kill only the relatives
> of Albert Einstein and to give pain through Hitler's vendetta.
> Hope you can help me to find the truth and to help the
> Italian state not bury the truth. Warm greetings.

But it was to no avail. On 22 August 2018, De Paolis wrote to Lorenza that 'We have completed the investigation initiated after your written statement and, unfortunately, have been unable to find any evidence to support your claims'. The file, he said, would now be sent to the archives, effectively closing the case. He then continued:

> I certainly do not intend to question your recollections and your passionate search for the truth on events so serious that they have marked your life since childhood. As you are well aware, I share your passion and frustrations. However, undoubtedly due to the difficulties linked to the considerable amount of time that has now elapsed and the impossibility of objectively matching the data you have provided with what we know (especially given the legal rules governing investigations and criminal trials), we have not been able to find the necessary evidence to support your statements [about Johann Riss]. I assure you that we did everything we could. Everything possible. I thank you most sincerely and send you my warmest regards.

What De Paolis did not share in his email was that he thought Lorenza Mazzetti was an unreliable witness. 'She was very old,' he would later say, 'she may have had dementia' – adding, for clarification, 'it was so many years later, too many years to recognize a suspect.' When asked whether it was possible that Lorenza and Paola had correctly identified Johan Riss as the perpetrator, he replied, 'It is not probable that [Riss] was the perpetrator. But it is possible' – he gave a small smile – 'in the same way that I am the mastermind of the 9/11 attacks.'

And with that, Italy's leading military prosecutor made it clear that he was unlikely ever to believe that Johann Riss was involved in the Einstein murders.

# 26. Munich, 2019

Lorenza Mazzetti was not someone to put all her eggs in one basket. Around the time that she felt cold-shouldered by the military prosecutor in Rome, Lorenza asked Barbara Schepanek, a television journalist in Munich, to help her look into the former German soldier Johann Riss. Barbara had more than twenty years' experience in television and was making a short news feature with Lorenza.

'I'm telling you, it's him,' Lorenza Mazzetti said down the phone. She had found the guy who murdered her family members and his name was Johann Riss. At this point, Barbara remembered getting goosebumps. It was thrilling to believe that the man responsible for the Einstein murders might at last be found. After the call ended, Barbara began looking for information on Riss.

According to his military records held by the Bundesarchiv in Berlin, Johann Robert Riss was born on 27 January 1921 in Emmering, a village of a thousand people fifteen miles west of the outskirts of Munich. Sometimes called 'Johann' and at others 'Hans', he was raised a Catholic by his carpenter father and mother who worked in laundry. As a boy, like millions of others, he belonged to the Hitler Youth, where he learned how to march, sang patriotic songs, took part in competitive sports and was taught how to use a gun. He liked gymnastics and alpine skiing and he was good at swimming (he had a life-saving certificate). At fourteen he left school and became an apprentice salesman. A little later, he began work in an electrics company. At some point he was involved in an accident resulting in a scar on his forehead. Now fully grown, he was five foot five inches tall, blond and with blue eyes. He also wore glasses. He married a local girl called Maria and together they moved into an apartment in Fürstenfeld-bruck, less than two miles from his parents in Emmering.

In December 1938, ten months before the start of the war, the seventeen-year-old Riss volunteered to join the Wehrmacht. On his enlistment documents, he gave his mother's name as the emergency contact. At first, Riss was assigned to an infantry signals company, where he underwent radio-operation and communications training. In late 1940, he was posted to German-occupied Poland, and he was still there when, in June 1941, the Nazis invaded the Soviet Union in Operation Barbarossa. Riss was serving with the 62nd Infantry Regiment in Army Group Centre, commanded by General Fedor von Bock. For days on end, they marched across eastern Germany and into Byelorussia. 'Along the roadside,' reported one of Riss's comrades, 'there were strewn stinking, bloated horse carcasses, shot-up vehicles and corpses of Soviet soldiers.'

On 14 July, after two weeks of non-stop marching, they came to Mogilev, east of Minsk. They soon heard about the fierce battles that had taken place here. 'From many sections came reports of cruel maltreatment and mutilation of the wounded, of massacres of prisoners,' reported a soldier from Riss's regiment.

Using knives and bayonets, a soundless mass murder was carried out against soldiers and horses. The guards had been silently slaughtered, the artillerymen found in their tents with their throats cut, the wounded mutilated in an inhuman way. The disgust at such acts generated a terrible rage that drove to even greater harshness in battle and to scepticism towards enemy groups willing to surrender.

Riss and his colleagues were told that the people they were fighting belonged to a 'lower level of civilization', that they had to be liberated from Bolshevism, and their land was needed to help feed the people back home in Germany. Moreover, they were instructed that Soviet soldiers often dressed in civilian clothes and that they should be 'dealt with'. They understood that this was a command to shoot civilians on sight, including women and children, even if unarmed. In addition, there was a competition between their regiment and the one close by. Whoever took more villages, killed more people, earned bragging rights. If that was not enough motivation, the soldiers were provided with pills that reduced fatigue and gave them a sense of invincibility.

During one battle, in mid-November, fourteen members of Riss's regiment were killed and fifty-nine wounded. One of his comrades described their situation:

So we attack again, march and attack, from village to village. Again and again we are told: 'The village in front of us is occupied by the enemy. Get ready for the attack.' We hauled the heavy equipment, the weapons, machine-gun ammunition boxes, grenade-launcher rounds. Then suddenly again shelling, artillery, *Ratsch-Bum*, the howling of Stalin's organ, taking cover, throwing oneself into the mud . . . and forward again . . . forward . . . and shoot! That's how it goes every day. They want the village. We have orders to take it, to destroy the enemy.

Over the following weeks, Johann Riss's regiment took part in a series of murderous assaults, setting fire to scores of villages, killing hundreds of civilians and taking few soldiers prisoner. Reports of rape and theft were widespread. The fighting was often savage. All the while, they were bombarded by barrages of Soviet artillery. It was a brutalizing, dehumanizing experience.

By mid-December, Riss and his comrades had reached Eremino, a small town twenty miles from the outskirts of Moscow. The temperature was now permanently below zero, the ground was frozen, yet they had no winter clothing. Soviet resistance had reached an even higher level of intensity, with casualties on both sides extraordinarily high. Then, just before Christmas, Riss became ill. According to his military records, he had 'an ear infection and a pimple on his arse', which may have been a euphemism for something more serious (perhaps that he'd been shot or hit by shrapnel there), or maybe it was just a medical orderly with a sense of humour. The fact he wasn't discharged for several months suggests he was indeed suffering from something fairly severe. He was transported back to a military hospital near Munich to recuperate. After a few months, he was discharged and then deployed for a relatively peaceful stint in France.

On 10 July 1943, Riss arrived in southern Italy. This

happened to be the same day that American, British and Canadian forces landed in Sicily, preparing the way for the Allied assault on the mainland. Riss was assigned to the newly formed 26th Armoured Reconnaissance Detachment (*Panzer-Aufklärungs-Abteilung*) which was attached to the 26th Panzer Division. There he remained until September, when he developed worrying symptoms included vomiting, lack of appetite, diarrhoea and yellow-coloured skin. He was diagnosed with jaundice and spent the winter in an Austrian hospital. Six months later, he was once again discharged, first spending time in the detachment's reserve 3rd Company, and then, in the spring of 1944, transferring back to 1st Company. The German military records ended in early September 1944, when Johann Riss was declared 'missing'. At this time, his rank was *Unteroffizier*, or sergeant.

According to US Army records, Riss was captured by the Americans near Rimini, on the Adriatic coast, on 3 September 1944. He was shipped across the Atlantic to the USA, where he was held in a series of prisoner-of-war camps, arriving first in Newport News, Virginia, on 9 November, before being moved to Camp Chaffee in western Arkansas, followed by Camp Maxey, just north of Paris, Texas. He was released after a bout of tonsillitis, in June 1946, almost two years since his capture and a year after the war's end, and returned to Germany.

Contained within these US Army records were two black-and-white photographs of Riss taken by the Americans on 14 September 1944, eleven days after his capture and just six weeks since the Einstein murders. These were the pictures that Lorenza and Paola had so confidently identified to the Italian prosecutors. Below the images were nine fingerprints.

223

According to the notes on the page, at the time the finger-prints were taken, Riss's right thumb was bandaged.

Riss's personal files were silent about his whereabouts during the summer of 1944 when the Einstein murders took place, but his regiment's casualty reports shed some light on the issue. From these, it was possible to establish that, on 11 July, a member of Johann Riss's 1st Company was killed in Montevettolini, a village forty-five miles northwest of Il Focardo. There was little information about the movements of the reconnaissance detachment, let alone of Riss's company, for the rest of July and the first week of August. This changed on 11 August, when two things happened. First, according to the casualty reports, Sergeant Michael Bonk of 2nd Company was killed near the small hamlet of Spicchio-Sovigliana, just thirty miles to the west of Il Focardo. And then, on the same day, Riss was transferred from 1st to 2nd Company, presumably to replace Bonk.

What did all this mean? At the time of the Einstein murders on 3 August 1944, Johann Riss was likely between thirty and forty-five miles from Il Focardo, less than a two-hour drive from the scene of the crime. What was not in Johann Riss's military records was his activity between 11 August and the time of his capture in early September. That did not stop the Bavarian television journalist Barbara Schepanek. She went online to see if she could find anything else. After trawling through various websites, she discovered something of significant interest: Johann Riss, the man Lorenza and Paola Mazzetti believed murdered their relatives, had been found guilty of committing another major war crime near Florence.

*

Early in the morning of 23 August 1944, just twenty days since the Einstein murders, Johann Riss's unit arrived in the marshes of Fucecchio, an area of flat wetland fifty miles west of Florence. By the day's end, they and other units belonging to the 26th Panzer Division had murdered 174 civilians, including elderly men, pregnant women and twenty-seven children. The Germans said this was a reprisal following the wounding of two soldiers by partisans in the days before. Italian historians would later conclude the killings were to create chaos in the local population, a form of terrorism.

Ulivero Baldi was seventeen years old when the soldiers arrived that day. At the time, he was living with his family. They kept horses, cows and pigs. A German officer had taken over the Baldis' house, so they were living in an outbuilding. They had become friendly with this officer, offering him milk. At around 6 a.m. on 23 August, this officer had come and warned them that a raid was imminent. They quickly fled towards the marshes and hid behind some tall reeds. From here, Ulivero watched the massacre unfold. He saw people shot just a few feet away, including a woman nursing a baby, and a young boy. Later, Ulivero learned that his cousin had been killed, along with scores of friends and distant family members. The bodies were buried in a mass grave. When asked what he would have liked to happen to those guilty of the massacre, he replied with a steeliness in his eyes, 'I would do to them what they did to us.'

In 2008, three years after the successful prosecution of the ten Germans for their role in the Sant'Anna di Stazzema atrocity, Marco De Paolis had opened an investigation into the Fucecchio massacre. As part of these efforts, he asked his counterparts in Germany to carry out certain inquiries.

A few weeks later, there was a loud knocking at the door of Johann Riss. At the time, he was eighty-seven years old, wheelchair-bound, and needing constant care. He lived with his wife Irene in the town of Kaufbeuren, southwest of Munich. When they went to see what all the noise was about, they were surprised to see a group of police officers standing on the threshold. The police said that they had a warrant to search the place as part of an Italian war crime investigation. The couple were shocked. There had been no warning before the police arrived. The search lasted more than an hour. The police officers were methodical, going through the house and examining boxes full of personal items and looking at photographs, but they found nothing of interest and took nothing away with them.

In June 2011, three years after the police turned up at his front door, Johann Riss was found guilty by a court in Rome of taking part in the massacre in the Fucecchio Marshes. He was sentenced to life in prison. He was not, however, in court to hear the verdict, his doctors having declared him medically unfit to travel. Two years later, on 17 March 2013, the military court in Rome's decision was upheld by the Italian Court of Appeals and a European arrest warrant was issued. The prosecutor in Rome then applied to the authorities in Munich to approve the extradition of Johann Riss to Italy. But, just as they had with the ten men found guilty of the massacre at Sant'Anna di Stazzema, the Germans rejected the request, saying that according to their constitution, German citizens had a right to be tried in their own country. As a last resort, the Italians requested that Riss's sentence be implemented in Germany, but this too was denied, on the grounds that Riss had not been found guilty by a German court. Despite being sentenced to life in prison in 2011, Riss had not spent a day behind bars.

Now, in April 2016, Barbara Schepanek contacted the police in Kempten, who had responsibility for crimes committed in the district where Riss lived. The case was assigned to Detective Norbert Bernhard, head of the murder investigations team. After reviewing the research and having consulted with his colleagues, the detective chose to open an investigation.

Such a decision might not have been made just a few years before, given the suspect's age, but recently the German authorities had developed an appetite for prosecuting elderly Nazi war criminals. Just five years earlier, in 2011, John Demjanjuk was sentenced, aged ninety-one, to five years in prison for being a guard at the Sobibor extermination camp. And the previous year, in 2015, Oskar Gröning, aged ninety-four, was sentenced for being accessory to mass murder during his time as a bookkeeper in Auschwitz.

In the spring of 2016, Bernhard began his investigation into Johann Riss. He tracked down his military and employment records. He then asked for an interview, but was told by Riss's doctor that his patient was physically unable to take part. Still not satisfied, the detective obtained a search warrant, drove to Kaufbeuren and, on 10 June 2016, turned up at Johann Riss's door along with seven other police officers. Once again Riss's house was searched. Once again nothing of interest was found.

Five days later, Lorenza travelled from Rome to Kempten to be interviewed by Detective Bernhard. As she stepped out of the car wearing a green sweater, matching green beret, blue trousers and bright red sunglasses, she smiled at the waiting media. 'I had a great breakfast,' she laughed happily. 'I'm being treated very well by my German hosts.'

Inside the police station, Lorenza was formally shown the photographs of Johann Riss taken shortly after he was captured by the Americans in September 1944. Once again she confirmed that this was the right person. She said she was 100 per cent certain. After the interview concluded, Lorenza was escorted out of the police station by Bernhard. They walked through the wide atrium hand-in-hand, smiling and laughing. 'I hope, that they can do something,' Lorenza told the television crew in English before she left the building. 'It's up to the police now to prove it's him, to research the case.'

Two months later, on 10 August 2016, Lorenza received a letter from Munich. 'The accused was found during a search of his home,' wrote the German authorities. '[He] is severely ill with dementia and is no longer fully aware of his surroundings. He could no longer be questioned about the facts.' This discovery was backed up by a copy of an insurance document, which stated that Riss had experienced 'a significant cognitive deterioration in the case of pre-existing dementia'. In addition, they had uncovered various reports confirming Riss's diminished cognitive state. In November 2012, for instance, he was found looking for his wife at a Christmas market and had to be escorted back home by the police. Not long after, he attracted attention because he overtook another car at a level crossing in a dangerous manner and then drove across the rail tracks while ignoring the red flashing lights. The following year, his wife reported him missing after he left her to go to the toilet and then wandered off. In summary, the letter concluded, 'The investigation had to be discontinued because the accused is no longer able to be questioned or to stand trial.' The police in Kempten were closing the case.

Later, Barbara asked Lorenza how she felt, given that Johann Riss would now never be charged with the Einstein murders, let alone spend time in prison. 'The first phase of remembering is over,' Lorenza told the TV journalist. 'The second phase of forgetting is also over. And the third phase of knowing who did it is also over. As for the man who I recognized, whose face I saw, I don't want him to go to jail. It's enough for me that I know who did it.'

There were some who did not believe that Johann Riss was the perpetrator. One of these was the Italian historian who had been looking into the case for more than a decade. 'It's ridiculous', said Carlo Gentile; 'it could never be Johann Riss.' He listed the reasons why: Riss was a junior non-commissioned officer and so would not have the authority to carry out the murders, there was no archival evidence linking him to the murders and, most importantly in his opinion, it was possible to locate Clemens Theis far closer to the crime scene. Others pointed out that various witnesses had testified that the commanding officer was a captain, whereas Johann Riss was a sergeant. For his part, the Italian prosecutor Marco De Paolis maintained his doubts about Lorenza's mental abilities given her age, and therefore felt her identification of Riss was unreliable. As for the German prosecutor, Hubert Ströber, when asked for this thoughts on Johann Riss, he said he did not have a view as the suspect did not live in his district and therefore he had never looked at his file.

Such concerns did not persuade Lorenza and Paola

Mazzetti, who had recognized Riss in the photographs, nor Barbara Schepanek. In their view, the evidence found in the archives was strong. Riss had opportunity (on the day of the crime, he was located within two hours' drive from Il Focardo), he had means (he had a gun and commanded soldiers with machine guns), and the crime fitted a pattern of behaviour (he took part in another appalling atrocity twenty days after the Einstein murders). His psychological profile was also a possible match to the crime (after experiencing extreme brutality on the Eastern Front, Riss had become desensitized to violence).

But there was one last piece of the puzzle that was missing: motive.

The question of motive had long perplexed those who had looked into the Einstein murders. In 1945, a clerk at the US War Crimes Office in Rome had written in the file: 'Likely reason is that [Nina's] husband is a Jew.' When Carlo Gentile had looked at the case in 2005, he determined that the murders were spontaneous; it was, he said, 'an episode of gratuitous violence'. This conclusion was rejected by both Hubert Ströber and Marco De Paolis, who both said that the German soldiers would have only come to Il Focardo if they had received strict instructions from their superiors.

Over the years, numerous eyewitnesses supported the view that the murders were well planned rather than being spontaneous. Among them was Eugenio Carrara, who lived on another estate a few hundred yards from the Einstein villa. He recalled that in the spring of 1944, just three or four months before the murders took place, German soldiers came knocking at his family's house specifically asking for the location of Robert Einstein. Eugenio's testimony echoes other witnesses, including the priest Don Giuseppe and the partisan Vasco Caldini, who both said that German soldiers were looking for Robert Einstein in the weeks and months before the murders.

'There was a strict chain of command,' the historian Christian Jennings said when asked about the Einstein murders. 'It is very unlikely it would have been a spontaneous act. Almost certainly this order came from Berlin. It would have been issued by Ernst Kaltenbrunner, deputy head of the SS and passed down the line.' A journalist for more than thirty years, Jennings has written extensively about war crimes in Italy. 'The order would most likely have been sent to Verona, to the desk of Friedrich Bosshammer', the senior SS officer in charge of the rounding up and deportation of Jews in Italy from January 1944 till the end of the war. The order would then have been dispatched to a local unit.

When investigators from Ströber's office looked into the case in 2009, they came to the same conclusion. 'The proximity to the approaching front,' they wrote in a letter following a conversation with an eminent historian, 'indicates that the murders were ordered from the very top, or could only be ordered from the very top.'

If it was an orchestrated assault, what then? Why were the Einsteins targeted? In his research in the German military archives, Prosecutor Ströber found that Jews in the Florence area were not being rounded up in the summer of 1944, and certainly not in the last days of the occupation. Furthermore, according to local testimony, there were other Jews living in the vicinity of Il Focardo at the time of the murders, and none of them had been attacked. The Einsteins, therefore, had been specifically targeted.

The view that the killings were pre-planned was held by the surviving members of the Einstein family. In her interview with Milton Wexler in 1944, Seba had stated, 'I think they wanted my brother-in-law and they didn't find him and it was the cruellest thing they could do, so they killed the wife and the children.' Robert had agreed, he said the Germans had come to Il Focardo 'to arrest me because I was a Jew'. Sixty-three years later, when Lorenza was interviewed under oath by the German policemen and Italian military investigators in 2007, she said, 'The Germans were certainly looking for my uncle because he was Jewish and because his cousin was famous [*ben noto*]'. When it was her turn to answer, Robert's god-daughter and niece Anna Maria Boldrini had affirmed this conclusion, 'I think that everything occurred exclusively due to the Jewish origins of my uncle and that his cousin was famous.'

According to those who lived near Il Focardo at the time of the murders, the crime was not only premeditated, it was driven by a thirst for revenge. Aldo Casino was living close to Il Focardo at the time of the murders and remembered the day his friends told him the shocking news. 'It was,' he stated unequivocally, 'a vendetta.' This word, 'vendetta', was often repeated by the local residents when they spoke about the Einstein murders. It was also used by the Jewish community. 'We all believe this to be a vendetta against Robert Einstein's cousin,' said David Liscia, former president of the synagogue in Florence.

Was it really credible that Nina, Luce and Cici Einstein were murdered as an act of revenge against Albert Einstein?

That this was a killing in retaliation against the most famous Jew in the world for his very public anti-Nazi proclamations and for his support of the US military? Some people believe this to be a stretch, arguing that the motivation for the killings lay elsewhere, either as a reprisal for helping the partisans or as an act of spontaneous violence. However, it was not unusual for the Nazis to punish people for the behaviour of their relatives, and the practice had particular currency in the summer of 1944. On 20 July, just two weeks before the soldiers arrived at Il Focardo, an attempt was made to assassinate Adolf Hitler in the briefing room of his Wolf's Lair military headquarters in Poland. The plot was led by Colonel Claus von Stauffenberg and had the support of many of his army colleagues, but it failed to kill the Führer. In the aftermath, it was announced that the Nazis would target the plotters' relatives. Within a short time, Stauffenberg's brother Berthold, who was involved in the plot, was tried and executed, Stauffenberg's wife was deported to Ravensbrück, his children were interned in special homes and a number of his adult relatives were also sent to concentration camps. The family members of other conspirators were similarly punished. News of both the assassination attempt on Hitler and the punishment that followed were widely reported and were well known to the German soldiers stationed in Italy at the end of July 1944.

Even if the Nazis were targeting the relatives of Albert Einstein, why would they focus on his family in Italy? At the time, Albert was living in Princeton, well beyond the reach of the Nazis. Who, then, was his closest relative? His parents were both dead, as was his second wife, Elsa. His son Hans Albert was working at the US Soil and Conservation Service in Pasadena, California, and was therefore also inaccessible. His other son, Eduard, first wife, Mileva, and cousin Edith were all in Zurich, all beyond the Nazis' grasp. Finally, his sister Maja was living with him in Princeton, taking her off the target list. That left one close relative living in German-occupied Europe: Robert Einstein. And when he was not available, they went after his wife and two daughters. It was, as Seba had told Milton Wexler, 'the cruellest thing they could do'.

And what of Johann Riss, was he capable of carrying out an act of revenge or vendetta ordered by his superior officers? From her research into the massacre in the Fucecchio Marshes, Barbara Schepanek could imagine that Riss was capable of obeying an order that resulted in the death of civilians, including women and children.

Considered collectively, all the evidence – the positive identification, the opportunity, the means, the pattern of behaviour, the psychological prolife and the motive – indicated that Johann Riss may well have been the person who committed the Einstein murders. And while much of this evidence was circumstantial, and eyewitnesses are notoriously bad at identifying perpetrators years after a crime, it deserved to be taken seriously. The problem was that it was too late.

On 10 October 2019, Johann Robert Riss died at his home in Kaufbeuren. According to the death notice published in the local paper, the *Allgäuer Zeitung*, Riss was survived by his wife, sons, daughter-in-law, grandchild and brother. The family, it said, was 'in deep mourning'. The announcement ended with the words: 'The farewell took place in peace and quiet.'

\*

Three months later, on 4 January 2020, Lorenza Mazzetti died at her home in Rome. Following her wishes, she was buried in Badiuzza Cemetery, a few yards from her uncle Robert, aunt Nina and cousins Luce and Cici. Her death was marked by various papers around the world, including the *New York Times*, which announced: 'Lorenza Mazzetti, Wartime Survivor and Seminal Filmmaker, Dies at 92'.

Two and a half years after that, on 21 July 2022, Paola Mazzetti died, also in Rome, five days short of her 95th birthday. She was buried next to Lorenza. 'Together with her twin sister Lorenza, she survived the massacre of the Einstein family,' wrote the mayor of Rignano sull'Arno on the town's website. 'Paola leaves us the important witness of memory. We are sure that our community will be able to collect it and pass it on to future generations so that the memory of what happened is not lost.'

# 27. College Park, Maryland, 2023

Now that Johann Riss was dead, it was impossible to prosecute him for his alleged role in the Einstein murders. There
was, however, one narrow path forward. If it was possible
to confirm Riss's presence at the crime scene, then it might
be possible to track down other members of his unit that
were still alive and file charges against them. To make any
case stick would require hard evidence. The most compelling would be anything forensic tests could provide, such as
DNA or fingerprints. There was a slim chance; but, to those
who ran the United States National Archives and Records
Administration (NARA), it was worth a try.

Twenty-five years earlier, in 1998, the US Congress
had passed the Nazi War Crimes Disclosure Act. It established a working group of academics and historians to set
about reviewing the files covered by the legislation. Their
efforts took more than a decade to complete and resulted
in the declassification of an estimated 8 million documents
which were housed in the large concrete-and-glass National
Archives building in College Park, Maryland, a forty-five-
minute drive from Washington DC.

Among the declassified documents were the German war crimes files compiled by American investigators between 1943 and 1945 in Italy. These made for gruesome reading. Twenty-nine civilians murdered in Poggiolforato. Forty-four partisans hanged on meat hooks in Fanano. A grenade thrown into a cellar in Podernovo, killing nine civilians. The shooting of eight Americans who were held as prisoners of war. An old man thrown down the stairs. Ten civilians killed near Ligonchio. Also included in these files was Milton Wexler's investigation file for the murder of the Einstein family at Il Focardo in 1944: case number 16-71.

On a mild and overcast Wednesday in October 2023, forensic expert Brian Dalrymple woke up early at his home in Toronto, Canada, drove to the airport and caught a plane to Washington DC. He was in his mid-seventies with glasses, closely cropped grey hair and matching moustache. With him was a small suitcase in which he had packed his equipment: safety goggles, a digital camera and, most importantly, a handheld laser. His task that day was to examine the notice left by the German perpetrators at Il Focardo for fingerprints and, if any were found, to compare them to those taken by the Americans from one of their prisoners of war: Johann Riss.

This would be the first time anyone had tried to use fingerprint analysis to identify the perpetrators of the Einstein murders. When he heard of the attempt, Marco De Paolis, who for more than a decade had been in charge of the Italian effort to solve the crime, said that he would have pursued this line of inquiry if he had known that the original documents were still available. When he was asked for his response, public prosecutor Hubert Ströber said that he wished that he had thought of doing this when he was running his investigation. A fingerprints expert who worked for the Carabinieri went further. 'It will be a desperate attempt and very likely it is a dead end,' he said. 'But because of the sensitivity of this case it should be done. It is important. Every effort should be made, not only for the family, but for the sake of history.' He paused for a moment. 'This is something that should have been done a long time ago.'

According to various criminologists who have written about the history of fingerprints, humans have been aware for thousands of years that they can be used to identify people. In ancient China, Babylon and Persia they were used to seal contracts. Then, in 1788, a German anatomist determined that fingerprints were unique to each individual. Just over a hundred years later, in 1892, fingerprinting was used for the first time when Francisca Rojas was found guilty of cutting the throats of her two sons in Buenos Aires Province, Argentina. At first, she accused her neighbour, who denied the crimes. The case was solved when police discovered a bloody thumb-mark on a door, which was identical with Rojas's prints. She then confessed to the murders. Soon after, fingerprinting became a regular tool in homicide squads around the world.

Fingerprints are impressions left on a physical object by a human finger's friction ridges, separated into arches, loops and whorls. Fingerprints contain water, salt, amino acid and greases (chlorides mixed with fatty acids and triglycerides). There are three types of fingerprints: those left in a soft material such as wax or paint ('plastic' prints); and those that are left on a hard surface, which are either visible ('patent' prints) or invisible ('latent' prints). To obtain latent prints from a piece of paper, police departments around the world typically use a chemical reagent such as ninhydrin; this turns violet when it comes into contact with the amino acids secreted by the skin. The problem with using ninhydrin, however, is that it leaves a permanent mark on the paper being examined and therefore is prohibited by the officials at NARA, whose mission is to preserve the objects under its protection. Fortunately, this was not the first time Brian Dalrymple had been faced with this problem.

In 1975, the US Department of Justice launched proceedings against Valerian Trifa, the former archbishop of the Romanian Orthodox Church of America. They said that when he applied for US citizenship in 1957, he had failed to disclose that during the war he had held a senior position in the Romanian Iron Guard, which had been responsible for the killing of thousands of Jews in Romania. Trifa denied the accusation vehemently. When confronted with a postcard that he had written to Heinrich Himmler on 14 June 1942, he denied that he was the author. To prove otherwise, the Justice Department asked the West German authorities to send the original of the postcard so that they could test it for fingerprints. The Germans said they would comply with the request, with one condition: the postcard could not be damaged or altered in any way. This appeared to be an insurmountable obstacle, given that both powder and liquid reagents would almost certainly damage the evidence. Luckily, someone at the Justice Department had heard of the work of a forensic expert in Canada.

Brian Dalrymple had spent the previous few years experimenting with the forensic use of laser technology. Though less sensitive than powder and liquid analysis, lasers possessed the clear advantage of not damaging evidence. Dalrymple agreed to help. The postcard was sent to the USA and, after thoroughly examining it, Dalrymple was able to develop a number of observable latent impressions, including a particularly clear image for the left thumb. He then compared this to the inked fingerprints that had been taken from Trifa; it was a good match. The trial of Valerian Trifa started in October 1982. Based on the overwhelming forensics evidence, Trifa admitted that he had been a member of the Iron Guard and that he had concealed this information when he entered the US. To avoid deportation, he flew to Portugal on 13 August 1984. He died three years later, aged seventy-two.

Since his success with the Trifa case in 1984, Brian Dalrymple had become a leading expert in laser fingerprint technology. He had served as an expert witness for all levels of the Ontario courts, as well as in Quebec, New York State and Bermuda. He had received multiple awards for his work, provided instruction to police forces and prosecutors in Canada, the USA, China, Australia, Israel and the UK, written in numerous academic journals and authored various books on the subject, including the aptly titled *The Skin of Murder Victims: Fingerprints and Other Evidence*.

When it came to the paper notice left by the perpetrators at Il Focardo in 1944, there were, however, several outstanding questions. First, if fingerprints were left, would they have survived all these years? 'Not impossible at all,' Brian said, before heading off to Washington DC. 'If the evidence is stable enough, there is no reason to consider the prints will not survive.' Would it be possible to isolate the suspect's marks, given the document had passed through so many hands? Again Brian was encouraging, explaining that if a person was in an elevated emotional state, such as that caused by a fight-or-flight situation, they typically left different fingerprints to people who were calm. The chemicals in their sweat included adrenalin, which could be detected. In other words, a perpetrator's fingerprints can often stand out, even if others have touched the object in question. But, he hastened to make clear, the odds of finding a positive match were still low.

So it was that, on 25 October 2023, Brian Dalrymple arrived by taxi at the National Archives in College Park. When asked why he had come all this way, he said that he 'had friends who lost people in the Holocaust, that's why'. He would not be charging a fee.

Heading towards the building, he carried his small suitcase in one hand and his coat in the other; it was ten degrees warmer here than in his native Toronto. After checking in at reception, he was escorted downstairs to a photographic lab, a clean windowless room with concrete floors, filled with the latest technological devices. Brian was shown a station he could work at and began assembling his equipment. He attached his camera to the metal copy stand hanging above the table, removed the lens cap, connected his handheld laser to a battery pack, put his goggles on and slid on a pair of white gloves. He was now handed the evidence.

This was the notice authorized by the German commander and left near the bodies of Nina, Luce and Cici Einstein. Since then, it had endured an extended chain of custody: first collected by the *fattore* Orando Fuschiotti, who had given it to Seba, who had handed it to Milton Wexler during his visit to Il Focardo, who had added it to the US

War Crimes Commission file, which had then been sent from Italy to the USA, and which had ended up here in the National Archives outside Washington. The paper was yellow with age, creased both horizontally and vertically, and it had two holes punched in the top. This suggested that at one time it had been folded up, and at another, probably later, filed in a two-ring binder. The text ran to six lines and was typed in purple ink. The word SECRET was stamped in red at the bottom and the top of the page. There was also a file number written in pencil, along with 'Exhibit A', both probably added by Wexler when he submitted the report. Brian carefully removed the notice from its protective cellophane folder and laid it on the table in front of him. The lights in the room were dimmed; he was ready.

But there was a problem, the laser would not power up. This was perplexing, as he had checked it the night before and everything was working as normal. To his not inconsiderable embarrassment, it appeared that he had travelled all this way and his equipment wasn't functioning properly. Then, after a few more minutes of fiddling and pushing buttons, the light came on. Sometimes that just happened. The notice was now illuminated in a bright green light. Brian focused the lens and carefully examined the document. A few minutes later, he tried a different coloured filter, and then another. Along the way, he took photographs. After an hour and a half, his work was complete. He packed up his equipment, thanked his hosts and headed back to the airport.

The next day, he wrote up his findings in a report. The bad news was that he had not been able to find any complete prints. The good news was that, after enlarging the images, he saw 'the slightest vestige of ridge detail'. It was not conclusive by any means, and was insufficient to allow a comparison with those Johann Riss had given the US Army in 1944, but 'it remains just a suggestion of something'. This left open the possibility that Riss did touch the notice, but frustratingly it couldn't be proved.

It appeared doubtful that forensics was going to crack the case. Finding any form of justice for the Einstein family appeared more hopeless than ever.

# 28. Florence, 2023

With the prosecutors in Italy and Germany having closed their investigations into the three main suspects, and the fingerprint examination in Washington having failed to turn up anything new, it was highly improbable that a criminal prosecution would ever make it to trial. But there was still a possible way of providing justice to the Einstein family: money.

The history of compensation for Nazi war crimes has been mixed and complicated. The issue was raised in the Potsdam Conference that took place between Stalin, Truman and Churchill in July 1945, but the focus was on state reparations – including the transfer of German industrial machinery, trains and ships to the Allies, and the confiscation of overseas investments – rather than individual victims.

Two years later, on 10 February 1947, Italy signed a treaty with the Allies in Paris. In Article 77, the Italian state waived on its own behalf and on behalf of its citizens claims against Germany including 'all claims for loss or damage arising during the war'. In future years, Germany would treat this waiver as a get-out clause when it came to individual claims connected to war crimes. Italy, on the other hand, would argue that Article 77 had no impact on individual claims. The issue came up again in 1952, during the German External Debt Conference held in London, but the question of money owed by what was then the West German government was 'deferred until the final settlement of the problem of reparations'.

Despite repeated efforts, this matter remained unresolved until 2 June 1961, when representatives of the Italian and West German governments met in Bonn and signed an agreement. West Germany would now pay Italy 40 million Deutschmarks (equivalent to £280 million today) as compensation for Italians who had suffered Nazi persecution during the war 'on grounds of their race, faith or ideology'. In turn, Italy agreed to indemnify West Germany against any future judicial proceedings by its citizens. As far as West Germany was concerned, this was meant to be a full and final settlement.

Meanwhile, the West German government established a system for financial restitution for Jews and other victims of Nazi crimes who lived around the world. Many criticized the process for being slow, bureaucratic and parsimonious, but the government was praised for at least having a system in place. In the decades since, the West German government and later the unified Federal Republic of Germany paid out more than $90 billion to survivors of the Holocaust. In addition, they have contributed more than $40 billion to the State of Israel, which is widely considered to be a supplementary form of reparations.

The issue remained, however, that the original 1961 agreement between Italy and West Germany made no mention of the hundreds of thousands of Italian men deported to Germany as forced labour after refusing to serve in the Wehrmacht. It also appeared to exclude the thousands of Italian civilians who were killed by German soldiers as part of so-called 'reprisal attacks' in places like Fucecchio and Sant'Anna di Stazzema. Perhaps most significantly, as far as Italian Jewish victims were concerned, no provision was made for the compensation of individuals' pain and suffering; they were able to claim only for the loss of capital assets such as real estate, works of art, and jewellery. As a result, Italian Jews and Italian non-Jews both continued to make claims over the next few decades, and one after another they were rejected by Italian courts declaring that Germany now had state immunity. That was until 1995, when a lawyer living in Florence filed a suit.

Joachim Lau was born in Germany, graduated in law at the University of Stuttgart and in the 1970s moved to Tuscany. One day, an elderly man walked into his office located a few steps from the Uffizi Gallery in Florence, introduced himself as Luigi Ferrini, and asked when he would receive compensation for being deported to Germany during the war and subjected to forced labour. The lawyer was intrigued and said he would get back to him. Over the next few days, he studied the case and found there was a hole in international law: it was not clear if individuals who were victims of Nazi war crimes in occupied countries could have legal recourse.

On 23 December 1998, Lau filed a claim against Germany in the civil court in Arezzo. It was the first case made on behalf of Italians deported by the Nazis. The claim was rejected by the court on the grounds of state immunity from individual prosecutions. Four years later, Lau appealed to the

Constitutional Court in Rome. Finally, after another six years, in June 2008 it ruled in his favour, declaring that Germany must pay Ferrini compensation. The case was extensively covered in both Italian and German media, triggering a wave of new legal applications which were granted by Italian courts. In response to these applications, the German government submitted an appeal to the International Court of Justice in The Hague, arguing that the Italian verdict overturned the long-agreed system of post-war reparations which had resulted in Germany paying out billions of dollars. The appeal took years to process. Eventually, on 3 February 2012, a decision was reached. The justices concluded that Italy's supreme court had violated Germany's sovereignty in 2008 by judging Luigi Ferrini was entitled to compensation, and that Germany was immune to being sued in foreign courts by victims of Nazi war crimes. They went on to demand that the Italian courts cease their 'unlawful practice to further infringe on Germany's sovereignty'. The case was widely covered by the world's media. The BBC, for instance, declared on its news website: 'UN Court Rules against Italy over WWII Compensation'.

By this time, however, even more plaintiffs had petitioned Italy's Constitutional Court. On 22 October 2014, Italy's highest court ruled on these other cases and declared that the decision by the International Court of Justice in The Hague to deny claims by victims of Nazi crimes in Italy was 'in breach of inviolable human rights' and therefore unconstitutional. The German government once again appealed the decision to The Hague. The fact that one member of the European Union was taking another to the international court was so unusual that once again it made headlines.

France 24, for example, reported that 'Germany Takes Italy to Court over Nazi Compensation Claims'.

Several observers were perplexed as to why Germany continued to refuse to make payments. After all, the crimes were not only well documented, they had been acknowledged by numerous senior politicians, including the president of the Federal Republic of Germany. It was not just about the money. 'It was partly a question of pride,' Joachim Lau explained. 'It was also a matter of principle. Germany felt that other countries had also committed war crimes and did not understand why it was the only one which had to make payments.'

As the cases pinged back and forth between Rome and The Hague, a major diplomatic rift became a real possibility. To avoid this, the German and Italian governments initiated a series of high-level discussions about how to resolve the matter. The negotiations dragged on for years until finally, in April 2022, Italy's prime minister Mario Draghi announced that an agreement had been reached. First, a fund would be created to make payments to victims of all Nazi war crimes in Italy. Crucially, this would be the first time that Italians could file a claim because of pain and suffering. Payments would be limited by capping the total amount of money available and by not accepting applications after a certain date. And second, Italian courts would no longer be able to take on any other German war crime compensation cases.

Initially, a deadline for compensation applications was set for the end of 2022. Following complaints from multiple lawyers representing victims that this was insufficient time, the deadline was extended. Victims and their families now had until 28 June 2023 to submit a claim.

\*

On 10 June 2023, Paola Mazzetti's daughter Eva Krampen Kosloski met the civil attorney Diego Cremona at his office in Florence. Like so many of his colleagues, with less than three weeks to go before the filing deadline, Diego was overwhelmed with preparing claims. But after speaking with Eva he agreed to represent the family.

The next eighteen days were spent hunting down original documents from archives and government sources – including birth, death and marriage certificates, affidavits and photographs – and preparing the necessary legal paperwork. With just hours to spare before the 28 June deadline, Diego filed a claim for up to €250,000 on behalf of the Einstein family at the district court in Florence. It was one of more than a hundred claims that he made, the vast majority of which were on behalf of Italian citizens who had been arrested for their political beliefs and then deported to Germany.

'It's a principle of fundamental law,' Diego said, when asked why these claims were important. 'These crimes must not be forgotten.' It was self-evident that filing a claim wouldn't 'bring someone back to life', but, if successful, it would provide financial compensation to the victims and a modicum of justice. With luck, it might also contribute to a sense of peace and reconciliation with the crimes of the past.

Diego was not the only one to file claims. In all, more than a thousand cases – representing more than 15,000 people – were submitted to courts across Italy. In July 2023, the Italian government announced that it had increased the fund to €61 million and that it would be administered by the Ministry of Finance and Economics. Diego found it 'very strange' and 'extraordinary' that it was the Italian government, not the Germans, who would be making payments to victims of German war crimes in Italy. 'It could be that there was some backroom deal,' he said, 'but we will never know as it would have been secret.' The source of the funds had an impact on some of his clients, Diego revealed. When some of the families discovered that the payments would come out of the Italian purse, they decided not to pursue claims. Typically, these were younger people. His older clients, who realized that this might be their last chance, made the decision and submitted their applications.

On 3 August 2023, the first compensation case was heard in the city of Trento, in northern Italy. This involved an Italian man who had refused to serve in the German Army and was deported to a hard labour camp in Germany. His had been one of the first claims to be filed, before the deadline had been extended. The decision was speedy. That same day, the president of the court announced that the Italian state must pay the victim €50,000. With the first case settled, the courts moved on to the next, and then the next. It is not clear how long it will take to process the rest of the cases. Two years perhaps, maybe three, from the date of the application. Diego expected that politics would not slow things down. 'I hope there will be no difficulties', he said, optimistically.

At the time of this book's publication, it is too early to say what decision the district court of Florence will reach on the Einstein case. But according to those involved, it is expected that the judge will find in favour of Eva and award her some if not all of the money that she requested. If she is successful, it will be noteworthy. For though no individual soldier or officer will have been found guilty – whether Clemens

Theis, August Schmitz or Johann Riss – it would be the first recognition by a court that the German state was responsible for the murder of Nina, Luce and Cici Einstein. More than this, the court will have acknowledged that the family suffered not only economic losses but horrendous pain and suffering and must therefore be compensated. A form of justice, however small, would at last have been served.

Does this mean that the crimes can now be forgotten? That the Einstein family can hope to have some peace? As far as Nina, Luce and Cici are concerned, it is of course too late for any hope of reconciliation. The same goes for Robert, whose grief and guilt drove him to suicide. The two nieces Lorenza and Paola lived longer, but they too are not around to appreciate the gesture from the state.

'I sued as a matter of principle,' said Paola's daughter Eva Krampen Kosloski, who made the claim. The application for compensation was the last best attempt at obtaining some kind of justice for Nina, Luce and Cici Einstein. 'This is not about the money,' Eva stressed. 'This is about the Italian and German governments finally acknowledging this terrible war crime. And the lasting damage it has caused my family.'

It's early in the morning and more than a hundred people are gathered in Badiuzza Cemetery. They are here to remember the brutal murder of Nina, Luce and Cici Einstein and the suicide of Robert Einstein. At the front of the crowd, holding handmade signs declaring 'never forget' and 'remember our history', are a class of thirty pupils and a teacher from the local primary school. The mayor of Rignano sull'Arno is present, as are members of the regional council, local representatives from the partisan remembrance group ANPI, the Red Cross, various police officers dressed in ceremonial uniform, and scores of other local people interested in this history. Also present is Paola's daughter, Eva Krampen Kosloski. Dedicated to remembering the Einsteins, the event was organized by the Rignano sull'Arno town council.

The cemetery is small; fewer than three dozen people are buried here. Among the graves are the two newer ones of Lorenza and Paola Mazzetti. In the far corner, a few steps away from the twin sisters, stands a pyramid-shaped monument, perhaps twenty feet tall. It juts into the clear blue January sky, its shiny metallic surface incongruent among the natural tones of the cobbled ground and the stone walls below it. At the memorial's base lie the graves of Nina, Luce, Cici and Robert Einstein.

First to speak is the teacher. She reminds the gathering that 'Jews were not allowed to go to school' during the fascist period and that this was 'the start of hell for the Jewish people'. Next up is the mayor. 'The Racial Laws of 1938 showed the inhumanity of people,' he says; 'we need to know what happened so it doesn't happen again.' He then states, 'This monument is to remember the Einstein family who were killed because they were Jewish.'

'They were not all Jewish,' shouts a man in a large brown trilby hat standing next to Paola's grave. He says he is a member of the Waldensian Church and that Robert's wife and daughters belonged to his community. He makes no mention that Luce and Cici would have been considered *Mischlinge* by the Germans or Nina considered to be a blood traitor, nor that many in the area believed the entire family to be Jewish and that somebody local probably betrayed the Einsteins.

Finally, it is the turn of Paola's daughter. Eva holds the microphone close to her mouth and speaks clearly and forcefully. 'These women were killed by the Nazis just because their surnames were Einstein,' she says. 'My mother and aunt survived because they did not have the Einstein surname.' She continues, 'My mother and aunt were in an upstairs bedroom. They were thinking about all the people they loved, and that they would not see them again.' The children standing nearby listened intently, gripped by the story.

With the speeches now ended, the group moves towards the memorial. Members of the regional council, the mayor and the other dignitaries lay wreaths. All the while, a policeman in navy-blue uniform and matching peaked cap keeps his hand raised smartly at his forehead, saluting the Einstein family. And then the crowd disperses, seeking shade and respite from the grim history.

The following day, Eva meets the local town council in Rignano sull'Arno. They discuss setting up a permanent exhibition about the Einsteins and their time in the community. This might include photographs of Nina, Luce, Cici and Robert. The letter that Robert wrote to the *fattore* Orando Fuschiotti just before his suicide. Paintings by her aunt Lorenza and her mother Paola, a copy of Lorenza's autobiographical novel. The family will not be forgotten.

# Epilogue

It was over drinks one evening with my neighbours Vito and Lucia that I first learned about this story. They lived near the villa Il Focardo, where the details had been passed down from one generation to the next. As we watched the red and pink hues of the sunset spread and then darken over the valley, Vito and Lucia told me what had happened: Robert hiding in the woods, Nina and the others trying to survive that terrible day, the murders, the suicide, the failure to solve the crime. I was deeply moved.

I wrote to Marco De Paolis, the military prosecutor in Rome who for more than a decade had investigated the case. I heard back that he was unable to help me; he no longer had the files. Next I contacted Hubert Ströber, the German prosecutor. Again I promptly received a reply, and again I was told that I could not be given access to the files, this time for reasons of confidentiality.

With the two main sources of information blocked, was there any point in pursuing my inquiry? To make matters worse, it was eighty years since the crime had taken place: most of the witnesses had died, the trail had long gone cold. Not to mention the difficulty of being an outsider; I had never lived in Italy, nor did I speak Italian.

But every time I pulled away from the story of the Einsteins, something seemed to tug me back: we shared a similar background. My family was also German Jewish, and was forced to leave Berlin in the 1930s. My grandmother was thrown out of Heidelberg University, where she was studying to be a journalist. Her father, Dr Alfred Alexander, had to shut down his business because Jews were not allowed to practise medicine. The Nazis stole our family home. Five of my relatives were murdered in the Holocaust.

The two families also knew each other. My grandmother used to tell a story from when she was a child in Berlin. One day, she would say, Albert Einstein and his wife Elsa came over for dinner to the family's apartment on Kaiserallee. She recalled peering through the keyhole of the dining-room door and seeing that the great scientist was wearing house slippers, confirming the rumours of his forgetful nature. After the meal, her father Alfred Alexander escorted Albert to the salon to take coffee, intending to quiz him about the theory of relativity. But when he climbed into bed later that night, Alfred confessed to his wife that he and his guest had become so engrossed in discussing the latest detective novels that he had forgotten to ask.

The two men also corresponded. On 27 April 1926, Albert Einstein wrote a letter thanking my great-grandfather for the medical treatment he had provided to his terminally ill uncle and aunt:

Dear and Esteemed Dr Alexander!

Words cannot express the good you have done for my family. You not only spared my uncle [Rudolf Einstein] whatever suffering he could be spared from after confirming the hopelessness of the situation. With the benevolence that emanates from your person you also made those difficult days easier for everyone, especially my kind-hearted aunt [Fanny Einstein], something which not many would have been capable of. The old woman is overcome with gratitude towards you, a sentiment we all share. I hope that you are able to get some of what you give others back yourself.

Clasping your hand in sincere gratitude,
A. Einstein

This direct connection with the Einstein family made the story real. It made it personal. And so I decided to look into it. A few bureaucrats saying 'no' was not going to stop me finding out what happened to the Einstein family in the summer of 1944.

I first wanted to speak to those with experience of what happened. I was fortunate to be able to meet a number of people who remembered the events of 3 August 1944. They generously shared not only the facts of the case but its impact, both emotional and social. Next I looked into the wider pattern of war crimes committed in Italy (the Einstein murders were listed as number 2,550 of 5,884 in the *Atlas of Nazi and Fascist Massacres in Italy*). Particularly heart-rending were conversations with those who had lived through the massacres at Sant'Anna di Stazzema and in the Fucecchio Marshes. They bravely told me what it was like to witness a loved one being killed right in front of you. The grief that follows, the pangs of survivor's guilt.

To understand the topography of the crime, I went to see the villa Il Focardo – which at the time of my visit was in poor condition, its current owner having gone bankrupt – as well as

Badiuzza Cemetery, the Incontro monastery and the villages and towns around. And from the archives in Florence, Rome, Berlin, London and Washington DC, I was able to gather the essential facts of the case, the What, When, How and Where.

Which left the Who: who were the perpetrators of the crime? There had been at least six investigations, carried out by people from four countries over a period of eighty years and, in the end, three possible suspects had been identified. Each effort had its advantages – for instance the Wexler investigation took place soon after the crime, Ströber's was extremely thorough and well resourced, while De Paolis's was on home territory. Each was backed up by compelling, though sometimes contradictory, evidence. All the witnesses said that the German commander wore spectacles, yet the first suspect (Clemens Theis) never wore glasses, while the other two (August Schmitz and Johann Riss) both wore glasses but could not be placed as close to the crime scene. Each of the investigations had its own advocates and detractors. Each had its own motivation and context. In the end, determining the identity of the perpetrators remained frustratingly elusive.

Just as I was putting the finishing touches to this book, the Imperial War Museum in London sent me footage of German prisoners of war captured by the British at the Incontro monastery on 8 August 1944. Like Pathé news reels from this time, it was made up of long sequences filled with grainy, black-and-white images and without sound. As the film spooled forward, a band of around thirty German prisoners trudged along a dusty Tuscan track followed by a British soldier with a gun held towards their backs. Many of the Germans were jackletless with their shirts undone. All of them had been stripped of their weapons. The film cut to the prisoners standing outside a single-storey hut, presumably where they were being held. A sergeant methodically went through one of the prisoner's pockets. The film cut to a wide shot, panning left to right across the prisoners. One or two of them looked defiantly at the camera. If Robert Einstein's testimony to Milton Wexler was correct, some of these prisoners had been at the villa Il Focardo five days before. These could well be the faces of the Einstein family killers.

None of the previous investigators or prosecutors tasked with looking into the murders had reviewed this footage. Perhaps, if this film had come to light a decade or two earlier, things would have been different. And maybe with advances in Artificial Intelligence and facial recognition technologies, it might be possible in the future to identify those in the film. Either way, with the vast majority of possible suspects dead, and barely any time left to file charges against those still alive, it is too late for prosecutions.

Does it really matter that we won't know who precisely pulled the trigger of the gun that killed Nina, Luce and Cici Einstein? Suppose we did find out, would it make our understanding of this history any better? In these types of war crimes, indeed, in the retelling of all crimes, it is possible to obsess on determining the names of the exact people responsible, for reasons both of justice and narrative completion. But in a way it's a distraction from remembering the broader historical forces: that three people were killed because they were related to Albert Einstein, that the family was Jewish, that the murders took place in the last hours of the German occupation of Florence, that Italians betrayed the family and that German soldiers and the German state were involved. It would be significant, of course, to know who was individually responsible, but not knowing does not diminish the power of the wider story.

Too often, perhaps, we think about the causes of a crime being either the fault of the individual or the fault of the collective: how much should we blame the perpetrators, how much do we condemn the nation? But in asking this question, it can let the middle off the hook. In Germany, the millions of people who voted Hitler into power, the thousands who helped transport the Jews and other victims to the camps; the vicious anti-Semitism that permeated Nazidom to a group of young German soldiers stationed in Tuscany who killed a Jewish family. In Italy, the millions of people who supported Mussolini, and the policemen, administrators and railroad workers who helped deport Jews out of the country; the collaborators who betrayed the identity and whereabouts of the Einstein family.

In the end, perhaps, it is not a choice between either/or; instead, there is a continuum of responsibility, from the individual to the collective, and by not knowing exactly who-dunnit, we are forced to examine the more complex root causes of this terrible crime, this difficult period of history.

This all begs perhaps a more important question. Why, just as the Allies were pushing into the area, did a small unit of German soldiers go out of their way to travel to a remote villa outside of Florence to track down Robert Einstein and his family?

Some historians argue that the murders were a reprisal against the Einstein family, others that the killings were a spontaneous act of brutality. A more likely motive, believed to this day by the vast majority of local residents as well as many of the police officers and investigators tasked with looking into the crime, is that the triple murder was an act of revenge, a vendetta. After all, the German soldiers chose not to kill Paula, Lorenza, Anna Maria or Seba; their last name wasn't 'Einstein'.

On 16 April 1953, the Milan newspaper *L'Unità* declared that 'the reprisal against the great Jewish scientist who had become a promoter of anti-Nazi propaganda in the USA, was ordered by Hitler'. Six decades later, this theory was still going strong, as indicated by a story on 23 August 2017 about the Einstein murders which ran in the German newspaper *Süddeutsche Zeitung* under the headline: 'The Man That Hitler Most Hated'. Lorenza Mazzetti also believed that the Führer ordered the killing. In late 2019, just months before she died, she was interviewed by the journalist Massimiliano Scuriatti:

Scuriatti: [Robert Einstein] was a Jew and Albert Einstein's cousin, do you think that this was enough reason to kill him?
Lorenza: Certainly. Hitler hated the Einstein family and this is known.

Five years later, on 3 August 2024, this theory was endorsed by Eugenio Giani, the president of Tuscany. During an event at Badiuzza Cemetery to mark the eightieth anniversary of the Einstein murders he said that '[Albert] Einstein was a big problem for Hitler' because of the scientist's work helping the US military. That this led to a 'vendetta' and, because 'it was impossible to kill Albert Einstein since he was living in the United States, [Hitler] decided to kill Robert Einstein and his family'.

Could this possibly be true? Could the Einstein murders be tracked back to Adolf Hitler? Hitler was the individual most responsible for the policies and actions of the

Third Reich; the person who for more than two decades had written about his hatred for the Jews and repeatedly and vehemently spoke out in public about the urgent need to eliminate them; and the man with a specific and terrier-like animus against the country's most famous Jew, Albert Einstein. He also had an extraordinarily tight grip on the country's intelligence and military apparatus, including the final say on high-profile operations. There is, however, no evidence to support the conclusion that Adolf Hitler personally ordered the hit on Robert Einstein. Or that the murder of Nina, Luce and Cici which followed could somehow be linked to the Führer. Indeed, if it was a vendetta carried out on behalf of the German state, it could just as easily have been ordered by Heinrich Himmler or his deputy Ernst Kaltenbrunner.

The president of Tuscany, Eugenio Giani, gives a speech at Badiuzza Cemetery to mark the eightieth anniversary of the Einstein murders, 2024.

Whoever it was exactly that initiated the kill order, among the people who live near Il Focardo, local and regional politicians, and surviving members of the Einstein family, one theory remains dominant: representatives of the German state murdered the wife and daughters of Robert Einstein, and they murdered them because of a vendetta.

There was another aspect of the story that fascinated me: what is the legacy of the fascist period today?

About a year into my research, I was walking to the bus stop in the town of Antella, just outside Florence, when something caught my eye. There, above the entrance of an ochre-coloured building, was painted in bold red letters: *Casa del Popolo* – literally, the 'People's House'. For more than a century, this building, like thousands of others up and down the country, had provided an alternative cultural hub to the local power of the Church. I looked closer at the writing. Behind the *Popolo* there were other letters, faded, but brushed in a darker red and clearly visible: *Fascio*. As in, *Casa del Fascio*, or the 'Fascist's House'.

I sent a message to Francesco Casini, the forty-something mayor of the local municipality. Did he know about the re-emerging letters? What was his plan? A few seconds later, he wrote back. 'You are the first to tell me.' He then suggested we meet the next day.

At 8.30 the following morning, I was waiting outside the Casa del Popolo. A tattered Italian flag hung limp and forlorn from the building. Next door, a rust-coloured railway carriage that had been converted into a restaurant was shuttered. It would open later for dinner. Parents parked nearby, delivering their children to the Santa Maria Primary School.

Francesco walked up. '*Ciao*, Thomas,' he said, beaming.

He was a youthful-looking man with a neatly cropped salt-and-pepper beard. He looked up at the building and nodded his head. 'The wind and the rain have removed the paint,' he stated; 'history has come to the surface.' He smiled at this insight. 'It needs to be painted,' he said, 'and quickly.'

I asked if it might be a better idea to leave it. Perhaps to keep the letters that spelled *Fascio*, and add a sign that explained the context. Otherwise, was he not erasing history? The mayor shook his head. 'The writing will be redone,' he proclaimed. 'It has to be covered up.'

Unlike Germany, which underwent a rigorous period of denazification in the late 1940s and where many of its leaders were put on trial (though many would say that both the denazification process and trials did not go far enough), Italian politicians made a collective decision not to confront their country's fascist period. They declared an amnesty protecting possible war criminals. And while the National Fascist Party itself was banned, former fascists were permitted to work in politics, business and the intelligence services. Today, this national amnesia is reflected in the numerous physical reminders from the fascist regime. Across Italy, there are buildings, arches, bridges, murals and other public structures, large and small, where fascist symbols have been left intact, including eagles, *fasces* (a bundle of sticks wrapped around an axe handle – an ancient Roman symbol), flaming torches, and excerpts from speeches made by Benito Mussolini. In Florence, for instance, the football stadium that was built in the shape of the letter 'D' – for 'Il Duce' – still stands, to the shame of many local football fans.

There is, of course, a more positive legacy, of which Italians are rightly proud. In the 1930s and 1940s, thousands of politicians, journalists and writers were imprisoned for their acts of defiance against the fascist regime. Later, the resistance became armed, with bands of partisans fighting the German occupiers and supporting the Allies, resulting in thousands of deaths and casualties. Throughout this time, thousands of Jews were offered help by their neighbours, including members of the Church.

There are many who say there is another legacy of Italy's failure to confront its fascist period: the resurfacing of extremist politics. With no consensus on the facts – who did what to who and with what upshot – the country has a divided history. Journalists and historians have warned that the failure to learn the lessons of the past will lead to the same terrible mistakes being made again. Others say that this is a simplistic analysis. The events before and during the Second World War are too far away, and the factors involved too complicated, to make a direct connection with what we see today. Italy, after all, is not the only place which has seen a rise in extremism.

There is, however, some cause for optimism. In July 2000, the Italian government enacted legislation that stated the country would henceforth hold a *Giorno della Memoria*, or Day of Remembrance, each year on 27 January, the anniversary of the liberation of Auschwitz. Since then, schools, community centres and town halls across the country have held events recalling the 8,564 Jews who were deported from Italian-controlled territory, along with the 600,000 Italians deported to Germany and the thousands of civilians killed by the Nazis.

Then, on 26 January 2024, at a ceremony in his official residence, the Palazzo del Quirinale, Italy's president Sergio Mattarella gave a momentous speech. In front of prime minister Giorgia Meloni, members of parliament and representatives from the Jewish community, he declared that the Holocaust was 'the most abominable of crimes in terms of gravity and size'. He then asserted:

> It must never be forgotten that our country, Italy, adopted during fascism – in a climate of overall indifference – the ignoble Racial Laws [of 1938]: the initial chapter of the terrible book of extermination; and that members of the Italian Social Republic actively collaborated in the capture, deportation and even massacres of the Jews. An inextinguishable burden of pain, blood, death on which we can never lower the veil of silence.

A final word about the people at the centre of the tragedy at Il Focardo, starting with Robert Einstein. By the time of his death, he had achieved so much. He overcame his father's financial failures and built his engineering business to a point where he could purchase a large estate near Florence where his extended family could enjoy the beautiful countryside. He was adored by his wife, daughters and nieces. A feeling which was reciprocated, so much so that he remained in the woods to protect his extended family, despite considerable physical hardship and mental anguish. He was respected by his *fattore* and deputy *fattore*, the *contadini* and the local priest. And, despite the overwhelming pain and guilt that followed the murders, he had the resilience to remain alive for eleven and a half months following the brutal murder of his wife and two daughters. Long enough for his three nieces to have their futures settled. Long enough to enable them to live another seven decades.

The record of the younger daughter, Cici, is less clearly defined. Her life was cut too short to know what she might have done. We know she liked to paint, and that she achieved

good grades at school. Perhaps she would have followed her
sister and father into the sciences. Or maybe she would have
pursued the arts, of which her mother was fond. What we do
know is that she was cherished by her family and by the local
residents, and with her murder came the singular, excruciat-
ing pain of losing someone so young. What we also know
is that Cici was the same age as her cousin Anna Maria Boldrini, who is, at the time of writing, ninety-eight years old
and still alive. Cici had so many days in front of her. She was,
said her aunt Seba, the 'flower of grace and innocence'.

Nina was aged fifty-nine when she was killed. She loved to
play the piano in the Sala Rossa, to paint, read poetry, walk in
the hills above the villa and entertain friends. She was, by all
accounts, kind and generous and full of the joys of life. And,
above all, she enjoyed being a mother. For even though she had
two daughters of her own, she took in her brother's two young
children, Paola and Lorenza, who quickly came to love her and,
later, she offered shelter to her sister Seba and niece Anna Maria.
She was also a heroine. When her husband was threatened, she
protected him by encouraging him to take refuge in the woods.
When soldiers broke through her front door, she kept silent for
as long as she could, to shield those held hostage in the villa.
And finally, in those last terrible moments, she held on tight to
her two daughters, her protective arms around them.

And then there is Luce, who was twenty-seven years old
when she was killed. We know that she was a smart and
strong young woman who had almost completed her final
year at medical school with excellent grades and was just
weeks away from qualifying as a doctor. For a woman in the
1930s to have studied to become a doctor was unusual; to
do so in conservative Italy was extraordinary. It spoke to her

sense of empowerment and fortitude, as well as to her commitment to public service and duty.

At 8.30 a.m. on 26 January 2024, eighty years after Luce Einstein was killed and on the same day that President Mattarella gave his speech at the Palazzo del Quirinale, the University of Florence held a ceremony in her honour. During the event, a passage was read out from the diary of Paola Mazzetti. This recalled the horrific events of 3 August 1944 at Il Focardo. It was around seven at night, Paola remembered, and they were still being held in the bedroom upstairs. With her was her aunt Seba, her sister Lorenza and her cousins Anna Maria, Cici and Luce. Nina was downstairs in the Sala Rossa and Robert was hiding away in the woods. It was then, Paola recalled, that Luce gave her necklace to Seba and said, 'Remember my love.'

> She took off her little necklace and, embracing aunt Seba from behind, placed it around her neck. Why did she do it just before going with her sister to face death? Luce knew she was going to die and wanted to give aunt Seba a sign of love and solidarity, as if to say, 'You, who will see what you will see, remember my love.' In her, courage turned into love and compassion.

This, then, is Robert, Nina, Luce and Cici's story. It is a reminder, as Luce suggests, to be grateful for what we have – a family's love, a necklace, a beautiful view, the taste of a ripe peach. It is also a testament to the power of memory and the central role that history continues to play long after events are over. And it is proof that choices can have profound consequences. As Robert Einstein said in the aftermath of the murder of his wife and two daughters: 'I shall be restless until the murderers and their hirelings have had the punishment they deserve.'

# Notes

## Abbreviations

AEA      Albert Einstein Archives, Jerusalem

COSJA    Central Office of the State Justice Administrations for the Investigation of National Socialist Crimes, Ludwigsburg: file on the Einstein murders investigation into Clemens Josef Theis (case number 518 AR 257/05, files B162 43704 to B162 43710)

FF       Frankenthal Files: nine bundles of documents from the Frankenthal public prosecutor's Einstein murders investigation (case number 5037 Js 23 137/13) which were disclosed to the author after a verdict by the Administrative Court of Neustadt an der Weinstrasse (case number 5 k 75/23.NW)

MCR     Military Court in Rome archive, Viale delle Milizie: references are to the Einstein murders file, case number 298/08 RGIP, unless otherwise stated

NARA    United States National Archives and Records Administration, College Park, MD: references are to the Einstein murders case file, RG 153, Entry 143, Box 528, Case 16-71, 'Incidents at Troghi', unless specified otherwise

TNA      The National Archives in Kew, London

## Part One. Crime

1 *It was such a night that one knew that human eyes . . .*: Primo Levi, *If This Is a Man* (Abacus, 1987), p. 21.

### *1. Il Focardo, 1944*

3 *two weeks earlier . . .*: German soldiers had been looking for Robert for months. Sometime in early spring 1944, a unit visited Nello Carrara and his wife Gaetanina Gattai, who lived on a nearby estate, and asked for the whereabouts of 'the engineer' (author's conversation with their son, Eugenio Carrara). According to the priest Giuseppe Agnoloni, a few weeks later a butcher was stopped by a truckload of Germans who asked where Robert's villa, Il Focardo, was. The butcher heard one of these Germans say in Italian, *'la stare grande ebreo molto cattivo?'* or, 'There stays a big very bad Jew' (the original German is likely to have been *Saujude* or *Judensau*, meaning 'Jew pig'): see Giuseppe Agnoloni's memoir, *Ricordi di guerra* (Archivio del Comune di Rignano, 1998). Rodolfo Paoli – a professor of German who was a friend of Robert and Nina Einstein and lived four miles from Il Focardo on Via Montisoni – also said that the Germans were looking for Robert Einstein in the weeks before 3 August 1944: see Paoli's memoir of the war, *Cronache di una guerra combattuta senza armi (1943–1946)* (Pagnini, 2014). During the summer, the villa Il Focardo was requisitioned by two separate German units, but they had gone by the end of July.

6 *Nina was fifty-nine years old*: I have used the date given on Nina's birth certificate: 24 March 1885 (Bergamo registry of birth certificates, no. 349, p. 1, 1885). In contrast, both her

gravestone and Robert's Munich police registration form state she was born in 1886 (though the handwritten number in the latter appears to have been altered from 1885). Also, Robert told the American war crimes investigator Milton Wexler on 17 September 1944 that his wife was 'fifty-eight' at the time of her death (NARA).

6  *his beard and hair were flecked with white* . . .: Of all the accounts I read, that of Eugenio Boldrini – nephew to Robert and Nina Einstein and brother to Anna Maria – was the only one to be negative about Robert. 'I cannot remain silent about Uncle Roberto, towards whose family my envy was directed,' he wrote. 'He was a rich German, who my aunt Nina, my mother's older sister, had married. A woman of great intelligence, Nina was overshadowed by the authoritarian "engineer", not surprisingly called "the devil". Perhaps he was pleased with this, cultivating the Mephistophelean beard. I never liked the meticulousness with which he treated the dogs, daughters and granddaughters entrusted to him, relegating the girls to their room with a nod at the slightest infraction: what a contrast to the cheerful anarchy of my family!' (Eugenio Boldrini's unpublished 'Dull Old Chronicles', provided by his sister, Anna Maria Boldrini).

7  *their villa – Il Focardo*: I was told by some locals that the villa was named after a previous owner, but I was not able to verify this.

7  *In front of her stood seven heavily armed German soldiers*: There is considerable disagreement on the number of soldiers at Il Focardo on 3 August 1944. In a 2007 interview with German police and Italian investigators, Lorenza Mazzetti said the Germans at Il Focardo 'numbered around 10–13 soldiers, but

certainly no more than around twenty men' (FF Bundle II, p. 262). She also said that four to five soldiers broke through the door at the start of the assault. Her twin, Paola, told Milton Wexler there were 'six or seven officers', including 'a captain and a lieutenant' (NARA). The word 'officers' may be a mistranslation of 'soldiers' because, when pressed, she said that 'we only knew a captain and a lieutenant'. A neighbour called Renzo Giorgetti, who lived at Il Manco, near to Il Focardo, told German investigators on 22 July 2009 that there were '6–8 soldiers' on the day of the massacre and 'only one truck drove away from the villa' afterwards (FF Bundle V, pp. 1240–41; unredacted version, MCR Volume V). In his statement given to Italian investigators on 14 November 1944, the estate manager, Orando Fuschiotti, said there were fifty soldiers (FF Bundle VI, p. 1191). Robert also told Wexler there were fifty soldiers, but he never saw the Germans up close (NARA). In their final summary of the case, 6 November 2013, the Baden-Württemberg police wrote that the number of soldiers at Il Focardo was 'around 10 to 13, at most 20 people' (FF Bundle IX, p. 2093). I have settled on Paola's number of seven, rather than using a range.

7 *She said she was Nina Einstein*: Nina's full name was Agar Cesarina Lucia Mazzetti (Bergamo registry of birth certificates, no. 349, p. 1, 1885).

7 *He asked where her husband was*: While the exact details of this part of the conversation are not known, eyewitness accounts all concur that the commander repeatedly questioned Nina as to her husband's whereabouts. See the accounts of Lorenza Mazzetti in her autobiographical novel about her time with Robert and Nina Einstein, *The Sky Falls* (Bodley Head, 1962), p. 144, and in her

self-illustrated investigation of the same story, *Album di Famiglia* (La nave di Teseo, 2011), p. 160.

7 *They had orders to arrest him, he said . . .*: For this part of the conversation, see Giuseppe Agnoloni's *Ricordi di guerra*, which provides a detailed account of the whole encounter.

8 *Cici . . . good grades . . .*: Cici's given name was Anna Maria, but I have used her nickname, Cici, to refer to her, in order to avoid confusion with her cousin Anna Maria Boldrini. When the Einsteins arrived at Il Focardo in 1937, Cici would have entered the Michelangelo *ginnasio inferiore*, or middle school, before moving on to the *liceo* (high school) in 1940. She attended both institutions with her cousins Lorenza and Paola Mazzetti. In 1942, Cici received *profito molto* (very good) for religion and *cultura militare* (military instruction), seven (out of ten) for both Italian and history, and sixes for mathematics and physics. Paola's grades were the best of all the girls; in 1943, for instance, she was given a nine (out of ten) for Greek, which is superb. Both Lorenza and Paola had to retake their science exam at the end of the summer term in 1944 (Michelangelo High School archives, Florence).

8 *followed by Anna Maria . . .*: Anna Maria Boldrini was born in Rome on 26 July 1926 (FF Bundle II, p. 262). According to her sons, she was baptized in St Peter's Basilica in Rome, and Robert and Nina attended as her godparents (conversation with the author, 2023).

## 2. Munich, 1884

9 *his father Jakob was 'Mosaic'*: From Munich City Archives, police records. Robert's father's name is spelled variously as 'Jakob' and 'Jacob'.

9 *Müllerstrasse 3*: According to the Munich address book of 1883, it appears that Jakob's apartment was in the front building ('I. Aufgang', or 'first staircase') while Hermann's apartment was in the rear building ('II. Aufgang'). The 1890 address book has both families living at Adlzreiterstrasse 14 (which was also the official address of the brothers' company), but Jakob is listed as living at number '1' (perhaps the first floor) and Hermann at number '0' (maybe the ground floor). However, the architectural sketch of Adlzreiterstrasse 14 does not appear to show the building split into two units, which suggests more fluid living arrangements (Alto Brachner et al., eds, *Abenteuer der Erkenntnis. Albert Einstein und die Physik des 20. Jahrhunderts*, Deutsches Museum, 2005, fig. 14, 'Plan über einen Anbau im Anwesen Rengerweg').

9 *solidly upper middle class*: Jürgen Neffe, *Einstein: A Biography* (Polity, 2007), p. 45.

9 *'inwardly inhibited and alienated'*: Albert Einstein diary, 6 October 1922 (AEA 29-129).

10 *... helped Albert with his mathematics*: 'Algebra is the calculus of indolence,' Albert's uncle Jakob once told him. 'If you do not know a certain quantity, you can call it $x$ and treat it as if you do know it, then you put down the relationship given, and determined this $x$ later.' From Alexander Moszkowski, *Einstein the Searcher: His Work Explained from Dialogues with Einstein* (Methuen, 1921), p. 224.

10 *a deep affection for each other*: According to *Il dolore di avervi dovuto lasciare* (ANPI Provinciale di Milano, 2015), written by students and teachers of the Giuseppe Parini High School with a preface by the historian Roberto Cenati.

10 *Hermann 'owing to his contemplative nature ...'*: This and other quotations of Maja's words in this chapter come from her

'Albert Einstein: A Biographical Sketch', trans. Ann Beck, in John Stachel et al. (eds), *The Collected Papers of Albert Einstein*, vol. 1 (Princeton University Press, 1987), pp. xv–xxii.

11  *an end to his religious exuberance*: According to some (for instance, Albrecht Fölsing, *Albert Einstein: A Biography* (Penguin, 1997), p. 21), Albert did not perform his bar mitzvah. However, the Einstein expert Barbara Wolff told me 'there is no original source to support this'.

12  *'discomfort spiraled toward depression'*: Walter Isaacson, *Einstein: His Life and Universe* (Simon & Schuster, 2007), p. 22.

12  *enrolled in a local school*: Robert attended the International School for Protestant Families (later merged with the Swiss School in Milan). See *Il dolore di avervi dovuto lasciare*.

12  *The two families once again lived together*: In Milan, the families lived near the city centre, at Via Bigli 21, while their factory was on Via Lecchi.

13  *Robert . . . fell in love with the Italian countryside*: Albert felt similarly. 'Italy made a great impression,' Maja later wrote, 'the way of life, the landscape, the art – everything attracted him, and later, from afar, became an object of longing' ('Albert Einstein: A Biographical Sketch', p. xxii).

14  *He died in Milan in 1902 . . .*: Hermann was cremated and then buried at the Milan City Cemetery, section V, plot 83. Albert returned from Berne to see his father a few days before he died. Robert likely attended the burial (AEA 29-157, 81-594, 81-595).

14  *Seven years later, Robert's parents divorced . . .*: It appears that Ida may have remarried. In August 1913, she wrote on a postcard from Osnabrück that she was visiting family ('meine Lieben') there with her husband and Edith. We do not know the name of this second husband. See Martin J. Klein (ed.),

*The Collected Papers of Albert Einstein*, vol. 5 (Princeton University Press, 1993), document no. 459.

14 *Robert and Edith were 'deeply shocked . . .'*: Memorial page for Jakob Abraham Einstein, Find a Grave (memorial no. 83746852). The funeral took place at 9.30 a.m. on 10 September 1912 at the Central Cemetery in Vienna. He had been working for an electrical firm in the city when he was struck down.

14 *Following in his father's footsteps . . .*: Trying to confirm what Robert Einstein did in his early adult life proved challenging. The only thing I could find was a letter written on 21 January 1994 by an unnamed correspondent from the Max Planck Institute in Berlin to the deputy mayor of Rignano sull'Arno. 'In case it might be of interest to you,' they wrote, 'I'm enclosing the little information I was able to gather about Robert Einstein and his family members.' The letter stated that Robert lived in Aachen, Germany, in 1901, before arriving first in Rome on 8 October 1901, and then in Naples on 19 August 1902, where, 'According to the recollections of Robert Einstein's nieces, it would seem that Robert Einstein and his future wife Agar Cesarina Mazzetti met as teenagers in Naples in the early years of the century' (FF Bundle V, pp. 1112–14). Fifteen years later, on 28 September 2009, the Rignano sull'Arno municipality forwarded the Max Planck Institute letter to the prosecutor in Rome (MCR N 211/08 RGNR, Volume V).

14 *he met Nina Mazzetti . . .*: Robert and Nina's niece Anna Maria Boldrini said they met in Rome (conversation with the author, February 2024). According to their nieces Lorenza and Paola Mazzetti, they met in Naples (see previous note).

15 *a count of the number of Jews . . .*: This was the so-called *Judenzählung*, or 'Jewish census'. It also found that 12,000

Jews died in battle and more than 30,000 were decorated for their bravery.

16 *his religion was Catholic*: According to Robert's birth certificate, both of his parents were Jewish (Munich City Archives, GU STAM I 1570 1884). His residence record for 1914 states his religion as 'Isr' or 'Israelite' (Munich City Archives DE 1992 PMB E 48). In a letter to the author of 7 December 2023, Dr Christian Freundorfer from the Munich City Archives wrote that 'Robert Einstein was of Jewish religion. Of course, it is not clear from the files whether he was a practising Jew. Only the documents of the Jewish community before the Shoah could give us information about this. But unfortunately they are no longer preserved.' He added: 'From our documents only the Jewish religion emerges. If [Robert] had been officially "Catholic," that would have been noted in the police registration form [which it is not]. The fact that "k" for Catholic was stated in the war logs you sent may well be due to a transcription error by the receiving soldier in the office.'

16 *the Royal Bavarian Light Infantry Regiment* . . .: The source documents for Robert's wartime service can be found in the Bayerisches Hauptstaatsarchiv in Munich (Abteilung IV Kriegsarchiv, Kriegsstammrolle, 1914–1918: Volume 2248, Kriegsstammrolle 4. Kompanie; Volume 4113, Kriegsstammrolle, Bd. 1; and Volume 4044, Kriegsstammrolle Bd. 3).

16 *'I'm curious what our cousin . . .'*: Letter from Maja Winteler-Einstein to Paul Winteler, 10 March 1917, in Diana K. Buchwald (ed.), *The Collected Papers of Albert Einstein*, vol. 16 (Princeton University Press, 2021), document no. 309a.

16 *They called her* . . .: According to her birth certificate in the Munich City Archives, Luce's middle name was 'Edith' or 'Edy', after Robert's sister.

### 3. Rome, 1921

20 *when they arrived back in Rome*: On 5 September 1921, Luigi Ansbacher (the son of family friends in Milan) wrote to Albert Einstein that 'I was pleased to hear through your cousin, who now lives in Rome, that you remembered me and inquired about me' (AEA 43-056).

20 *They rented a small apartment . . .*: They lived at Via Bartolomeo Bossi 31 (MCR N 211/08 RGNR, Volume V).

20 *'travelling incognito'*: Postcard from Albert Einstein to Maja Einstein, written Berlin, 8 October 1921 (sold by Christie's, London, on 9 May 2018; AEA 97-148). Maja lived at Via Marsilio Ficino 8 in Florence from 1921 to 1924.

20 *Robert and Nina travelled to Berlin . . .*: Robert and Nina's visit to Berlin was mentioned in a note from Albert Einstein's stepdaughter Ilse to Maja in which she said, 'Last week Robert Einstein (Buvi) [*sic*] and his wife were in Berlin, we also spoke of you' (AEA 97-151, p. 2). The letter was written on Sunday, 23 April 1922, so 'Letzte Woche' could refer to any time between 10 and 20 April. As Albert was away from Berlin earlier in April, and returned in the evening of 14 April, there is a good chance he saw Robert and Nina during their visit.

20 *'Bubi'*: On 24 April 1922, Albert wrote to Sebastian Kornprobst (a former colleague of Jakob and Hermann Einstein), saying that 'Yesterday Robert E., formerly Bubi, who lives in Rome, was with us'. Jette Koch (Albert's grandmother) told Fanny Einstein (Elsa's mother) in a letter dated 2 March 1884 that she'd heard that 'Ida [Robert's mother] with her Bubi is quite lively' – 'Ida mit ihrem Buben ganz munter [sei]' (AEA 143-346).

21 *Over the next few years, Nina and Robert . . .*: On 31 December 1929, a story appeared in the Bavarian newspaper *Der Bund* reporting that Robert Einstein had been the cause of a car accident the previous day on Rome's Piazza della Libertà in Rome resulting in injuries to Senator Vittorio Scialoja (Italy's leading delegate to the League of Nations since 1921). The paper said the senator's injuries were 'not of a dangerous nature'.

22 *Would she be able to look after the twins?*: It has been challenging to determine exactly when Lorenza and Paola started living with Nina and Robert. It certainly happened before they moved to Perugia in 1935. According to Paola's daughter, Eva Krampen Kosloski, her mother and aunt moved in with Nina and Robert Einstein in 1933 or 1934, when the girls would have been six or seven years old (conversation with the author, 2024). In its obituary of Lorenza Mazzetti, *The Times* in London reported that the twins' 'father, Corrado, an insurance agent, entrusted them first to a family friend, the futurist painter Ugo Giannattasio, before they were adopted at seven by their father's sister, Nina' (*The Times*, 20 January 2020). In the documentary *Because I Am a Genius! Lorenza Mazzetti* (dir. Steve della Casa and Francesco Frisari, 2016), which explores her life and work, Lorenza said that she and her sister didn't want to go to live with Robert and Nina.

22 *Robert's electrical engineering business . . .*: In the short biography written by the Max Planck Institute, it was reported that 'during [Robert's] residence in Rome he carried out his activity as an electrical engineer in a radio factory, perhaps owned by him' (FF Bundle V, pp. 1112–14). According to Anna Maria Boldrini, however, Robert worked for a radio manufacturing company called Phonola (conversation with the author, February 2024).

22 *a horse farm near . . . Corciano*: Robert purchased the Monte-malbe horse farm near Corciano. Franziska Rogger, in her biography *Einsteins Schwester. Maja Einstein – Ihr Leben und ihr Bruder Albert* (Neue Zürcher Zeitung, 2005), reported that Maja 'paid a lengthy visit' to the family when they lived there. In 2000, the municipality of Corciano created the 'Robert Einstein Park' 500 yards northwest of the farm.

22 *where Luce would start her . . . medical studies*: According to Lorenza, both she and Paola were members of the Italian fascist youth group. When Lorenza wrote to Mussolini and received a postcard in reply with his signature, she ran to Robert and shouted: 'Uncle, uncle, Il Duce has written to us!' (*Because I Am a Genius! Lorenza Mazzetti*).

22 *'Here life continues as usual . . .'*: Letter from Robert Einstein to Nello (no last name provided), 22 December 1935, exhibited at Rignano sull'Arno town hall, 3 August 2024. The letter was typed on letterhead with 'Montemalbe Estate' printed on the top left corner and the telephone number 'Perugia 3-39' along the left-hand edge.

24 *'To bed, to bed! . . .'*: Lorenza Mazzetti, *London Diaries* (Zidane Press, 2018), p. 69.

25 *Enrico Bürgisser had inherited the estate . . .*: Enrico Bürgisser inherited Il Focardo from his father, Rodolfo, in 1922. Rodolfo's bank was called Il Piccolo Credito; it would later become Credito Toscano and later still Banca Toscana. Information on the purchase of Il Focardo comes from the Agenzia delle Entrate Ufficio Provinciale del Territorio in Florence (Referenza conservatoria Volume 1442, Articolo 4882, 19-10-1937 F1786 n.89).

26 *the yellow and red peaches . . .*: Peach farmers I spoke with told me that the most likely varieties grown at Il Focardo would

have been Burrona di Rosano and Cotogna di Rosano. According to the annual bulletin of the Royal Tuscan Horticultural Society in 1899, 'the municipality of Rignano sull'Arno supplies Florence with *Rosano* peaches'.

27 *equivalent to £515,000*: In 1937, £1 was equal to about 100 lire. The value today of £6,000 in 1937 from website measureingworth.com.

### 4. Il Focardo, 1944

31 *With Orando and Erenia . . .*: The Fuschiottis had three children: Marinella and Antonello (who were four years and nine months old at this time); and Mauro, who would be born in 1950. According to Marinella, 'My father had a good relationship with the Einstein family and especially with Robert, who was a very generous man and cared about the people who worked for him. They were friends. Robert did not act like a boss to my parents.' She then stated that Robert did not treat her mother as a '*fattoressa* [estate manager's wife] but as a friend' as well. In 1955, the Fuschiotti family moved to Florence, where they took over the management of a hotel on Piazzale Donatello, and lived nearby on Via Alfieri for three years. In the run-up to the 1960 Rome Olympics, they left Florence to open a hotel in Rome where they remained. (Conversation with the author, 2023.)

31 *the deputy estate manager, Pipone . . .*: The deputy *fattore*'s given name was Egisto Galante and he was born in 1898. According to his granddaughter, Francesca Salomoni, Pipone was 'very close' to Robert, who he called 'Signor Robert'. Francesca also told me that, at one point, the author Ernest Hemingway stayed at Il Focardo.

## 5. *Il Focardo, 1938*

35 *he remained both a committed atheist . . .*: According to Lorenza Mazzetti in an interview included in the documentary film *Because I Am a Genius! Lorenza Mazzetti* (2016).

36 *two of the country's prime ministers were Jewish . . .*: Alessandro Fortis (1905–1906) and Luigi Luzzatti (1910–11). The prime minster of Jewish descent was Sidney Sonnino (1906 and 1909–10): his father was Jewish and he was brought up Anglican.

37 *Hitler was said to have been impressed by its magnificent view . . .*: Some say that because Hitler so greatly admired the Ponte Vecchio it was later protected when the retreating Germans destroyed the city's other bridges on 3 August 1944. Alternative explanations for the bridge's survival include the theory that two workers might have disconnected the wires attached to the explosives, or that the German commanding officer of the city was an art lover.

37 *home to memorials . . .*: Florence Nightingale, who was born in the city in 1920, also has a memorial in Santa Croce.

38 *. . . stripped of his Italian citizenship*: On 24 August 1937 – a few weeks before Robert purchased Il Focardo on 15 October – Robert, Nina, Luce and Cici registered with the Rignano sull'Arno municipality. In the top right corner of Robert and Luce's registration form, their nationality was written as German (they were both born in Munich), which was then crossed out, and under which was added 'now Italian'. It is not clear when they first acquired Italian citizenship. On Robert, Luce and Cici's form, it was later recorded that their Italian citizenship was withdrawn following the Racial Laws of 1938. Further down Robert's form, a note was inserted

stating that his Italian citizenship was returned to him following King Vittorio Emanuele III's decree Number 25 revoking the Racial Laws on 20 January 1944. On Luce and Cici's forms the withdrawal of their Italian citizenship was crossed out. On 3 August 2024, Paulo Banci, head of the local chapter of the partisan remembrance group ANPI, told me that Robert never learned that he regained his Italian citizenship. Presumably, his daughters also did not find out. I saw copies of the four registration forms at an exhibition held at the Rignano sull'Arno town hall on 3 August 2024, titled *Gli Einstein a Firenze e dintorni* ('The Einsteins in and around Florence').

38 *'di razza Ariana' . . . 'Israelita'*: For this enrolment form, and more information on Luce Einstein's student days, see her file in the University of Florence archives.

38 *Maja . . . purchasing a boat ticket to the USA*: On 14 December 1938, Albert Einstein wrote to Maja: 'I think you should come over to visit me soon and wait for how things develop . . . Once you have the visa, or at least know that you will receive it soon, let me know when you can travel. I will then look after everything and send you everything to [a Swiss address]' (AEA 29-428 and 123-58 [translation]). That same day, he wrote to the Swiss consul in New York: 'I have invited my sister, Mrs. Marie Winteler-Einstein, to visit me here in Princeton and kindly ask you to grant her this visit by issuing a visitor visa' (AEA 29-429). According to the Einstein expert Barbara Wolff, Maja left Le Havre on board the SS *Paris* on 1 March 1939 and arrived in New York on the 8th.

39 *'Infiniti auguri . . . Roberto'*: Telegram from Robert Einstein to Albert Einstein, 14 March 1939 (AEA 30-775). According

to his birth certificate, his first name was Robert (Munich City Archives, birth certificate GU STAM I 1570 1884). For the sake of consistency, I have employed this form of his name, except when speakers refer to him as 'Roberto' in quoted speech, or when he signs himself thus in letters.

39 *Cosimo I de' Medici, announced a law for the Jews . . .*: Some historians say that he had no choice as the pope had declared his own anti-Jewish laws in the bull *Cum nimis absurdum* of 14 July 1555 (although Tuscany was not part of the Papal States and Cosimo's legislation was more than a decade later), or that he received the title of grand duke from the papacy in 1569 in exchange. Others argue that Cosimo saw the ghetto simply as a money-making opportunity, rather than as persecution. Whatever his motivation, the antisemitic decrees and the suffering that resulted were of Cosimo's creation.

39 *. . . a single ghetto in Florence*: The history of the Florentine ghetto in this chapter is based in part on the exhibition *Gli ebrei, i Medici e il Ghetto di Firenze* (*The Jews, the Medici and the Ghetto of Florence*) at the Palazzo Pitti, October 2023– January 2024.

40 *Piazza Vittorio Emanuele II*: In April 1947, the square would be renamed Piazza della Repubblica.

## 6. Florence, 1943

45 *Living in Pisa at this time was Nina's sister Ada . . .*: Ada and her family had moved there in 1932, to Viale Bonaini, and then later to Via Risorgimento.

46 *Villa La Selva*: The villa was confiscated from its Jewish owner, Silvio Ottolenghi, who fled to Palestine. At first,

the villa served as an internment camp for opponents of the state; but then, starting in early 1943, it became a transit camp for more than 200 local Jews who had been rounded up. Today, there is no mention of this history at the villa, though there is a memorial about 500 yards away, on the road leading to the house.

46 *Half the raiding party . . .*: The Italian fascists in the raiding party belonged to the Reparto Servizi Speciali della Milizia, an official organization based in Florence that ultimately reported to Mussolini. It was led by Mario Carità and was colloquially known as 'Banda Carità' (Carità's Gang). Its members were well known for torturing the people they arrested.

46 *between twelve and twenty Jews . . .*: The exact numbers are unknown. For a detailed investigation into the number of victims, their names and backgrounds, along with the wider story, see Marta Baiardi, 'Persecuzioni antiebraiche a Firenze: razzie, arresti, delazioni' and its appendices, in Enzo Collotti (ed.), *Ebrei in Toscana tra occupazione tedesca e RSI. Persecuzione, depradazione, deportazione (1943–1945)* (Carocci editore, 2007).

47 *'The following police order . . .'*: Quoted from the copy of Police Order Number 5 in Archivio Centrale dello Stato, Rome, Categoria A5G (II Guerra Mondiale), Busta 151. One of those to be rounded up under the new decree was the chemist Primo Levi from Turin. On 13 December 1943, he was arrested in Valle d'Aosta in northern Italy, transferred to the concentration camp in Fossoli, seventy-five miles north of Florence, and then transported on to Auschwitz in February 1944. Later, in 1947, he would write the book *If This Is A Man* about his terrible experiences in the camp.

49 *Miriam Cividalli Canarutto . . .*: When I visited the ninety-two-year-old at her apartment in Florence in 2023, she told me: 'There are two types of Italians. The *fattore*, who saved us, and the others who arrested and killed the Jews.' I asked if she believed that Italians had fully confronted their history. She smiled and replied, 'Few people have learned. They declare that "the past is the past".' She added that she was very worried that young people in particular knew so little of their country's actions during the fascist period. As for her own father, she was incredibly grateful. 'Without him,' she stated, 'I would not have lived such a long life.'

### 8. Princeton, New Jersey, 1944

55 *a 'notorious organisation of Nazi killers' . . .*: According to the newspaper, the organization in question was called the *Fehme* and was led by Edmund Heines.

55 *'I do not fear danger' . . .*: *Le Soir*, 8 September 1933.

56 *and stripped him of his German citizenship*: Albert became a Swiss citizen in 1901. Between the wars, his status was a matter of much dispute. This ended on 7 February 1924 when he accepted that he was both a German citizen and a Swiss citizen. In March 1933, he applied to relinquish his German citizenship. However, the German government wanted to be seen as the one in control and announced it had withdrawn his citizenship on 29 April 1933. For an excellent discussion of this matter, see Barbara Wolff, 'Albert Einstein German, Swiss and American?', available online at Google Arts and Culture. Value in British pounds today from measuringworth.com.

56 *'We must strike hard . . .'*: *New York Times*, 30 December 1941.

56 *'on several mathematical physical problems . . .'*: *New York Times*, 25 June 1943.

57 *Einstein had donated the manuscript . . .*: According to the *New York Times* article, Albert had thrown out the original manuscript after publication, so the 'relativity manuscript was especially re-copied by Dr. Einstein for this occasion'.

57 *a 'nuclear chain reaction . . .'*: Letter from Albert Einstein to President Roosevelt, 2 August 1939 (original in the Franklin D. Roosevelt Presidential Library and Museum, Hyde Park, NY).

### 9. Il Focardo, 1944

59 *'If the partisans eat the calves . . .'*: Nello Dino's account in this chapter comes from his memoir, *Ricordi di quei giorni* (Giuntina, 1975).

### 10. Il Focardo, 1944

63 *'Raus!' A soldier barked . . .*: This quotation, along with Nello Dino's other testimony in this chapter, taken from his *Ricordi di quei giorni* (Giuntina, 1975).

63 *'Who are the Einstein family members?'*: From Nello Dino, *Ricordi di quei giorni*.

64 *'You are accused . . .'*: This quotation, along with Seba Mazzetti's other testimony in this chapter, is taken from her statement to US war crimes investigator Milton Wexler on 17 September 1944 (NARA).

64 *Orando and Pipone . . . were pushed outside . . .*: For Orando Fuschiotti's and Pipone Galante's accounts of the events in this chapter, see the former's statement to Italian investigators,

14 November 1944 (FF Bundle VI, p. 1191), and the latter's statement to Milton Wexler, 17 September 1944 (NARA).

67 *Nina showed him her identity documents*: From Camillo Arcuri's account of the massacre and its aftermath, *Il sangue degli Einstein Italiani* (Ugo Mursia Editore, 2015), p. 77.

67 *'We were worried'* . . .: Unless stated otherwise, Lorenza's testimony in this chapter is taken from the interview she gave in late 2019, just before her death, to the Italian journalist Massimiliano Scuriatti, published as *Una vita, mille vite. Conversazione con Lorenza Mazzetti* (La nave di Teseo, 2021), which included an in-depth conversation around the events of 3 August 1944 and their aftermath.

68 *'The piano,' cried Luce* . . .: Quotations in this paragraph taken from Lorenza Mazzetti, *The Sky Falls* (Bodley Head, 1962), p. 147.

68 *The oil painting of Albert Einstein* . . .: Paola's daughter, Eva Krampen Kosloski, told me in 2023 that this painting of Albert was stolen from the villa after the war. Her mother had said she saw it later in an antique dealer's, but she was too intimidated to challenge the owner. When, in June 2024, I asked Eva whether the painting was hung above the fireplace, she wrote back: 'Unfortunately I don't know and I don't know if it was a big drawing. I know that it was hung in the living room and was visible.' In his memoir, Robert and Nina's friend and neighbour Rodolfo Paoli confirmed that there was a painting of Albert Einstein hanging in the Sala Rossa: *Cronache di una guerra combattuta senza armi (1943–1946)* (Pagnini, 2014), p. 15.

69 *'We found this in the cellar'* . . .: According to Lorenza Mazzetti, in Massimiliano Scuriatti, *Una vita, mille vite. Conversazione con Lorenza Mazzetti*, p. 125. It is conceivable that a member of the

Einstein family, or one of the *contadini*, helped the partisans by storing or supplying weapons. However, the accusation has been vigorously denied by numerous witnesses over the years. In his statement to Milton Wexler on 17 September 1944, Robert said it was 'impossible' that dynamite had been stored at Il Focardo (NARA). Lorenza asserted to Scuriatti: 'I am convinced that the dynamite wasn't at our house. It was a set-up.' The priest Giuseppe Agnoloni told war crimes investigators on 23 January 2008: 'It was also said that [Robert Einstein] was involved with the partisans, but I exclude it absolutely' (FF Bundle III, pp. 658–60). As was the case with the massacres at Sant'Anna de Stazzema and the Fucecchio Marshes, the Germans often used accusations of helping partisans as the excuse for violent reprisals.

## *11. Il Focardo, 1944*

71  *Nina decided to tell him the truth . . .*: Details of the interrogation of Nina, and then those of Luce and Cici, come from Seba's statement to US war crimes investigator Milton Wexler (NARA).

71  *'Roberto, Roberto' . . .*: This quotation, along with Franco Giorgetti's other testimony in this chapter, come from his unpublished memoir, 'I ricordi di Franco' (pp. 19–24), given to the author at a meeting on 27 February 2023.

72  *'I'm going, I'm going' . . .*: Part of Nello Dino's testimony in this chapter derived from his memoir *Ricordi di quei giorni* (Giuntina, 1975).

72  *'They will kill all of us . . .'*: Quoted from Camillo Arcuri, *Il sangue degli Einstein Italiani* (Ugo Mursia Editore, 2015), p. 77.

74 *'Remember my love'*: Recorded by Paola Mazzetti in her unpublished diaries, parts of which were read out by her daughter Eva Krampen Kosloski at an event to commemorate Luce Einstein's posthumous graduation, held on 26 January 2024 at the University of Florence. Luce's full words were: 'Tu che vedrai quello che vedrai, ricorda il mio amore.'

75 *'Never had my sister . . .'*: Seba's words in this paragraph are quoted from the statement she gave to a US soldier on 14 August 1944 (NARA).

75 *they heard the sound of gunfire*: Some witnesses described the shooting as machine-gun fire, yet Lorenza said she heard distinct shots. It is therefore not clear exactly what type of weapon was used.

75 *'There was a shot and a scream . . .'*: From Lorenza Mazzetti, *The Sky Falls* (Bodley Head, 1962), p. 149.

### 12. Il Focardo, 1944

78 *thirteen-year-old Franco Giorgetti . . .*: The details about Franco Giorgetti in this chapter come from his unpublished memoir, *I ricordi di Franco* (pp. 19–24), given to the author at a meeting on 27 February 2023.

78 *'No, you mustn't give satisfaction . . .'*: As remembered by Franco Giorgetti, 'I ricordi di Franco'.

79 *'His plan was to find death . . .'*: From Franco Giorgetti, *I ricordi di Franco*.

80 *as the last explosion could be heard across the valley*: When asked if it was possible for the people at Il Focardo to hear the bridges being blow up in Florence, Marinella Fuschiotti, Orando's daughter, said, 'Of course, we could hear it' (conversation with the author, 2023).

80 *Born less than an hour's drive from Il Focardo* . . .: Giuseppe Agnoloni was born in Montemignaio in the province of Arezzo on 4 August 1914 (interview with war crimes investigators, 23 January 2008, FF Bundle III, pp. 658–60). In his memoir about these events, *Ricordi di guerra* (Archivio del Comune di Rignano, 1998), Agnoloni does not mention that this was his birthday.

81 *'Go . . . get out of here . . .'*: This and subsequent quotations in this chapter come from Giuseppe Agnoloni's *Ricordi di guerra*.

## Part Two. Aftermath

83 *'Once the experience of evil has been endured . . .'*: Natalia Ginzburg, 'The Son of Man' (1946), in *The Little Virtues* (Arcade, 1989), p. 49.

### 13. Il Focardo, 1944

86 *Nello Dino recalled in later testimony* . . .: Nello's account is taken from his memoir, *Ricordi di quei giorni* (Giuntina, 1975).

87 *'Call Washington . . .'*: In his *Ricordi di quei giorni*, Nello Dino said that the young man asked that the message be conveyed directly to President Truman. The obvious problem with this story is that Harry S. Truman did not become president of the United States until 12 April 1945, eight months later. Most probably the incorrect naming of the president was due to a memory lapse or slip of the tongue; it was unlikely to be malicious. On 2 July 2007, the former partisan Vasco Caldini gave his own version of the episode, stating: 'The

story of this family [the Einsteins] was followed particularly by the Americans. Even the president himself personally inquired with an American officer on the spot about how things had gone. Indeed, the Americans had prepared a plan to make the family escape which would have been possible before the massacre.' He then revealed that 'My brother-in-law told me that he had witnessed a telephone conversation between an American officer and the president on this topic' (FF Bundle II, p. 258).

89 *Ali the dog was killed*: In the available evidence there is nothing that says who found the dead dog or what had happened to it. All Lorenza said about this in her interview with Massimiliano Scuriatti, *Una vita, mille vite. Conversazione con Lorenza Mazzetti* (La nave di Teseo, 2021), is that 'they killed our dog'.

89 *'As the hours passed'* . . .: Unpublished remembrances written between 2010 and 2016 by Anna Maria Boldrini, provided by her family.

90 *There he reported the deaths* . . .: See the death certificates of Nina, Luce and Cici Einstein at Rignano sull'Arno town hall. Those of Luce and Cici are shown in the 2001 German TV documentary *Der Fall Rignano – Die Mörder der Letzten Tage*.

90 *the Convento dell'Incontro*: According to testimony from a Franciscan priest in Fiesole given to German investigators in September 2009, the Convento dell'Incontro was founded around 1700 and was closed in the 1970s. At the time of the battle in August 1944, there were mostly men living there (FF Bundle V, pp. 1265–80). In their various wartime accounts, the Allies typically described Incontro as a 'monastery', with the exception of US war crimes investigator Milton Wexler's

interviews with Seba and Robert, where *convento* was translated as 'convent'.

90 *two days after the murders, long columns . . .*: For a detailed description of the battle at Incontro, see 'Report of the attack on Incontro Monastery by 2 Battalion, Duke of Cornwall's Light Infantry' (TNA WO 204/8047).

91 *'The fury of war . . .'*: Giuseppe Agnoloni's account of the siege of Incontro comes from his *Ricordi di guerra* (Archivio del Comune di Rignano, 1998).

93 *the young man introduced himself . . .*: For details of Robert's encounter with Alberto Droandi, see the latter's article, 'Agosto 1944. Quei cinque giorni di Robert Einstein', *Notizie di Historia*, December 2004.

95 *It was 9 August 1944*: There are differing accounts of how Robert spent his time after he left Il Manco. In his article 'Agosto 1944', Alberto Droandi says that Robert spent just one night in Montevarchi (8 August). In his testimony to the US war crimes investigator Milton Wexler in September 1944, Robert Einstein says that Alberto Droandi 'held me there for three days because I had an idea to kill myself' (NARA). I have followed Alberto's account as he was less volatile during the events described.

96 *a number of small notices . . .*: An original copy can found in the official investigation dossier of the US War Crimes Commission (NARA), where it is labelled 'Exhibit I'. Also in this dossier is a report by Wexler and his fellow investigator Edwin Booth which calls the notice a 'note of execution left by the German commander'. In her testimony to Wexler, Seba said, 'There were several notes' (NARA) and that she was given her copy by a 'farmer', presumably Orando (NARA). On 27 July 2009, at the local Carabinieri station in

Sesto Fiorentino, Bruno Giorgetti, a former neighbour of the Einsteins who lived at Il Manco, gave a signed statement to German investigators. He said that he, his brother Franco and cousin Renzo were with Orando Fuschiotti when they went to the villa the day after the shootings. They entered through the terrace (all except Franco who entered through the front door). It had been Franco, Bruno said, who discovered the notices left by the Germans 'in front of the entrance to the villa.' The names of Bruno and the others were redacted in the files I was given by the German prosecutor (as was the case for almost all the names in the documents), but they were unredacted in the files in Rome (FF Bundle V, pp. 1098–1102; MCR Volume V).

96 *'The family was executed . . .'*: As a fluent German and Italian speaker, Robert would have noticed that the phrasing in the last line, 'passata alla fucilazione' (literally, 'passed to the firing squad') was unusual. Typically, a native Italian would say 'passata per le armi' ('sent for execution'). This suggested that one of the German soldiers had written the notices rather than a local resident.

97 *his statement was now taken down . . .*: The 14 August statement by Robert Einstein, along with one given by Seba Mazzetti on the same day, are preserved in the Einstein murders case file (NARA). They were typed in both English and Italian, signed by Robert and Seba and submitted to the War Crimes Commission for Florence. It is likely that these statements were taken by a US soldier but this is not recorded anywhere. They were labelled as 'Exhibit C' in the investigation summary prepared by Wexler and Booth on 22 September 1944 and described as 'copies of reports of this incident upon which this investigation is based'.

98 *Robert was adamant: 'both of these accusations . . .':* The local police had come to the same conclusion. On 30 August 1943 – before the start of the German occupation – the Questura di Firenze (Florence central police station) wrote a memo to the Ministry of Interior Political Police Division: 'Subject: Einstein, Roberto, son of Jakob and Ida Einstein, born in Munich on 27/02/1884 [sic], residing in Rignano sull'Arno, Florence. Stateless engineer. The Jew Roberto Einstein, owner of the "Focardo" estate, in the hamlet of Troghi, Municipality of Rignano sull'Arno, has always been closely guarded by the Carabinieri of that locality and has never given rise to suspicions of contacts with British or American spies. He is very rarely absent.' The document was briefly shown on screen during the 2001 TV documentary *Der Fall Rignano – Die Mörder der Letzten Tage.*

## 14. Il Focardo, 1944

99 *four other members of the newly formed United States War Crimes Commission . . .:* These were commissioners Major Edwin Booth, Major Carl Cundiff, along with private first class Robert Passigli, who was the translator, and technician fourth grade Adrian Stehouwer, who took notes.

99 *Wexler was here to investigate . . .:* Wexler's Einstein murders case file can be found at US NARA, RG 153, Entry 143, Box 528, Case 16-71, 'Incidents at Troghi'.

100 *Three months later, he received orders from General Clark's office . . .:* Information on Wexler's early war crimes work in NARA, RG 153, Entry 143, Box 528, Case number 16-54.

100 *the murder of fifty-two civilians in Bellona*: The figure of fifty-two comes from the US War Crimes Commission case file

at NARA. Since then, historians using different methodologies have provided a range of figures, including fifty-four (Gabriella Gribaudi, *Guerra totale. Tra bombe alleate e violenze naziste. Napoli e il fronte meridionale, 1940–1944*, Bollati Boringhieri, 2005, p. 381) and seventy-six (Carlo Gentile, *I crimini di guerra tedeschi in Italia, 1943–1945*, Einaudi, 2002, p. 133).

101  *the so-called Moscow Declarations*: Copies of the declarations are available online at the Avalon Project and other sources.

102  *up to 560 people had been killed*: Historians, investigators and witnesses have provided a range of estimates for the numbers killed in this massacre, from 400 to 560. The confusion is partly due to uncertainty about the number of refugees living in the village at that time.

102  *'I saw the Germans rounding up . . .'*: US War Crimes Commission file on Sant'Anna di Stazzema, NARA, RG 153, Entry 143, Box 528, Case 16-62.

103  *a Nazi 'Black List'*: See the letter of 22 January 1943 from Washington Field Office to the director of the FBI, included in the more than 1,400-page declassified FBI file on Albert Einstein (Bufile 61-7099, 'Albert Einstein, Part 3 of 9', p. 5, available online at FBI Records: The Vault). While Hoover was concerned about Einstein posing a security threat to the USA as a pacifist and alleged communist, it is not clear whether he was concerned about threats in the other direction, against the scientist from the German government or other Nazi organizations.

107  *the entire Einstein family was Jewish*: In a conversation with the author in 2022, Aldo Casino, the oldest surviving resident in San Donato in Collina, said, 'People in the area believed the mother and daughters were Jewish. They were killed because they were Jewish.'

111 *he had provided them with fruit . . .*: Nina, Luce and Cici all denied that Robert had given food to the partisans. Either he kept them entirely in the dark or they deliberately withheld the information from the Germans.

111 *'I heard from a priest at the Incontro [monastery] . . .'*: The monks at Incontro kept a chronicle of the fighting that summer, a copy of which was given to German investigators in September 2009. It included this passage: 'The English approached having learned that there were Germans up here and therefore began to shoot at us with cannons, which continued day and night until August 8; on that day they occupied Incontro and captured the Germans. Both we and the evacuees [local civilians taking refuge from the fighting] survived a terrible time locked in the cellar' (FF Bundle V, pp. 1265–80).

112 *Seba said she was fifty-six . . .*: According to Seba's gravestone in the Cimitero Evangelico agli Allori in Florence, she was born on 12 January 1888. She died on 23 January 1953 and was buried in the same grave site as her brother Corrado (plot V III). The cemetery website states that she was born in Naples. In her unpublished remembrances written between 2010 and 2016, Anna Maria Boldrini said her aunt Seba was born in Bergamo.

114 *'she had her spectacles'*: None of the photographs that have survived show Nina wearing glasses. This suggests that the spectacles Nina was holding were reading glasses.

115 *'the Germans had violated . . .'*: There is some dispute as to whether the three women were sexually assaulted by the German soldiers. In his memoir, *Ricordi di quei giorni* (Archivio Giutina, 1975), Nello Dino recalled that 'the girls showed evidence of [sexual] violence'. Similarly, in his account *La*

*rappresaglie nazifascist sulle popolazioni toscane* (ANFIM, 1992), the local historian Ugo Jona, wrote that 'they seemed to have been raped'. In the 2001 German TV documentary *Der Fall Rignano – Die Mörder der Letzten Tage*, the narrator says that 'Luce, the older of the two sisters, was raped before the execution'. When I asked the director, Tilman Spengler, about this, he replied: 'As far as I remember, it was Lorenza who told me about the rape very early and later [after the film was aired] denied ever having told me so.' On 3 July 2007, in an interview at her home in Verona, Anna Maria Boldrini was asked by German police officers, 'Did the German soldiers, both before and during the day of August 3, sexually abuse women from Villa Il Focardo?' She replied, 'I am not aware of any such details' (FF Bundle II, p. 262). When asked the same question, Lorenza was definitive. 'Absolutely not,' she said. 'Maybe some farmer might have told it, but it's just a rumour' (FF Bundle I, p. 40). When also asked the same question by the German police on 17 January 2008, Paola said, 'No nothing of the sort' (FF Bundle III, p. 568). Given the above, I have chosen not to include the sexual violence in the main narrative.

### 15. Il Focardo, 1944

120 *Albert described the accident to a friend . . .*: Letter from Albert Einstein to Otto Juliusburger, 6 September 1944, written at No. 6 Knollwood, Saranac Lake, NY (sold by Christie's, London, on 23 May 2019; AEA 38-221).

120 *'My dear Doctor Einstein, I take this occasion . . .'*: Letter from Milton Wexler to Albert Einstein, 17 September 1944 (AEA 55-48).

121 *'I received the news of the tragedy . . .'*: Letter from Maja Einstein to Bice Besso Rusconi, 17–23 September 1945 (Biblioteca Nazionale Centrale di Firenze, 'Fondo Besso', cassetto 5, inserto 5, n. 13; copy in MCR Volume V). Presumably the 'cousin' that Maja refers to is Robert and the 'American person' is Milton Wexler. Neither of the letters Maja mentions has survived.

122 *'Dear Albert, I don't know if you have heard . . .'*: Letter from Robert Einstein to Albert Einstein, 27 November 1944 (AEA 55-49).

124 *Maja and Albert wrote directly to Robert . . .*: Their letter writing was reported in an article in *Il Nuovo Corriere* on 28 July 1945. Anna Maria Boldrini confirmed that Albert and Maja wrote letters of condolence to Robert and the others in Florence (interview with the author, February 2024). The original letters have not been found in the archives.

124 *'I wrote you a card . . .'*: Letter from Maja Einstein to Paul Winteler, 31 March 1945 ('Samedi avant Paques') (AEA 73-659).

126 *extremely rare for them to be killed in Italy*: In October 2009, the Frankenthal prosecutor Hubert Ströber asked the researcher Nina Staehle to look at the files in the National Archives in Kew. After an extensive exploration, Staehle found one potentially similar case to the Einstein murders, which took place on 24 August 1944 when three Jewish women were killed by German soldiers in Rufina, eight miles northeast of Il Focardo (TNA WO 310/219). In a letter dated 17 November 2009, Staehle wrote that 'there is no apparent direct connection' between the two crimes. Later, Ströber's investigators discovered that the Rufina murders had previously been looked into by the Mannheim prosecutor's office,

starting on 31 June 1967. That earlier investigation had determined they were probably carried out by members of 754th Grenadier Regiment, 334th Infantry Division, which, on the day of the Einstein murders, was located in Cascia near Regello, just seven miles southeast of Il Focardo. However, it had also concluded that the Rufina murders were a 'spontaneous action near the front' – in other words, they had not been ordered, and were therefore unlikely to be part of a wider campaign against Jews in the area. Ströber's team therefore ruled out a link between the two war crimes (FF Bundle V, p. 1355).

### 16. Il Focardo, 1944

130 *'I was very puzzled'* . . .: This and the rest of Giuseppe Agnoloni's testimony in this chapter come from his memoir, *Ricordi di guerra* (Archivio del Comune di Rignano, 1998).

130 *Robert was suffering a strong sense of guilt*: Another person to note Robert's guilt was his friend Professor Rodolfo Paoli. In his memoir *Cronache di una guerra combattuta senza armi (1943–1946)* (Pagnini, 2014), Paoli reported Robert telling him several times that 'if they [the Germans] had found me they would have spared them [his wife and daughters]'.

131 *'I could not face the memory . . .'*: Lorenza Mazzetti, *London Diaries* (Zidane Press, 2018), p. 157.

131 *Lorenza was tormented by nightmares* . . .: Details of Lorenza's dreams are taken from her *London Diaries*, pp. 64, 132 and 135.

131 *Lorenza would later describe her emotional state* . . .: Details taken from Mazzetti, *London Diaries*, pp. 137, 29 and 136.

132 *'It was terrifying . . . it was the end of the world . . .'*: Taken from an interview Paola gave for the documentary *Attraverso l'amore. Paola Mazzetti si racconta* (Ronin Film Productions, 2021).

132 *More analytical than her twin . . .*: Anna Maria Boldrini said that while her cousin Lorenza was like a 'volcano', Paola was like a 'mountain lake'. Unless otherwise stated, information from Anna Maria Boldrini in this chapter comes from an interview with the author in Verona in February 2024, when she was ninety-seven years old. Anna Maria said that she had not spoken about the murders with a journalist before because it made her feel anguished (*angosciata*); but now, with the passage of time, the events were in the past and 'what happened was so terrible it was important to speak about it and remember'. She said that she still prayed every night for Nina, Luce, Cici and Robert, and thanked them because she was saved from the dangers of being bombed in Pisa.

132 *She remembered certain moments more sharply than others . . .*: These details come from Paola's interview with German police officers on 17 January 2008 (FF Bundle II, pp. 565–9).

133 *'I pretend to laugh and joke . . .'*: Mazzetti, *London Diaries*, p. 63.

134 *sleeping in his eldest daughter's narrow bed . . .*: This was reported in *Il Nuovo Corriere*, 28 July 1945.

134 *'My uncle was deeply depressed . . .'*: In her unpublished remembrances written between 2010 and 2016, Anna Maria described Robert as experiencing *'terribile scoramento'*, or 'terrible despondency'.

135 *'They were very friendly . . .'*: *Il Nuovo Corriere*, 28 July 1945.

135 *'The Florence that we . . .'*: Herbert L. Matthews, 'Italian Art under Shellfire', *Harper's Magazine*, May 1945.

136 *'How is it possible that our dead . . .'*: Mazzetti, *London Diaries*, p. 134.

### 17. Il Focardo, 1945

139 *He brought along his son . . . Giancarlo . . .*: The information about the Bürgisser family was sent to me by Carmen Bürgisser (Rodolfo Arnoldo Bürgisser's great-granddaughter, and granddaughter of Enrico's brother Luigi). She began researching the Einstein family story after finding an old postcard, written by Enrico to her grandfather Luigi in 1924, with a picture on its front of the villa Il Focardo. 'It's really true,' she told me, 'that what you don't write . . . you lose!'

141 *'Is it all right if I take a peach?' . . .*: Marinella Fuschiotti told me that the best peaches on the estate were to be found near Pipone's house, Casa Bella (conversation with the author, 2023).

142 *'. . . as if it was the last I ever ate'*: This story was told to me by Pipone's granddaughter Francesca Salomoni, who was still living at Casa Bella. As she relayed it, tears flowed down her cheeks.

### 18. Il Focardo, 1945

143 *Robert was lying on his bed, gasping*: The account of this episode comes from the priest Don Giuseppe Agnoloni's memoir *Ricordi di guerra* (Archivio del Comune di Rignano, 1998). In an interview with the author in 2023, Orando's daughter Marinella (who was four years old at the time) remembered some of the details differently: in particular, that it was her mother, not her father, who found Robert Einstein. 'After the murder, Robert always came to eat with us,' she said. 'That morning he didn't come for breakfast, so my mother

went to call him, and found him having taken a whole box of sleeping pills.'

143 *'We have to drive the engineer to the hospital'*: Newspaper article by Luciano Masini, 'Ho cercato di salvare Einstein con la mia Balilla' ('I Tried to Save Einstein with My Balilla Car'). Orando's daughter Marinella provided a cutting of the article, which does not have a date or the name of the newspaper.

145 *who named it after the city of Verona*: According to a letter by Dr Kurt F. Behne, his former teacher Mering had been on vacation in Verona when he received a telegram from Fischer saying that he had successfully synthesized the drug. Mering was so pleased by this that he called it veronal. See 'Correspondence', *Journal of the American Medical Association*, vol. 97, no. 3 (1931), p. 198.

145 *the Austrian writer Stefan Zweig*: So many Jews around this time committed suicide using veronal (including Zweig) that the author Victor Klemperer noted in his diary that he thought 'veronal should now be called "Jewish drops"'' (19 July 1942). In a couple of later entries, he also lamented that he did not have any (6 May 1944, 27 February 1945). See Victor Klemperer, *I Shall Bear Witness: A Diary of the Nazi Years, 1942–1945* (Modern Library, 2001), pp. 103, 313, 424.

146 *Anna Maria reminded the priest that she had been baptized*: According to Anna Maria, both her great-grandfather Ludovico Conti and her grandfather Lorenzo Mazzetti 'played an important role in the history of the Waldensian Church in Italy', so when her Waldensian mother, Ada, had married her Catholic father, she 'received a lot of criticism from the Mazzetti family'. Their disapproval worsened when they learned that Ada, 'had undertaken that the children would

be educated in the Catholic religion' (unpublished remembrances written between 2010 and 2016 by Anna Maria Boldrini).

146 *Robert Einstein was declared dead*: Robert's death was registered at the town hall in Rignano sull'Arno on 16 July 1945 in front of the mayor, Ferdinando Castiglioni Sessi (Rignano sull'Arno municipal archives).

### 19. Il Focardo, 1945

149 *Robert had known he would kill himself . . .*: Rodolfo Paoli, who wrote an article about Robert and his murdered family which appeared in *La Nazione del Popolo* on 23 July 1945, said that Robert waited until early July before committing suicide so that Lorenza and Paola could complete their end-of-year exams the week previously. In an interview with the author in 2023, Pipone's granddaughter Francesca Salomoni said her grandfather believed that Robert had killed himself in July (rather than later) in order to avoid the first anniversary of the murders, which was coming up on 3 August. According to some other accounts, Robert killed himself on the anniversary of his wedding to Nina. This is not correct, as they were married in October 1913. 'It is a legend,' Robert and Nina's great-niece Eva Krampen Kosloski told me in 2023, 'something to make the story sound good.'

149 *'My Dear Orando . . .'*: Letter from Robert Einstein to Orando Fuschiotti, 30 June 1944, courtesy of Eva Krampen Kosloski private archive; published in Camillo Arcuri, *Il sangue degli Einstein Italiani* (Ugo Mursia Editore, 2015), p. 91.

150 *'Dear Picchia . . .'*: Letter courtesy of Anna Maria Boldrini. Anna Maria told her son Andrea Bellavite that 'Picchia stood

for Piccola [small] and that's what they called her because she was smaller in stature than the cousins' (email to the author, June 2024).

151 *Anna Maria was profoundly moved . . .*: Anna Maria's response to Roberto's letter was relayed to the author by her son Andrea in a phone call.

155 *'Someone must have betrayed the Einsteins'*: Beniamino Morandi's story was told to me by Vito Maiorano, whose family Beniamino worked for from time to time. Numerous other people have spoken about a betrayal. 'My brother remembers our mother talking about an Italian [who betrayed the Einsteins],' Orando Fuschiotti's daughter Marinella told me, 'but I don't know the name.' Similarly, Eugenio Carrara – who lived with his parents, Nello and Gaetanina, close to Il Focardo in 1944 – said that 'All the local people knew where the Einsteins lived. One of them likely gave the family away to the Germans.' While a former partisan called Vasco Caldini told German police officers in 2007, 'I can report that one of the [Einstein] employees was engaged to a *repubblicano* [a fascist who supported Mussolini's Italian Social Republic] who frequented their home' (FF Bundle II, p. 258). Another to believe there was a betrayal was David Liscia who, as president of the Florence synagogue, spoke at commemoration events for the Einstein family. 'Robert was thinking that the local people supported him,' he told me in 2022, 'they were not against him. The problem was it took only one person to betray them, so that they could be found. An Italian probably betrayed them.' In the eight decades since the murders, however, no definitive proof has surfaced that any Italian provided information to the Germans which led to the capture and ultimate killing of Nina, Luce and Cici Einstein.

155 *'time had not healed . . .'*: Alberto Droandi's testimony in this chapter is taken from his article, 'Agosto 1944. Quei cinque giorni di Robert Einstein', *Notizie di Historia*, December 2004.

156 *'Forgive me, if I was a bit annoying . . .'*: In her book *Album di famiglia* (La nave di Teseo, 2011), Lorenza wrote that Robert left the letter for her and her sister (p. 164). I was unable to find an original copy of this letter, however the article about the Einsteins in *Il Nuovo Corriere* of 28 July 1945 confirmed that Robert 'left a letter to his sister-in-law [Seba], one to his brother-in-law [Corrado], one to each of his nieces [Lorenza, Paola and Anna Maria]'. The article added, 'That's why they heard him, some evenings, typing so much in his room.' Variations of Robert's letter to Lorenza and Paola can be found in Lorenza's *London Diaries* (Zidane Press, 2018), p. 43, and *The Sky Falls* (Bodley Head, 1962), p. 154, the key difference being that these do not include the final line about him 'leaving everything' to his nieces.

156 *'A wall of water tumbles over me . . .'*: Mazzetti, *London Diaries*, p. 141.

158 *a 'day of mourning' . . .*: Quotations from Piero Calamandrei's speech at the event to commemorate Luce Einstein at the University of Florence on 26 January 2024 are from the original, held in the University of Florence archives.

158 *Corrado had written to the rector . . .*: Letter from Corrado Mazzetti to the rector of the University of Florence, 5 November 1945 (University of Florence archives).

159 *'. . . torn from the affection of his loved ones'*: Notice of death, *La Nazione del Popolo*, 28 January 1946. According to Corrado's granddaughter Eva Krampen Kosloski, he died in a bicycle accident (conversation with the author 2023). Coincidentally,

his death occurred a year to the day after the liberation of Auschwitz (27 January 1945).

159 *Afterwards, a small gathering was held . . .*: The notice in *La Nazione del Popolo* stated that a reception for Corrado would be held at 10 a.m. on 29 January at 'the home of the deceased', i.e. Robert's apartment at Corso dei Tintori 21. Corrado was buried in plot V III in the Cimitero Evangelico agli Allori, where he was joined seven years later by his sister Seba. His age when he died is derived from his gravestone, which states that he was born on 4 July 1892, in Naples.

159 *'We were saved by people . . .'*: Paola Mazzetti interview from the documentary *Attraverso l'amore. Paola Mazzetti si racconta* (Ronin Film Productions, 2021).

## 20. Princeton, New Jersey, 1945

161 *Perhaps as much as six or eight weeks*: We know that Albert and Maja must have heard about Robert's death by the end of September 1945 as she referred to it in the letter she wrote to her friend Bice Besso Rusconi, dated 17–23 September (original in Biblioteca Nazionale Centrale di Firenze, 'Fondo Besso', cassetto 5, inserto 5, n. 13; copy in MCR Volume V).

162 *'Had I known that the Germans . . .'*: Albert Einstein, quoted in 'Atoms: Einstein, the Man Who Started It All', *Newsweek*, 10 March 1947, p. 58. Shortly after the bombings, in an interview given to the *New York Times* on 12 August 1945, Albert refused to talk about Hiroshima: 'I will not discuss that,' he said. He was more open in the article 'Atomic War or Peace?', which appeared in the November 1947 issue of *Atlantic Monthly*, where he called atomic energy 'a menace'.

162 *'My mother died a week ago today ...'*: Letter from Albert Einstein to Heinrich Zangger, 27 February 1920 (AEA 39-732).

163 *'Although I saw him for such a brief time ...'*: Letter from Albert Einstein to Hans Albert and Frieda Einstein, 7 January 1939 (AEA 75-904). Albert wrote with condolences to other people following their bereavement, for instance, after a friend lost his eleven-year-old son to polio, Albert wrote: 'A human being is part of the whole world, called by us "Universe", a part limited in time and space. He experiences himself, his thoughts and feelings as something separate from the rest – a kind of optical delusion of his consciousness' (Letter from Albert Einstein to Robert Marcus, 12 February 1950, AEA 60-424).

163 *'homesick for Italy ...'*: Letter from Maja Einstein to Bice Besso Rusconi, 17–23 September 1945 (Biblioteca Nazionale Centrale di Firenze, 'Fondo Besso', cassetto 5, inserto 5, n. 13; copy in MCR Volume V).

164 *'Now he has again preceded me ...'*: Letter of Albert Einstein to Bice Besso Rusconi Vero Besso, 21 March 1955 (AEA 7-245.1).

165 *'develop a peaceful sense ...'*: See Walter Isaacson, *Einstein: His Life and Universe* (Simon & Schuster, 2007), p. 536.

165 *'Brief is this existence ...'*: Words spoken by Albert Einstein at the funeral service for Rudolf Landenburg, 1 April 1952 (AEA 5-160).

165 *his stepdaughter Margot*: Margot Einstein was the forty-four-year-old daughter of Albert's second wife, Elsa, who had died in 1936.

166 *the twenty-four most prominent Nazis ...*: Originally there were twenty-four individual defendants. Of these, Martin Bormann was tried *in absentia*, Robert Ley died before standing

trial, and Hermann Göring was convicted but killed himself before execution. In all, nineteen were convicted.

## Part Three. Justice

169 *'The important thing is not to stop questioning'*: Albert Einstein, quoted in William Miller, 'Death of a Genius', *Life*, 2 May 1955, p. 64.

### 21. Rome, 1994

172 *close to 22,000 Italian civilians . . .*: From *Atlante delle Stragi Naziste e Fasciste in Italia, 1943–1945*, online database (INSMLI and ANPI, 2016).

172 *the Evil Germans . . . the Good Italians : . .*: A number of Italian historians have investigated this idea, including David Bidussa, Filippo Focardi and Angelo Del Boca.

173 *the heroics of Italian resistance fighters . . .*: For instance, *Un giorno da leoni* (*A Day for Lionhearts*, 1961), *Le quattro giornate di Napoli* (*The Four Days of Naples*, 1962) and *Il partigiano Johnny* (*Johnny the Partisan*, 2000). Examples of films that feature bumbling Italian soldiers include *Mediterraneo* (1991) and the Anglo-American production *Captain Corelli's Mandolin* (2001).

175 *'I was told by many people . . .'*: Carlo Carli's words in this chapter come from a conversation with the author in 2023.

177 *'disappeared along the way . . .'*: The lost file was recently discovered by the military prosecutor in Rome (*La Repubblica*, 27 January 2025). The file includes a transmission page with the word 'OSS'. The link to the Office for Strategic Services (forerunner to the CIA) is unclear.

## 22. Cologne, 2002

179 *'I grew up in an area . . .'*: Email to the author, 13 October 2022.

179 *a book about war crimes in Italy . . .*: The book was Ugo Jona's *Le rappresaglie nazifasciste sulle popolazioni toscane* (ANFIM, 1992) which contains a day-to-day chronology of German violence in the region.

181 *After methodically looking through hundreds of pages . . .*: See Carlo Gentile, *Wehrmacht und Waffen-SS im Partisanenkrieg. Italien, 1943–1945* (Ferdinand Schöningh, 2012), pp. 374–9.

182 *Captain Clemens Josef Theis . . .*: In the source documents, his name is spelled variously 'Clemens' and 'Klemens', as well as 'Theis' and 'Theiss'. I have used 'Clemens Theis' as that is what he used (see his handwritten letter: COSJA B162 43170, p. 1285).

## 23. Ludwigsburg, 2005

185 *'For me the history was always present' . . .*: Quoted in Tom Lamont, 'The Race to Catch the Last Nazis', *GQ*, 12 September 2023.

185 *'Murder is not subject . . .'*: Quoted in Tilman Blasshofer, 'Race Against the Clock for Germany's Top Nazi Hunter', Reuters, 27 January 2023.

186 *'After we have found* [*the perpetrators*] *. . .'*: Quoted in Tom Lamont, 'The Race to Catch the Last Nazis'.

186 *Judge Will was a tall, thick-set man . . .*: I met Judge Will at his office in 2023, when he courteously provided me with the files I requested, but declined to speak in detail about the Einstein murders case.

186 *As one feature writer observed . . .*: See the description of Judge Will in Tom Lamont, 'The Race to Catch the Last Nazis'.

186 *In his first note on the case . . .*: COSJA B162 43704, p. 2.

187 *In December 2005, Judge Will travelled to London . . .*: On 8 March 2006, Judge Will made a file note (COSJA B 162 43704, p. 223) in which he summarized the progress of the case so far, including the documents he found at the National Archives in Kew. Among these was an entry in 4th Infantry Division's headquarters war diary on 3 August 1944, by a staff intelligence officer, which stated that '30 Germans after shooting two women in a house at 896594 were reported to be proceeding down the road, but a patrol failed to make contact with them' (TNA WO 170/408; quoted in COSJA B 162 43704, p. 223). The implication being that this British Army unit spotted the Germans as they left Il Focardo. In a conversation with the author in 2022, Carlo Gentile questioned whether the field report referred to Il Focardo. The grid reference does not appear to match the location of Il Focardo on contemporary Allied maps; the report mentions two women, not the three that were killed; and local witnesses do not mention Allied soldiers arriving till the following day.

188 *Theis's dog, named 'Stolg'*: Mentioned in 'Report of the attack on Incontro Monastery by 2 Battalion, Duke of Cornwall's Light Infantry' (TNA WO 204/8047; quoted in COSJA B162 43704, p. 63). This might be *Stolz* in German, meaning 'pride'.

188 *the vast majority had remained in Germany . . .*: Some had left the country, including Alfred Gerlach, who relocated to the UK, dying there in 1997 (COSJA B162 43704, pp. 95–6).

189 *'I am sending you the file . . .'*: Letter from Thomas Will to Hubert Ströber, 29 January 2007 (COSJA B162 43709, p. 1163).

### 24. Frankenthal, 2011

193  *In a note inserted in the file on 26 February 2007 . . .:* This, and much
of the information in this chapter, comes from the case files
of the Frankenthal prosecutor's office, which I won access
to with the help of Berlin-based lawyer Christoph Partsch.
The case was heard on 7 November 2023 at the Administrative Court of Neustadt an der Weinstrasse (case number: 5 k
75/23.NW). The judges ruled in our favour, explaining that
we had demonstrated not only that there was considerable
public interest in this case but that the inquiry was of 'outstanding importance [ . . . ] due to the historical dimension
of the criminal investigation of crimes from the Nazi era'. I
was told that this was the first time in German history that a
journalist had been granted access to a prosecutor's murder
files. The *Frankfurter Allgemeine Zeitung* on 13 November 2023
called the verdict a 'spectacular victory'. *Die Rheinpfalz*, on
21 November, quoted Andrea Wohlfart, chairwoman of
the Rhineland-Palatine branch of the German Journalists
Association, as saying that the decision was 'pioneering' and
'immensely important for media freedom'.

193  *'The American investigations . . .':* Author's conversation with
Hubert Ströber directly after the verdict in the trial to obtain
access to the Frankenthal Files, November 2023.

195  *Since that brief interview . . . she hadn't spoken to anyone . . .:* When
comparing his mother's response to the events at Il Focardo
on 3 August 1944 to those of her cousins Paola and Lorenza,
her son Andrea Bellavite wrote in a blog post on 13 January 2024: 'My mother Anna Maria faced those events with
a different spirit, keeping them silently in her memory and
entrusting them to the memory of her children.'

195 *According to the transcript* . . .: Interview with Anna Maria Boldrini, 3 July 2007 (FF Bundle II, p. 262).

197 *'Do you remember that the soldiers mentioned ranks* . . .': It is worth noting that the ranks suggested by the German police officers were from the SS, not the Wehrmacht.

198 *on separate occasions, the police officers showed* . . .: Lorenza was interviewed on 25 April 2007 and Paola on 17 January 2008 (Identity parade: FF Bundle I p. 380–88. Testimonies: FF Bundle I, p. 283, and Bundle I, p. 565).

200 *'I was aware of the historic dimension'* . . .: This quotation, and biographical details in this paragraph, come from an interview I had with Hubert Ströber in the corridor outside the courtroom, minutes after the court case in November 2023 was decided. The prosecutor's response to the court decision was both phlegmatic and pragmatic.

201 Bild . . . Der Spiegel . . .: Both newspapers published their articles on 18 February 2011.

204 *born on 22 October 1907* . . .: According to August Schmitz's birth certificate, his father Karl Joseph August Schmitz was a dental technician and, like August's mother Antonia Christina Schmitz (née Höffgen), a Catholic. They lived in Grevenbroich, but August Schmitz was born at his grandmother's house (Luise Höffgen, 'a widow and without occupation') in Krefeld, about twenty miles to the north (Krefeld town council archives). His full name as given on his birth certificate was August Jakob Ludwig Schmitz, while his military records have him as August Ludwig Jacob Schmitz (Bundesarchiv B563/1 KARTEI/S-3375/107).

204 *First, they travelled to Verona . . . Next, they drove to Rome* . . .: The police officers met Anna Maria Boldrini on 10 May 2011 and

Lorenza and Paola Mazzetti the following day (FF Bundle VIII, pp. 1980–98).

206 *'It seems an obvious conclusion . . .'*: Ströber sent his final report to Judge Will on 5 January 2014. It can be found in COSJA B162 43710, p. 1312, and in FF Bundle IX, at p. 2189. Ströber's conclusion was supported by the Baden-Württemberg police. On 6 November 2013, they wrote an 'Investigative Report' which stated that 'On the whole, everything points to the fact that the crime was rather committed by members of the parachute assault gun brigade alone' (FF Bundle IX, p. 2093).

206 *August Schmitz died in San Martino Buon Albergo . . .*: It appears that on 26 April 1945, August Schmitz took part in a war crime at the village of Ferrazze near San Martino Buon Albergo where twenty-six people were murdered. He was killed shortly afterwards by approaching American tanks and buried in an unmarked grave. This information was provided to me by Sergio Spiazzi, a local historian from San Martino Buon Albergo. 'At the time of the collective burial of the group of Germans at the cemetery,' Sergio said, 'no one had identification documents.'

208 *Reinhold Hanning . . .*: According to a Reuters report on 4 May 2016, Hanning again admitted to his crime in court. He 'offered an apology, stating that he was "sincerely sorry" and "ashamed" that he had belonged to a criminal organization that committed mass murder and countless atrocities, and that he had never done anything to prevent such actions' (Andrew Nagorski, 'Long Overdue, a Nazi Finally Says Sorry', Reuters, 4 May 2016). Sometimes admissions are too good to be true; for example, the one published by the *Daily Mail* on 28 August 2015 under the headline: 'Nazi Gold Train

Is FOUND: Deathbed Confession Leads Treasure Hunters to Secret Location as Polish Officials Claim They Have Seen Proof on Radar'. No train was ever found, nor any gold.

208 *A classified intelligence report . . .*: I found this in the Central Office archives (COSJA B162 43705, p. 35). The document was one of those discovered by Judge Will at the National Archives in Kew (TNA WO 204/8047, 'Report of the attack on Incontro Monastery by 2 Battalion, Duke of Cornwall's Light Infantry').

### 25. Rome, 2016

210 *One of these was Adele Pardini . . .*: Adele Pardini was eighty-two years old when I met her with her son Graziano at the Sant'Anna di Stazzema Museum (which was the village primary school at the time of the massacre). 'I was four years old at the time. I remember we were having breakfast. It was warm, so we were eating outside. I was just drinking milk from a cup when it was knocked violently from my hand. I looked up and saw German soldiers.' She said that among the armed men were people with masks covering their faces who spoke Italian. 'We and our neighbours were lined up against the wall of our house. They took out a machine gun and started shooting.' In the next few moments, her mother was hit in the head and died instantly. Her sister Maria (sixteen years old) and sister Anna (twenty days old) were also shot but were still breathing. More than ten others were killed. Just before the shooting started, Adele's elder sister pulled her into a nearby open door, saving her life. The next few moments, Adele said, were a blank. The Germans set fire to the house, and as the flames grew higher, Adele's sister screamed they

had to go back outside. 'For years I could not remember what happened next,' Adele explained. 'I knew that my mother's body was lying across the doorway, but I could not imagine how I could have climbed over her with my small legs.' It was only recently that she was able to piece together what had happened. To go outside, she was forced to walk on top of her mother's body. As she said this, almost eighty years later, Adele struggled with this most difficult of moments. 'I could not sleep last night,' she confided. 'I was nervous about talking about this with you.' After the war, several Italians were tried by the Courts of Extraordinary Assizes for their role in atrocities in Italy, although none was ever held to account for the Fucecchio massacre. For more information, see the *Atlante delle Stragi Naziste e Fasciste in Italia, 1943–1945*, online database (INSMLI and ANPI, 2016).

211 *On 24 February 2016 . . .*: Two and a half months earlier, on 7 December 2015, Lorenza wrote to Ruth Dureghello, president of the Jewish community in Rome, and said that she had identified the man responsible for the Einstein murders. This is the earliest reference I could find to Lorenza's suspicion falling on a specific individual (FF Bundle IX, p. 2123).

211 *'I want to be interviewed . . .'*: Letter from Lorenza Mazzetti to Marco De Paolis, 24 February 2016 (MCR Volume VI).

211 *she moved in her twenties to London . . .*: In her *London Diaries*, first published in Italy in 2014, Lorenza said that 'with my suitcase I flee in search of some unhappiness'. This line is quoted by Ali Smith in her novel of 2020, *Summer*. At the chapter's end, Smith writes that when the English and Scottish soldiers arrived they 'find a couple of shellshocked children sitting beside some newly filled graves [presumably Paola and Lorenza]. The first thing they do is teach those

children to sing some songs, in English. The first song they teach them? "You Are My Sunshine".'

211 *made a name for herself . . .*: Lorenza teamed up with three of her contemporaries: Lindsay Anderson, Karel Reisz and Tony Richardson. Together they became known as the Free Cinema Movement whose manifesto began: 'No film can be too personal.' While in London, Lorenza made a number of films, including *Country Doctor* (1953) and *K* (1954) – both of which were inspired by Kafka – and *Together* (1956), which received a 'Mention au film de recherche' at Cannes Film Festival.

212 *a prestigious Italian literary award*: *Il cielo cade* (*The Sky Falls*) won the Viareggio Award in 1962. In 2000, it was made into a film with Isabella Rossellini.

212 *She was well known for her parties . . .*: The documentary director Francesco Frisari told me that Lorenza's home was an 'open house' (conversation with the author, 2023).

212 *Some even called her 'obsessed'*: This is the word her niece Eva Krampen Kosloski used (conversation with the author, 2022).

212 *Lorenza Mazzetti arrived for interview . . .*: Details of Lorenza's interview are taken from MCR Volume VI, pp. 8–16.

213 *The photograph was not entirely dissimilar . . .*: It is not known if Lorenza made this point to the Italian investigators during her interview.

215 *'I don't know how we managed . . .'*: Interview given by Paola in her home in Rome to Salvatore D'Angelo and Salvatore Alfano on 27 November 2021 (available on the diocese of Nocera Inferiore-Sarno's website).

215 *Paola was questioned . . .*: Details of Paola's interview are taken from MCR Volume VI, pp. 17–25.

217 *Lorenza described ... as 'so kind' ...*: Quotations from the correspondence between Lorenza Mazzetti and Marco De Paolis are taken from MCR Volume VI.

217 *'I showed you the* Daily Mail *article ...'*: The article was by Allan Hall, 'The Nazis Who Were Never Brought to Justice', *Daily Mail*, 15 July 2015, which included photographs of Johann Riss.

218 *'She was very old ...'*: Interview with the author in De Paolis's office in Rome, 2023.

218 *'she may have had dementia'*: Lorenza's friends and family do not agree. Her niece Eva Krampen Kosloski told me in 2023 that she was 'certain' that her aunt didn't have dementia when she first identified Riss as the culprit in 2016. Francesco Frisari, who spent three years making a documentary with Lorenza between 2013 and 2016, told me in 2023 that 'She was 100 per cent sure that Riss was the guy. I don't think she was making it up. And I'm 100 per cent sure of that. She was not lying.' Francesco remembered the moment when Lorenza told him about her discovery; it was three weeks after they had presented their film at the Venice Film Festival. 'I have to show you something,' he recalled her saying. She took a creased piece of paper from her purse and showed it to him. 'That's the guy!' It was the picture of Johann Riss. She was excited. But she said that she was not looking for revenge. 'I just want the truth and to be taken seriously,' she told him. 'My grandmother had dementia,' Francesco continued, 'so I am very familiar with the symptoms. I can tell you categorically that Lorenza did not have dementia when she showed me the picture of Riss in 2016.' During a meeting with me in his office in 2023, Joachim Lau, the family attorney, confirmed that 'Lorenza's memory was absolutely fine. Certainly

in 2016 when she gave the testimony about Riss to the military court.'

### 26. Munich, 2019

219 *'I'm telling you, it's him'*: Conversation reported by Barbara Schepanek to the author in 2023.

219 *According to his military records* . . .: For Johann Riss's military records, see Bundesarchiv, Berlin, B563/1 KARTEI/ R-682/373 (central personnel military card); B578/295441 (medical records); ZA 12/62250 (basic personnel records as US prisoner of war, including photographs and fingerprints); B562/ALT.REG RISS (personal and family background); B563/107609 (regiment's casualty reports); B563/71766 (14th Company, 62nd Infantry Regiment records) and B563/60193 (7th Infantry Signals Reserve Company, Munich, records). See also the investigation into Riss's role in the Fucecchio massacre, which contains the only interview I found with Johann Riss, conducted on 23 November 2006, in which he confirmed to the Italian authorities that he had volunteered for military service in 1939 and later served in the Russian campaign (MCR N 19/08/Mod 40 ROG, p. 72).

220 *he belonged to the Hitler Youth* . . .: Riss's military records do not state that he belonged to the Nazi Party, but this is not definitive proof that he was not a member.

220 *'Along the roadside* . . .': Quotations of Riss's comrades taken from Emanuel Selder, *Der Krieg der Infanterie. Dargestellt in der Chronik des Infanterie-Regiments 62 (7. Infanterie-Division), 1935–1945*, Part IV: *Unternehmen Barbarossa – Der Russlandkrieg*, Part V: *Angriff auf Moskau ab 1. Okt. 1941* and Part VI: *Das Kriegsjahr 1942* (privately printed, 1985–9).

221 *the soldiers were provided with pills . . .*: See Peter Andreas, 'How Methamphetamine Became a Key Part of Nazi Military Strategy', *Time*, 7 January 2020.

222 'Ratsch-Bum*, the howling of Stalin's organ*: *Ratsch-Bum* was German soldiers' slang for the Soviet ZiS-3 76 mm field gun, and 'Stalin's organ' was the nickname of the Katyusha multiple rocket launcher.

225 *Riss's unit arrived in the marshes of Fucecchio . . .*: For more on the various investigations into this massacre, see the British Army's case files 'Fucecchio Marshes, Pistoia, Italy: German War Crimes against Civilians' (TNA WO 310/104), also the archives held by the military court in Rome, including key statements by General Eduard Crasemann (commander of 26th Panzer Division) and Josef Strauch (commander of 26th Armoured Reconnaissance Detachment) about Riss's unit being free to roam the area in early August 1944 (MCR N 211/08 RGNR).

225 *'I would do to them what they did to us'*: Ulivero Baldi recounted the events of the massacre to me when I visited his home near Fucecchio in 2022.

226 *medically unfit to travel*: On 18 April 2011, Riss was examined by a court physician in Kempten. They found that the then ninety-year-old was in failing health. He had experienced a stroke. He had near total hearing loss, walked unsteadily with a cane (he had a tendency to veer to the left), and had recently undergone prostate resection and hormonal therapy. In addition, Riss had medium-grade dementia. After three minutes, he was unable to repeat a series of five numbers which were shown to him. He could not remember his wife's maiden name, his birthday, wedding date or date of retirement. 'From a medical point of view,' the physician had

written, 'Mr Riss is not and will not, now or in the future, be able to travel and participate in the trial at the military court in Rome' (MCR N 211/08 RGNR).

227 *The German authorities had developed an appetite . . .*: This trend towards more aggressive prosecution of elderly Nazi war criminals would continue. In 2018, the ninety-four-year-old Johann Rehbogen was charged as being an accessory in the murder of hundreds of people at Stutthof concentration camp. This was followed in 2020 by Bruno Dey, ninety-three, who was charged for assisting in the murder of 5,230 people in occupied Poland. Then, in 2021, Irmgard Furchner, ninety-six, was charged with her actions while a secretary at the Stutthof camp. Also in 2021, an unnamed 100-year-old man was charged with accessory to murder during the time he served as an SS guard at Sachsenhausen camp. For many, however, this has all come too late.

228 *'I had a great breakfast . . .'*: Statement included in Barbara Schepanek's TV feature in Bayerischer Rundfunk's *Kontrovers. Die Story*, 22 March 2017.

228 *'The accused was found . . .'*: Letter from Munich public prosecutor's office to Lorenza Mazzetti, 10 August 2016, file number 114 Js 194479/16 (copy provided to the author by Lorenza's lawyer).

229 *'It's enough for me that I know who did it'*: Despite her words of optimism, Lorenza asked Viktoria von Schirach to contact the Central Office in Ludwigsburg to reopen the case. Viktoria was a literary agent and friend who lived in Rome. Her grandfather was Baldur von Schirach, the notorious head of the Hitler Youth who was found guilty at the Nuremberg Trials and sentenced to twenty years in prison. 'Whenever she wanted something,' Viktoria told me, 'Lorenza used my

sense of guilt. She manipulated me.' Which was why Viktoria travelled to Ludwigsburg and gave the investigators Lorenza's statement plus a photograph of Johann Riss. A short while later, someone from the Ludwigsburg office contacted Viktoria and said the photo had been doctored: it was a photocopy of Johann Riss to which had been added an officer's cap. They couldn't reopen the case. 'I was shocked,' recalled Viktoria. 'Lorenza made the whole thing up. It was quite upsetting.' Eva Krampen Kosloski, Lorenza's niece, told me in 2023 that she remembered the fiasco with the altered photograph, but not the way that Viktoria recounted it. Yes, her aunt had added the cap to the photograph, but she had never claimed that it was original and she certainly hadn't attempted to defraud the investigators. 'She just wanted to see what he looked like with a cap on,' Eva said. 'She made the collage because she remembered him like that. It was not intended to convince them. She was not trying to cheat in any way.'

229 *'It's ridiculous . . .'*: Conversation with the author, 2023.

229 *Lorenza and Paola Mazzetti, who had recognized Riss . . .*: In an interview with the author in February 2024, Anna Maria Boldrini did not recognize the photograph of Johann Riss.

230 *'an episode of gratuitous violence'*: Conversation with the author, 2023.

230 *. . . strict instructions from their superiors*: Marco De Paolis said that the Einstein murders were 'not randomly committed'; instead they were an 'intentional homicide'. Like members of the Einstein family, but unlike the historian Carlo Gentile, De Paolis believed that the perpetrators were members of the SS not the Wehrmacht. He also said that the crime was 'racially motivated' – in other words, the Einsteins were

killed because Robert was Jewish. Interview with the author, 2023.

230 *Among them was Eugenio Carrara . . .*: I met the ninety-one-year-old Eugenio Carrara at his house not far from Antella, five miles west of Il Focardo. 'My parents told Robert to leave in the spring [1944] when they heard rumours that the Germans were looking for him,' Eugenio told me. 'He said that there was no reason to leave, that he was protected as he was of German origin.' Why were the Germans looking for Robert? I asked. 'First, because they were seen as Jewish family,' Eugenio said. 'Second, because he was the cousin of Albert Einstein, so vendetta. This was not a casual killing. It was probably an order from higher up. They were looking for Robert for months.' I asked Eugenio about Robert's decision to hide in the woods while leaving his wife and daughters at the villa. He replied, sadly, 'I don't know what I would have done in his shoes.'

231 *'There was a strict . . .'*: Conversation with the author, 2023.

231 *'. . . ordered from the very top'*: Letter from Baden-Württemberg police to the prosecution office in Landau, 8 April 2009 (FF Bundle IV, p. 968). The letter is heavily redacted (like the rest of the Frankenthal Files) and so does not reveal the historian's name, but it does say that he or she has been 'working for more than thirty years almost exclusively on the Second World War'. The writer of the letter prefaces the historian's comment by saying that it is 'important information'.

231 *other Jews living in the vicinity of Il Focardo . . .*: I was told this by a number of local residents who were alive during the war, including Eugenio Carrara, Franco Giorgetti and Giovanna Marchi (whose family owned an estate near Il Focardo).

232 *'The Germans were certainly looking...'*: Interview with Lorenza Mazzetti, 25 April 2007 (FF Bundle II, p. 283).

232 *'It was ... a vendetta'*: Conversation with the author, 2022.

232 *This word, 'vendetta', was often repeated*: In Italian, according to the *Grande Dizionario Italiano* (considered by many Italians to be definitive), the word *vendetta* has a variety of meanings. At its simplest, it means 'revenge'. It also means 'punishment inflicted by divine justice'. And from Corsica came the idea of endless cycles of violent retribution between two families. In the mid-twentieth century, however, the meaning of *vendetta* in Italy widened to include unilateral acts of revenge against family members, perpetrated, for instance, by the Mafia and criminal gangs.

232 *'We all believe this to be a vendetta ...'*: Conversation with the author, 2022.

233 *the Nazis would target the plotters' relatives*: The concept of *Sippenhaft* – blaming family members for an act or crime committed by their relative – had existed in medieval German law. It was revived by the Nazis.

233 *his children were interned in special homes*: For more on the punishment of the 20 July plotters' children, see the television documentary *Hitlers Zorn – Die Kinder von Bad Sachsa* (dir. Michael Heuer, 2019).

235 *on 4 January 2020, Lorenza Mazzetti died ...*: In the interview Lorenza gave to Massimiliano Scuriatti just before her death, she again said that Johann Riss was the perpetrator. When the journalist challenged her about her memory, she pushed back: 'I can't forget that face. That thin, gaunt [*asciutto*] face with pale clear eyes, with round glasses, that will be in my head forever. I can't forget the crimes against my family' (*Una vita, mille vite. Conversazione con Lorenza Mazzetti*, La nave di

Teseo, 2021, p. 132). This detail about the shape of the glasses contradicts her earlier statement to German police when she said that the commander 'was wearing glasses with almost rectangular lenses and a transparent frame' (FF Bundle VIII, pp. 1980–98).

### 27. College Park, Maryland, 2023

237 *to those who ran . . . it was worth a try*: In May 2023, I contacted NARA and asked if they would allow me to carry out a fingerprint examination of the notice left at Il Focardo which they had in their archive. They replied: 'Unfortunately, NARA does not perform this type of work nor do we allow outside laboratories nor agencies to perform such work on records in our holdings.' Through an online search I found Brian Dalrymple, who said that he was willing to fly from his home in Canada to Maryland to conduct the examination and that his laser was small enough to carry as hand luggage. When I relayed this information to the head of NARA, William 'Jay' Bosanko, he generously invited Brian to visit. After the inconclusive results from NARA, I contacted the Italian authorities in September 2023 and suggested they might examine the other surviving notice held by Eva Krampen Kosloski. A few days later, the Carabinieri arrived at her door without warning and asked her for the notice. 'I was very frightened!' she told me shortly afterwards. 'But they were very nice.' In the end, the results of this second fingerprint analysis by the Italian authorities generated no new information.

239 *'It will be a desperate attempt . . .'*: Conversation with the author, 2023.

242 *he 'had friends who lost people in the Holocaust . . .'*: Conversation with the author, 2023.

243 *he wrote up his findings in a report . . .*: Sent to the author on 26 October 2023.

243 *. . . he had not been able to find any complete prints*: 'I wasn't surprised,' Brian said. 'I've been at this a long time and I know it's the exception rather than the rule to find this stuff.' Conversation with the author, 2023.

### 28. Florence, 2023

246 *this was meant to be a full and final settlement*: Italy and Germany signed a second agreement, also in 1961, determining compensation to Italy for 'certain property-related, economic and financial questions'. Germany paid a further lump sum of 40 million Deutschmarks to settle these 'outstanding questions of an economic nature'.

249 *'It was partly a question of pride . . .'*: Conversation with the author, 2023.

249 *in April 2022 . . . an agreement had been reached*: On 30 April 2022, the Italian parliament passed Decree Number 36/2022, which was then enacted as Law Number 79/2022 on 29 June.

250 *'It's a principle of fundamental law' . . .*: Conversation with the author, 2023.

250 *Diego found it 'very strange' . . .*: According to subsequent investigations, it became clear that the money originally came from the European Commission as part of a multi-billion-euro reconstruction package following the Covid-19 pandemic. Many suspect that Germany made a contribution to the European Commission via a back-door arrangement.

252 *'I sued as a matter of principle'* . . .: Conversation with the author, 2023.

253 *First to speak is the teacher* . . .: I noted down these speeches during the event.

## Epilogue

256 *the great scientist was wearing house slippers* . . .: The Einstein expert Barbara Wolff told me that she is sure this story is a 'concoction': Elsa would have made sure her husband did not leave his home still wearing slippers. In my grandmother's defence, she was known for telling the truth, if anything too much.

256 *'Dear and esteemed Dr Alexander!* . . .': Letter from Albert Einstein to Dr Alfred Alexander, 27 April 1926 (AEA 97-348). Rudolf Einstein and Fanny Einstein (née Koch) were also Albert's father-in-law and mother-in-law as he married his second cousin Elsa. Rudolf died on 27 April 1926 and Fanny died on 10 November 1926. This letter was included in a book of remembrances by various grateful patients and former patients, collected for Dr Alfred Alexander's fiftieth birthday in 1930, and including contributions from famous artists, scientists, writers and theatre directors.

257 *This direct connection with the Einstein family* . . .: I had another link to the Einsteins: like Robert, my great-grandmother Elsa Hirschowitz killed herself following Nazi persecution. Elsa was Jewish and fled to London in 1938. She was horrified by the situation in Germany and deeply distressed that so many of her relatives were unable to leave. Over the next few months, she tried to kill herself a number of times. Finally,

on 18 December 1938, she was admitted to Wyke House, a small private clinic licensed under the Lunacy Act 1890. According to the doctor's notes, she was 'suffering from profound melancholia with persecutory delusions, and hallucinations and suicidal tendency'. She died on 14 March the following the year. Her records said the cause was bronchial pneumonia; many in my family believe it was suicide. Such deaths are typically not included when counting the victims of the Holocaust.

257 *I went to see the villa Il Focardo . . .*: This was an unannounced visit. I went with Lorenzo Grassi, his wife Francesca Fantappiè and cousin Lucia Torrini. The front door was locked, so Lorenzo and I walked around to the rear. We were just approaching the back gate when Lorenzo heard a whizzing sound close to his head. He looked up and saw an old lady leaning out of a window. He shouted at her as she pulled her gun inside. It was probably an air rifle, he said, trying to laugh it off. A few months later, Lorenzo secured permission for us to go inside the villa. Thankfully, we were able to look around without being shot at.

258 *There had been at least six investigations . . .*: This number includes a very brief investigation that was carried out by the Carabinieri a few months after the murders. On 13 November 1944, a non-commissioned officer named Sergeant Major Maresciallo took down the testimony of Seba Mazzetti and Orando Fuschiotti in Rignano sull'Arno. He attached their single-page statements to a brief summary of the crime which stated that the suspects were '36 German soldiers [illegible] probably of the SS' (FF Bundle V, pp. 1185–90). The pages were included as part of a file on war crimes carried out by *Nazifascisti* in Tuscany submitted by the

Carabinieri in Florence to headquarters in Rome, and later included in a national list titled 'Second World War Evidence of Acts of Barbarism in Tuscany-Umbria', compiled on 21 July 1945 under the auspices of the commander-in-chief of the Carabinieri. In it, the murders of Nina, Luce and Cici Einstein were given the crime numbers 161, 162 and 163. I found no evidence that any action was taken by the Italian authorities following this report being submitted beyond sharing it many decades later with the German prosecutor's office.

259 *'Hitler hated the Einstein family . . .'*: Massimiliano Scuriatti, *Una vita, mille vite. Conversazione con Lorenza Mazzetti* (La nave di Teseo, 2021), p. 135. In her *London Diaries* (Zidane Press, 2018), Lorenza also wrote of 'the execution of a precise order against Einstein's relatives' (p. 168). A paragraph later, she added: 'During the negotiations with the Germans on the terms of surrender, the Americans and the British had precise orders to thwart Albert Einstein's attempt to shed light on the massacre of his cousin Robert's family'. She provided no evidence of this and I was unable to substantiate it.

259 *this led to a 'vendetta'*: Both Eugenio Giani and the president of the municipality of Rignano sull'Arno, Grazia Di Dio, in their speeches at the memorial event, called the Einstein murders a 'vendetta'. The quotations in this paragraph come from an interview the author carried out with Giani after his speech.

262 *this national amnesia . . .*: Many of those I spoke with, especially in the Jewish community, argue that one legacy of fascism is the prevalence of antisemitic language in Italy today. *Rabbino*, or 'Rabbi', means someone who is tight with their money. *Ebreo*, or 'Jew', can be used to mean 'a bad person' – as in, if

you are lying late in bed when you should have got up, someone might say, *Non essere un ebreo*, or, 'Don't be a Jew.' The
word *giudeo* can also be used as a general derogatory term for
a Jewish person. Jewish schoolchildren are told, 'Go burn
in the oven.' Pictures of Anne Frank are held up at football
matches to intimidate the opposition. Many people still use
the word *Cristiano* instead of 'person' – as in, 'Look at that
Christian on his bicycle' – the implication being that non-
Christians are not people. According to the Milan-based
foundation, the Centre for Contemporary Jewish Docu-
mentation, antisemitic incidents in Italy increased by 10 per
cent between 2021 and 2022. This included two assaults, ten
threats of violence, and one serious act of vandalism against
Trieste's synagogue. The threats against Senator Liliana
Segre – Holocaust survivor and perhaps the most famous
Jew alive in Italy – are considered of sufficient concern that
she is provided with a full-time bodyguard.

262 *the football stadium . . . in the shape of the letter 'D'*: Some have
argued that the Stadio Artemio Franchi was not built in this
form to honour Mussolini but for architectural reasons.

262 *thousands of Jews were offered help . . .*: There are numerous
incidences of the local population supporting their Jewish
neighbours. Just in Tuscany, for instance, Cardinal Elia
Angelo Dalla Costa, Archbishop of Florence, encouraged
the priests and nuns under his authority to provide safe
haven to more than 300 Jews. Another example was the Florentine priest Don Leto Casini, who assisted Jews by carrying
messages and forged documents. For their efforts, both men
were later recognized by Yad Vashem (the World Holocaust
Remembrance Center in Jerusalem) as 'Righteous Among
the Nations'. On the other hand, there are several cases of

Italians persecuting the Jews: Florentine police provided lists of Jews to the German occupiers; local villagers betrayed Jews living with their neighbours; and some members of the Tuscan Church refused to help Jews.

263 *the 8,564 Jews who were deported . . .*: The figure of 8,564 Jews deported from Italy, Italian-occupied France, Kos and Rhodes is provided by the United States Holocaust Memorial Museum. Of these, 1,009 survived, 107 died in transit camps in Italy and 196 were killed in Italy. Of the 7,879 Jews deported from mainland Italy, 263 came from Siena and Florence. These figures do not include Robert Einstein, as Holocaust-related suicides are rarely included. They also do not include Nina's, Luce's and Cici's deaths, as they are considered by most researchers not to be Jewish, even though their killings were racially motivated. The proportion of Jews who died in German-occupied Italy was around 18 per cent. This was much lower than some countries, such as Hungary (69 per cent), the Netherlands (73 per cent) and Poland (90 per cent), closer to that of Estonia (21 per cent), France (22 per cent) and Austria (35 per cent), and far higher than Denmark (1 per cent).

264 *Cici had so many days in front of her*: When asked what she thought Cici's life would have been, her cousin Anna Maria Boldrini said: 'She would have had a normal life; she would have married a rich man and had kids' (interview with the author, February 2024).

266 *'She took off her little necklace . . .'*: From Paola Mazzetti's unpublished diaries, read out by her daughter Eva Krampen Kosloski at an event to commemorate Luce Einstein's posthumous graduation, 26 January 2024, at the University of Florence.

# Bibliography and Sources

*English Editions*

Bassani, Giorgio, *The Garden of the Finzi-Continis* (Everyman, 2005)

Bettina, Elizabeth, *It Happened in Italy: Untold Stories of How the People of Italy Defied the Horrors of the Holocaust* (Thomas Nelson, 2009)

Browning, Christopher, *Ordinary Men: Reserve Police Battalion 101 and the Final Solution in Poland* (Penguin, 2001)

Clark, Ronald W., *Einstein: The Life and Times* (World Publishing Co., 1971)

Einstein, Albert, *The World As I See It* (Dead Authors Society, 2020)

Farrell, Nicholas, *Mussolini: A New Life* (Orion, 2003)

Focardi, Filippo, and Klinkhammer, Lutz, 'The Question of Fascist Italy's War Crimes: The Construction of a Self-Acquitting Myth (1943–1948)', *Journal of Modern Italian Studies*, vol. 9, no. 3 (2004)

Fölsing, Albrecht, *Albert Einstein: A Biography* (Penguin, 1997)

Gilbert, G. M., *Nuremberg Diary* (De Capo, 1995)

Goldhagen, Daniel, *Hitler's Willing Executioners: Ordinary Germans and the Holocaust* (Abacus, 1997)

Isaacson, Walter, *Einstein: His Life and Universe* (Simon & Schuster, 2007)

Jennings, Christian, *Anatomy of a Massacre: How the SS Got Away with War Crimes in Italy* (History Press, 2021)

Kemp, Anthony, *The Secret Hunters* (Coronet, 1998)

Kershaw, Ian, *The End: Hitler's Germany, 1944–1945* (Allen Lane, 2011)

Kertzer, David I., *The Pope and Mussolini: The Secret History of Pius XI and the Rise of Fascism in Europe* (Oxford University Press, 2014)

Krampen Kosloski, Eva, *After Images: The Massacre of the Einstein Mazzetti Family – Visual Resonances* (Sellerio Editore Palermo, 2024)

Levi, Primo, *If This Is A Man* and *The Truce* (Abacus, 1987)

Levi, Primo, *The Periodic Table* (Everyman,1995)

Mazzetti, Lorenza, *London Diaries* (Zidane Press, 2018)

Mazzetti, Lorenza, *The Sky Falls* (Bodley Head, 1962)

Mulisch, Harry, *The Assault* (Pantheon, 1985)

Neffe, Jürgen, *Einstein: A Biography* (Polity, 2007)

Pezzino, Paolo, *Memory and Massacre: Revisiting Sant'Anna di Stazzema* (Palgrave Macmillan, 2012)

Rigg, Bryan Mark, *Hitler's Jewish Soldiers: The Untold Story of Nazi Racial Laws and Men of Jewish Descent in the German Military* (University Press of Kansas, 2002)

Smith, Ali, *Summer* (Hamish Hamilton, 2020)

Stille, Alexander, *Benevolence and Betrayal: Five Italian Jewish Families under Fascism* (Picador, 2003)

*Italian Editions*

Agnoloni, Giuseppe, *Ricordi di guerra* (Archivio del Comune di Rignano, 1998)

Arcuri, Camillo, *Il sangue degli Einstein Italiani* (Ugo Mursia Editore, 2015)

Baiada, Luca, et al., *La giustizia civile Italiana nei confronti di stati esteri per il riscarcimento del crimini di guerra e contro l'umanità* (Editoriale Scientifica, 2023)

Bidussa, David, *Il mito del bravo italiano* (Saggiatore, 1994)

Casella, Luciano, *La Toscana nella guerra di liberazione* (Carrara, 1927)

Cenati, Roberto, *Il dolore di avervi dovuto lasciare* (ANPI Provinciale di Milano, 2015)

Ciardi, Marco, and Gasperini, Antonella, *Il pianoforte di Einstein. Vite e storie in bilico tra Firenze, Europa e America* (Hoepli, 2021)

Del Boca, Angelo, *Italiani, brava gente?* (Nerri Poza, 2005)

Dino, Nello, *Ricordi di quei giorni* (Giuntina, 1975)

Droandi, Alberto Mario, 'Agosto 1944. Quei cinque giorni di Robert Einstein', *Notizie di Historia*, December 2004

Focardi, Filippo, *Il cattivo tedesco e il bravo italiano. La rimozione delle colpe della seconda guerra mondiale* (Editori Laterza, 2016)

Frullini, Giovanni, *La liberazione di Firenze* (Pagnini e Martinelli, 2000)

Gentile, Carlo, *I crimini di guerra tedeschi in Italia, 1943–1945* (Einaudi, 2022)

Greco, Fabiola (ed.), *La forza della memoria* (Regione Toscana Consiglio Regionale, 2006)

Jona, Ugo, *La rappresaglie nazifasciste sulle popolazioni toscane* (ANFIM, 1992)

Mazzetti, Lorenza, *Album di famiglia* (La nave di Teseo, 2011)

Mazzetti, Lorenza, *Il cielo cade* (Garzanti, 1961)

Mazzetti, Lorenza, *Diario Londinese* (Sellerio, 2014)

Mazzetti, Lorenza, *Mi può prestare la sua pistola per favore?* (La nave di Teseo, 2016)

Mazzetti, Paola, *Di che segno sei? L'oroscopo per tutte le stagioni* (Fefè, 2010)

Mazzetti, Paola, *Un pensiero al giorno* (Ginevra Bentivoglio Editoria, 2014)

Mazzetti, Paola, *Un viaggio insolito* (self-published, 2013)

Paoli, Rodolfo, *Cronache di una guerra combattuta senza armi (1943–1946)* (Pagnini, 2014)

Pezzino, Paolo, *Anatomia di un massacro. Controversia sopra una strage tedesca* (Il Mulino, 2013)

Pezzino, Paolo, *Sant'Anna di Stazzema. Storia di una strage* (Il Mulino, 2013)

Salmon, Elio, *Diario di un ebreo fiorentino, 1943–1944* (Giuntina, 2002)

Scuriatti, Massimiliano, *Una vita, mille vite. Conversazione con Lorenza Mazzetti* (La nave di Teseo, 2021)

Tognarini, Ivano, *Storia a memori. Il sangue degli Einstein* (Instituto ligure per la storia della resistenza e dell'eta contemporanea, 2011)

Vinay, Paola, *Testimone d'amore* (Claudiana, 2009)


*German Editions*


Gentile, Carlo, *Wehrmacht und Waffen-SS im Partisanenkrieg. Italien, 1943–1945* (Ferdinand Schöningh, 2012)

Rogger, Franziska, *Einsteins Schwester. Maja Einstein – Ihr Leben und ihr Bruder Albert* (Neue Zürcher Zeitung, 2005)

Staiger, Georg, *26. Panzer-Division. Ihr Werden und Einsatz, 1942 bis 1945* (H. H. Podzun, 1957)


*Online Sources*


*Atlante delle Stragi Naziste e Fasciste in Italia, 1943–1945*, online database (INSMLI and ANPI, 2016)

*Films, Documentaries and TV shows*

*Aktenzeichen XY . . . ungelöst* (TV show), episode 443, broadcast ZDF, Germany, 23 February 2011, 8-minute segment on the Einstein case

*Attraverso l'amore. Paola Mazzetti si racconta* (documentary feature), directors Lulli and Claudio Costa, distributed Ronin Film Productions (2021), 23 minutes

*Because I Am a Genius! Lorenza Mazzetti* (documentary feature), director Steve della Casa and Francesco Frisari, distributed Istituto Lice Cinecittà (2016), 62 minutes

*Der Fall Rignano – Die Mörder der Letzten Tage* (TV show), director Tilman Spengler, episode 335 of *37 Grad*, broadcast ZDF, Germany, 18 December 2001, 30 minutes

*Einsteins Nichten* (documentary feature), director Friedemann Fromm, distributed Cinefattoria et al. (2017), 90 minutes

*Il cielo cade* (feature film), directors Andrea Frazzi and Antonio Frazzi, distributed Parus Film et al. (2000), 102 minutes

*Kontrovers. Die Story* (TV show), director Barbara Schepanek, broadcast BR Bayerischer Rundfunk, Germany, 22 March 2017, 19-minute segment on the Einstein case

*Together with Lorenza Mazzetti* (documentary feature), director Brighid Lowe, distributed BFI (2023), 54 minutes

# Acknowledgements

In writing this book, I collected letters, diaries, photographs, military records and other documents from various archives and research centres. Thank you to all those who assisted me, including: in Italy, the community library in Rignano sull'Arno, the Convento del Carmine in Florence, the Biblioteca Nazionale Centrale in Florence, the Archivio di Stato in Florence, the Tuscan Resistance Archive in Florence, the archive at the Liceo Michelangiolo, the University of Florence archives, the Deportation Archive in Prato, the museum in Sant'Anna di Stazzema and the Historical Institute of the Resistance and the Contemporary Age in Pistoia; in the USA, the National Archives and Records Administration (NARA) in Maryland, and the Collected Papers of Albert Einstein at Princeton University; in Israel, Yad Vashem in Jerusalem, the Central Zionist Archives in Jerusalem and the Albert Einstein Archives in Jerusalem; in Switzerland, the Albert Einstein Archive at the Literaturarchiv in Bern and the Archiv für Zeitgeschichte at ETH in Zurich; in Germany, the Bayerisches Hauptstaatsarchiv in Munich, the Albert Einstein museum in Ulm and the Bundesarchiv in Berlin; in the UK, the Wiener Holocaust Library in London and the National Archives in Kew.

As this is a cold case, many of the relevant documents were held by investigators and prosecutors, who typically jealously guard their materials. I would therefore like to thank the following in particular for being so generous and helpful: Judge Thomas Will and his staff at the Central Office of the State

Justice Administrations for the Investigation of National Socialist Crimes in Ludwigsburg, and Marco De Paolis and his team at the Italian Military Justice Court in Rome, both of who were instrumental in helping navigate their archives. In addition, I would like to thank Hubert Ströber at the Frankenthal Public Prosecutor's Office for providing me with his files, the first time these have been given by a German prosecutor to a journalist or writer.

Many witnesses who remembered the murder of the Einstein family agreed to speak with me, often telling their stories publicly for the first time. Finally, many brave men and women who survived other atrocities perpetrated against civilians in the Tuscan region during the war shared their personal stories with me. Their testimonies speak for many.

I would like to thank all the witnesses, historians, academics and others who kindly helped me with my research, including: Kristen Ackerman Piech, Marta Baiardi, Jordan K. Baldassini, Oliviero Baldi, Paolo Banci, Andrea Bellavite, Paolo Bellavite, Silvia Cristina Benzi, Anna Maria Boldrini, William Bosanko, Richard Breitmann, Camilla Brunelli, Silvia Brunelli, Carmen Bürgisser, Carlo Carli, Miriam Cividalli Canarutto, Eugenio Carrara, Francesco Casini, Massimo Casprini, Juanita Cox, Frank Crispino, Brian Dalrymple, Marco De Paolis, Anthony DePalma, Jader Di Nocera, Peter Einstein, Mark Featherman, Filippo Focardi, Annie Fraser, Francesco Frisari, Friedrich Fromm, Marinella Fuschiotti, Antonella Gasperini, Carlo Gentile, Franco Giorgetti, Marion Godfrey, Matteo Grasso, Gabriella Gribaudi, Michael Hemmler, Edmund Jacoby, Jainer Jahreis, Christian Jennings, Lutz Klinkhammer, Christiane Kohl, Eva Krampen Kosloski, Brett Lalonde, David

Liscia, Piergabriele Mancuso, Kani Marceau, Alberto Mariotti, Franca Mazzarella, Lorenzo Mechi, Lionello Viterbo Neppi Modona, Michele Morabito, Gianna Morandi, Sylvia Naylor, Chiara Nencioni, Blake Oliver, Allison Olson, John Owen, Sara Valentina Di Palma, Adele Pardini, Ada Partsch, Christoph Partsch, Paolo Pezzino, Liliana Picciotto, Hella Pick, Anthony Polonsky, Giacomo Quinti, Eli Rosenbaum, Francesca Salomoni, Barbara Schepanek, Viktoria von Schirach, Piero and Piera Sgherri, Tilman Spengler, Nina Staehle, Shlomit Taaseh, Andrea Tatini, Eric Van Slander, Stefano Velotti, Daniel Vogelmann, Sister Maddalena and Sister Tarcisia. A particular note of appreciation to Barbara Wolff, who so generously helped me navigate the documents, history and intricacies related to Albert Einstein, and to Lisa Graziani and Jannik Noeske for their fabulous help with research, translation and fact-checking.

A huge thank you to our open-hearted Italian neighbours who welcomed us into their lives, shared their stories and introduced us to the local history (including many eyewitnesses and survivors) as well as the local culture (especially the food): Giovanna Marchi, Lucia Torrini, Vito Maiorano, Lorenzo and Francesca 'Fanta' Fantappiè, Cecca, Leo, Peppo, Buba, Mattia, Giovanni and Anna Maria – and Anna (always). Though I am still wondering . . . *Dove è Catozzo?*

To my remarkable research assistant Margherita Piccioli, who worked with such good humour and grace as she diligently organized, arranged, translated and investigated this challenging story.

To my early readers: Niall Barton, Lynn Medford, Amelia Wooldridge, Lucy Baring, Kate Harrod, Rupert Levy, Gill Morgan, Amanda Harding, Zam Baring and Nick

Viner – thank you again. Also to Keith Lowe for his extremely helpful comments and for Mark Steitz for his messaging.

It takes a large number of people to produce a book and I'm incredibly grateful to everyone at Penguin Michael Joseph. In particular, thank you to my wondrous editor Jillian Taylor for her thoughtful input, brilliant support and encouragement; Paula Flanagan for expertly guiding the ship into harbour; Sukhmani Bhakar for her innovation and diligence in bringing the story to life through pictures; Serena Nazareth and Audrey Curl (Production); Ciara Berry (Publicity); Mubarak El Mubarak (Marketing); Jon Kennedy (jacket design); Roy McMillian (audio producer and narrator); Ruth Ellis (index); Christina Ellicott, Kelly Mason and Bronwen Davies (Sales); Sarah Scarlett and Lucy Beresford-Knox (Rights); Ian Moores (cypress trees icons); Stephen Hickson (family trees); Nicola Evans (Legal team); and to everyone at Penguin Random House who worked on the book. In addition, an enormous thank you to the superb Kit Shepherd for his incredible copyediting and Darren Bennett for his fabulous maps. To Alan Samson, an early supporter and reader. And to my incredible agents Sarah Chalfant, James Pullen, Claire Devine and Maria Calinescu.

To my daughter Sam, whose excellent editing skills extended even to this sentence, and who I appreciate, always.

And finally, to my extraordinary wife Debora Harding, who has patiently provided me with invaluable support and feedback for all my books, including this one, and to who I don't give sufficient credit.

# List of Illustrations

Readers will note that there are no pictures in the book of Robert's parents Jacob and Ida Einstein in the book or of Robert and his sister Edith as children. This is not an oversight. I reached out to all the obvious archives along with various members of the Einstein family but was unable to track down the images. If anyone does have these pictures, please let the publisher of this book know and we will try to include them in a later edition.

The author and publisher gratefully acknowledge the permission granted to reproduce the copyright material in this book. Every effort has been made to trace copyright holders and to obtain their permission. The publisher apologizes for any errors or omissions and, if notified of any corrections, will make suitable acknowledgment in future reprints or editions of this book.

## Integrated images

## Plate Section 1

1c. Albert and Maja Einstein: Heritage-Images / TopFoto
1d. Jakob and Hermann Einstein's business in Italy: Courtesy of Pavia Chamber of Commerce
2a. Robert and Nina Einstein: Courtesy of Anna Maria Boldrini
2b. Nina with Luce, Cici and twin babies, Paola and Lorenza: Courtesy of Anna Maria Boldrini
2c. Robert Einstein: *Il Nuovo Corriere* newspaper, published 28 July 1945
3a. Nina Einstein with her two young daughters: Courtesy of Anna Maria Boldrini
3b. Cici Einstein when older: Courtesy of Anna Maria Boldrini
3c. Luce Einstein when older: Courtesy of Anna Maria Boldrini
4a. Paola, Robert, Anna Maria, Lorenza, Eugenio and Seba in front of the entrance to Il Focardo: Courtesy of Anna Maria Boldrini
4b. Nina, Lorenza, Paola, Cici, Seba and Luce in Perugia: Courtesy of Anna Maria Boldrini
5a. Postcard of Il Focardo: Courtesy of Anna Maria Boldrini
5b. Front entrance to Il Focardo: Thomas Harding
6a. 'Pipone' Galante with Paola, Lorenza and others: Permission granted by Francesca Galante (Pipone's granddaughter)
6b. Alberto Droandi: Permission granted by Robert Giulio Droandi (Mario's son)
6c. Orando Fuschiotti: Permission granted by Marinella Fuschiotti (Orando's daughter)
7a. Albert Einstein under armed guard: Bettmann / Getty Images / Contributor
7b. Albert Einstein and his sister Maja Winteler-Einstein: © SZ Photo / Scherl / Bridgeman Images
8a. Hitler and Mussolini meeting: Photo 12 / Alamy Stock Photo
8b. Hitler and Mussolini's parade: Sueddeutsche Zeitung Photo / Alamy Stock Photo

**Plate Section 2**
9a. Notice left by Germans at the crime scene: Permission granted by the National Archives and Records Administration (NARA)
9b. Ponte Alle Grazie: IWM / Getty Images / Contributor

10a. Letter to Albert Einstein from Milton Wexler: © The Hebrew University of Jerusalem, Israel. Digital image photographed by Ardon Bar Hama

11a. Johann Riss's military card: Permission granted from Bundesarchiv, reference number: PA 2 2022/S-67

11b. August Schmitz: Permission granted from Bundesarchiv, reference number: MA 5 2024/KW09#0315#0001

11c. Clemens Theis: Permission granted from Bundesarchiv, reference number: MA 5 2024/KW09#0315#0001

12a. Milton Wexler: *New York Times*, 13 August 1949

12b. Carlo Gentile: Courtesy of Ann Büttner

12c. 'Einstein's Executioner Discovered': *Il Secolo XIX*, 10 February 2007

13a. German police investigators: Permission granted from the Military Prosecutor's Office of Rome

13b. Fireplace near where the victims were shot: Permission granted from the Military Prosecutor's Office of Rome

13c. Bullet holes in the wall: Permission granted from the Military Prosecutor's Office of Rome

14a. Judge Thomas Will: dpa picture alliance / Alamy Stock Photo

14b. Hubert Ströber: dpa picture alliance / Alamy Stock Photo

14c. Barbara Schepanek: Courtesy of Barbara Schepanek

14d. Marco De Paolis: Image Courtesy of Imagoeconomica

15a. Brian Dalrymple looks for fingerprints: Courtesy of the National Archives and Records Administration

15b. Notice left by the Germans examined using laser technology: Courtesy of the National Archives and Records Administration

15c. Anna Maria Boldrini with her sons (l-r) Paulo and Andrea: Thomas Harding

16a Gravestone of Nina, Luce and Cici: Thomas Harding

16b. Gravestone of Robert Einstein: Thomas Harding

Additional design elements, including stamps, extracted from the official investigation dossier of the US War Crimes Commission courtesy of the National Archives and Records Administration (NARA).

# Index

Page numbers in *italic* indicate illustrations

memory, Italian words for xxi
Mering, Josef von 145, 302
*mezzadria* 26
Milan 12, 13, 138
*Mischlinge* 107–8
Mogilev 220–1
Moiorano, Vito 305
Monroe, Marilyn 145
Montevarchi 93
Morandi, Beniamino 154–5, 305
Moscow Declaration 100–1
Mossad 183
Munich
    Robert Einstein's childhood
        9–12, 274
    Robert Einstein's home during
        1910s 15, 16
Mussolini, Benito 20–1, 36–7, 43,
    44, 45, 138, 280

Nagasaki 162
Nathan, Otto 165
National Archives and Records
    Administration (NARA)
    237, 325
National Archives, College Park
    237–8, 242–3
National Fascist Party 20, 36, 264
Nazi hunters 183–4
Nazi War Crimes Disclosure Act
    237–8
nuclear bomb development 57
Nuremburg, International
    Military Tribunal 166
Nuremburg Laws 107–8

Okinawa, Battle of 140
Operation Barbarossa 220–2
Ostler, H. L. 102–3

Pacifici, Wanda 46
Paoli, Rodolfo 153–4, 270, 300, 304
Pardini, Adele 210, 315–16
partisans 59–60, 68, 93, 111, 265,
    289
Partsch, Christoph 312
Pavia, Robert Einstein's
    childhood 12–13
peaches 26, 31, 141–2, 280–1, 302
Petacci, Clara 138
Pisa 44–5, 49
Pius XII 140
Poste Italiane 161
*Potente* (partisan leader) 60
Potsdam Conference 245
Priebke, Erich 172, 174
Princeton 56

race traitors 108
Raisi, Enzo 176
Rehbogen, Johann 321
reparations 245–6
Restone 93
Rignano sull'Arno 27, 251–3
Ripp, Josef 202
Riss, Johann
    appearance 213, *216*
    background 219–20
    Bernhard investigaton 227
    De Paolis doubts about
        involvement 218, 229

# About the Author

Thomas Harding is a bestselling author whose books have been translated into more than twenty languages. He has written for the *Sunday Times*, the *Washington Post* and the *Guardian*, among other publications.

He is the author of *Hanns and Rudolf*, which won the Wingate Prize for Non-Fiction, and *The House by the Lake*, which was shortlisted for the Costa Biography Award. His book *Blood on the Page* won the Crime Writers' Association Golden Dagger Award for Non-Fiction, while *White Debt* was longlisted for the Moore Prize for Human Rights Writing. More recently, his biography of the publisher George Weidenfeld, *The Maverick*, was selected by the *New York Times* as a Critic's Pick for 2023. Thomas is also the author of three picture books for children, including *The House by the Lake*, which was nominated for the Kate Greenaway Medal. He lives in Hampshire, England, with his wife, the author Debora Harding. You can follow Thomas on X @thomasharding and his author website www.thomasharding.com.